Penguin Books

Don Whillans : Portrait of a Mountaineer

Don Whillans was born in Salford in 1933, and began climbing on the gritstone edges of the Pennines in 1950, while serving his apprenticeship as a plumber. He graduated to the granite cliffs of the Lake District, Snowdonia and Scotland, pushing the standard of British rock climbing into a new sphere. His notable climbs in the Alps include the West Face of the Dru, the Central Pillar of Frêney and the West Face of the Blaitière.

In 1957 he was invited to join an expedition to Masherbrum, a 25,600-foot peak in the Himalayas, and later he took part in further expeditions to the Argentine, Chile, Nepal, Karakoram and Peru. After his ascent of the South Face of Annapurna in May 1970 he was asked to join an international expedition to scale the unclimbed South Face of Mt Everest in 1971.

Don Whillans is a member of the Rock and Ice Club, the Alpine Club and the Himalayan Club, and a Fellow of the Royal Geographical Society. He is married and lives in Rossendale, Lancashire.

Alick Ormerod is a 33-year-old lecturer in English Literature and Liberal Studies at Rossendale College of Further Education. He lives in Accrington, Lancashire, with his wife and three children.

D1643377

Don Whillans:
Portrait of a Mountaineer

Don Whillans and Alick Ormerod

 Penguin Books

Penguin Books Ltd, Harmondsworth,
Middlesex, England
Penguin Books Australia Ltd, Ringwood,
Victoria, Australia

First published by Heinemann 1971
Published in Penguin Books 1973
Copyright © Don Whillans and Alick Ormerod, 1971

Made and printed in Great Britain by
Richard Clay (The Chaucer Press) Ltd
Bungay, Suffolk
Set in Linotype Pilgrim

Contents

List of Illustrations

Authors' Note

The structure of the narrative needs some explanation: Don Whillans's own words are linked together by passages by Alick Ormerod, and the latter have been italicized to distinguish them from Don's account. This is an attempt to bring some objectivity into what otherwise would have been a purely subjective account of one man's life.

We have tried to reconstruct each incident as authentically as possible. We have also attempted to record Don's thoughts and feelings as they were at the time of each incident and not as they may be now.

Don kept a reasonably detailed series of diaries from 1951 onwards, so we hope that as far as dates, places and companions go, we are accurate.

We would like to thank the staff of the Commerce Department of Rossendale College of Further Education, the girls of the Full-Time Secretarial Course 1969–70, at the same establishment, and Mike Daniels, Rachel Bailey and of course our wives, for their invaluable help with the manuscript.

1 | City Child

Today, the grimy brick terraces of Lower Broughton, Salford, are poetically called 'twilight' housing. The excavators, the bull-dozers, the fires of wooden beams and window frames are only just round the corner; towering grey blocks of flats watch hungrily, waiting for the rubble to be flattened, as if eager for their species to propagate.

In 1933, down Nora Street where front doorsteps and win-dow sills were sand-stoned until they stood out like gold braid-ing, Donald Desbrow Whillans was busily finding his adven-turous feet.

My world was the backyard and the entry and a set of rail-ings where the river flowed past and I could see the footbridge that crossed the river and was forbidden. My world was as far as I could see and as far as I was concerned anybody who went farther than that dropped off the end of the earth.

Don's earliest memory of his father is of watching him set-ting off to work with his bicycle clips on. His father had a white-collar job – unusual for Nora Street – in an old-fashioned, long-established grocery business almost in the centre of Man-chester. Times were hard, even for grocers, and although Don himself was not aware of it, money was tight.

His first school was St Matthias's Infant School in the Adel-phi district of Salford, a small, overcrowded, dirty building, remarkable only for the fact that it housed a collection of some of the roughest, toughest kids in northern England. The disci-pline imposed on these children was probably the only really successful attempt at controlling them to be made during their whole lives.

I couldn't grasp the fact that I had to stay in one place all day. I can remember looking through the railings of the playground and feeling like some animal in a cage. I thought: 'Well, what they got me blocked up in here for?'

My mother used to come and collect me from school. I remember thinking: 'I can make it home on my own.' So one day I tried it. I hung about for a bit, waiting for my mother, half hoping she wouldn't come but I knew she would so I buggered off early and wound my way through all these streets – my first bit of route finding – and I was really pleased and relieved when I got to the bridge and I could see the house.

I thought this was a really worthy effort because I couldn't think of anything bigger. My mother was very upset about it; she lectured and gave me a clout or two and I couldn't work this lot out at all. I thought it was a real big effort on my part.

The chance came of a house on a council estate and Don's father eagerly took it, even though for him it meant a longer journey to work. Nora Street and its environs was not the ideal place in which to bring up two children – for by this time Don had a sister, Edna. The journey to his new home is clearly remembered by Don.

We went on a bus – a number 13 it'd be – and there were rows of houses with gardens. I kept running out and stopping outside each one: 'Is this ours? Is this ours?' There were trees in some of the gardens, big trees not bushes, and when we came to our house it had a grass patch in front of it. The door was at the side as we only had the top part of the house. I always wanted the door at the front.

A new school and a new start. Lower Kersal Council School was a larger, cleaner edition of St Matthias's.

You've no mates, you know you're on your own, and then the standard stuff for a new kid, first thing you get: 'D'you want a fight?' Then they gave us the old diphtheria jab and I thought: 'Well, if this is a sample of what they're doing here, I don't want to know.'

Lower Kersal School backed straight on to the River Irwell. Strangely enough, Don now lives almost at the rise of this same river up on the Rossendale Moors, but a vast change comes over the Irwell as it moves from tumbling stream to torpid river. The filthy effluent from dozens of factories pours into it as it winds sluggishly to Manchester and the Ship Canal. By the time it passes through Lower Kersal, it is the colour and consistency of thick, black ink. In this malodorous murk, Don learnt to swim.

We used to go in about five or six times a day. No towels, no trunks. I just sort of walked out of my depth and then I had to swim. I did some daft things there. I used to come out with my feet cut by broken bottles and there were hundreds of bloody black leeches that stuck on you. We used to have some good fun diving into great lumps of foam: 'Here's a big 'un,' and we'd dive right in 'em.

The war came and Don's father joined up. This meant another upheaval in the family as Don's mother had to go out to work. Her work at a factory manufacturing gas capes entailed very early rising. Don and his sister were taken to school for breakfast. Then the Germans turned their attention in earnest to Manchester Docks, and Anderson shelters sprang up in the back gardens of the council estate.

There was no point in going to bed and then having to trog back down in the middle of the night. There were two bunks my dad had made in the shelter; we slept in them and my mother slept in a deck-chair. I used to lie awake and watch the condensation on the walls. People said that you could be killed but it never bothered me, as far as I was concerned it was just good fun. I used to watch the searchlights and the bombs and mam used to grab me and drag me back in, telling me that I'd get hit with shrapnel.

*Closeted in a stuffy classroom all day, imprisoned in the
claustrophobic bomb shelter at night, Don found physical re-
lease hard to come by. At dinner times and in the after-school
hours he spent most of his time exploring the Irwell and its
banks.*

One of the teachers told us that there used to be fish in the
river and I couldn't see why there weren't any now. Then we
found some and proved him wrong. Little tiddlers in some
pools round an island. We used to explore down the river.
There was a big log just off the bank and when the river was
high it was covered. We played hours on that thing at 'King of
the Castle'. Jumping on and off, scrapping, getting filthy and
wet. You couldn't see the street from around the log and suddenly some kid'd shout, 'Hey, your mam's coming,' and there'd
be panic, charging round after your shoes and socks. If my
mother had found out that I swam in the Irwell she'd'd've killed
me. Farther up the river there was a weir. That was a place
that frightened hell out of me because there was a lot of water
coming over and the river was wide at that point and you
couldn't hear yourself speak. The water was churned up white
and the kids said there were knives under it. I was scared stiff
of the place. Later, there was one kid drowned there.

*All the various features on that stretch of the Irwell were
given names; one such was the 'Roman Bridge'. This was a
huge, brick buttress in the middle of the river – all that was left
of the bridge – with an inviting layer of grass on the top of it.
The water swirled around the base of the buttress and it was
irresistible to the adventurous spirit.*

I'd think : 'Can I do this?' And if I thought I could – even
going all out – I'd do it. But there were certain things that I just
wouldn't attempt and swimming out and trying to climb that
buttress was one of 'em. An expedition along the river bank
was a risky undertaking. If the guards patrolling the War Department dump didn't get you, there were the golfers on the
coures which backed right onto the river's edge. One of the

holes was on top of a hill. They had to play up a slope to the
green. We used to wait on top and pinch the balls as they
landed. Beyond the golf course were allotments guarded by
dogs and zealous amateur gardeners: then came the Red Rock,
a sandstone outcrop on which I did my first bit of climbing – a
traverse high over deep black sludge. The real snag in the in-
vestigation of the Irwell, however, was neither the interference
of the adult world nor the natural hazards. The thing was that
we were on new territory and there was always marauding
bands of Arabs – other kids, other gangs. I remember once
being stopped by a gang. I was dead small and very scared.

'What you think you're doing?' a big lad said.

'Why?' I asked, right back in his teeth.

'Because I want to know,' he said.

I thought: 'Well, I'm going to get clobbered anyway so I
might as well get in first.' So I cracked the lad and laid him flat.
That did it: I was in with that gang, the lad I flattened was
their chief tough.

*Don as an adult barely reaches a height of five feet three
inches; as a child he was incredibly tiny but incommensurately
pugnacious. Whenever violence seemed inevitable, Don's first
instinct was, and still is, to meet it before it met him. The
Irwell bank and the streets of Salford were the assault courses
which prepared Don for the battles with rock, ice and un-
appeasable elements he was later to face time and again.*

*Over the years, Don has had to prove himself to people who
have failed to reconcile his legendary toughness with his size
and physique. Even in childhood, his tenacity and courage
were bywords in an area where these qualities were essential if
a child was to survive to maturity.*

There was a mate of mine called Jimmy. I remember calling
for him once. I was just going to knock at the door when it
flew open and Jim came hurtling out. Right behind him, wing-
ing through the air as if it had come out of a gun, came an axe.
They were a hard lot that family.

Shortly after I moved up to the Junior department at school, a new headmaster arrived. He proceeded to behave like a new broom. He'd been a professional footballer and he could hit all right. Jimmy was the first to get it. He came out like he'd had the third degree. I was the next and I was nearly dying of fright. Swish! My eyes nearly came out of my head. I shot off to the toilet, flushed it and stuck my hands in the water – this was the magic cure. He really hurt me.

The bombing in Manchester had forced the authorities to resort to evacuation. The Germans were doing a thorough job and the bombs fell night after night on houses, factories and docks alike. To Don, it was still an exciting time. Bits of shrapnel were swopped for comics and stamps, and once the family emerged from the Anderson shelter on a dull, wet morning to find a land mine had dropped a hundred and fifty yards from the house and had blown the front door out. To his bewilderment, Don was taken away from all this entertainment, and with a pillow-case containing his essentials, he was separated from his mates and left the familiar streets for unknown territory. He arrived in Crawshawbooth, a tiny industrial settlement high on the moors between Rawtenstall and Burnley. Substantially-built stone cottages squat grimly against the windswept hills, which are filmed with the grime and soot dropped by the smoke from the Rossendale Valley.

My mother went with me. I'd no idea where we were going or in what direction. I remember meeting a woman in her house.

'I've been expecting you,' she said. 'I've got some of your favourite lemon cheese for you.'

'How d'you know I like lemon cheese?' I asked her.

'A little bird told me,' she said.

A little bird? I thought: 'This is a real set-up, this. How could a little bird have told her?' My mother went and that was it. I thought she'd gone for good.

For six months, Don had his first taste of being away from home. Naturally withdrawn and taciturn, he kept himself very much to himself and waited for things to get back to normal.

*When the blitz on Manchester abated, Don went thankfully
back to his old haunts and his confederates. Things got back
into the old routine: playing truant from school and sneaking
in at various cinemas, then having to run hell-for-leather to
buy the bread and milk before his mother got home for tea;
Saturday mornings spent down on the river with his best
friend, Bill Holland.*

*On the opposite bank of the Irwell was Manchester Race-
course, a green, inviting place which seemed like another
world to Don. The bank itself, rarely visited by anyone, was
infested with rats. Don and Bill Holland, full of adventure tales
about big-game hunting, decided to declare war against the
rats, so they armed themselves with catapults.*

These things were works of art. I always took great care
about mine, it had to be just right. We'd walk down some of
the streets that had privet hedges in the gardens and look for
good, forked branches. Mine had to be a perfect 'Y' and when I
found one, I'd go back when it was dark and hack some poor
bloke's hedge to bits to get at it. These catapults were lethal
weapons. We pinched the rubber from a garage that had a pile
of tyre inner-tubes dumped in the yard. It had to be red rubber,
black was no good. We made the slings out of bits of leather
and bound the whole thing up with shiny, copper wire. We
rarely used stones as ammunition, instead we swiped a packing
case full of big ballbearings from the W.D. dump and used
them. We plastered that racecourse bank with these things. I
don't remember ever hitting any rats but it was great to see the
sand and mud fly up just as if we'd been firing guns. One
favourite trick was when people left milk bottles standing on
window-ledges. The big thing was to break the bottle without
breaking the window. I could do this easily.

*Bill Holland, Ian Thompson, Jack Wedge, Eric Worthington:
these were the boys who played a part in shaping Don's future.
Their adventures were often hair-raisingly dangerous, and
always just that little bit more violent than the normal boyish*

escapades. *By the age of eleven, Don could look after himself in situations which were enough to cause the average boy to faint clean away:*

At home, his mother did her best to keep Don under some sort of control. Mrs Whillans had her hands full with work, running the house and looking after young Edna. Don was very often left to his own devices, and this helped to mould him into a self-reliant, independent character.

At school, his lack of interest in the business of learning didn't endear him to his teachers.

They used to say: 'Right, Whillans, you sit there where I can see you.' Right on the front row because I was as dumb as hell, they could get nothing through to me. I didn't like girls sitting next to me – especially if it was one I didn't fancy much. They used to make girls sit next to boys to cut out any possible trouble. I was extremely lucky with one or two of the girls I got. One was very bright, she came from a very scruffy home but she was always top of the class. She helped me a lot. On the other hand, I once had to put up with a girl who was thicker than I was. What made it worse was that she had a kind of crush on me. I used to pray for a change-round because I wasn't making any progress in my lessons at all.

It was not through any lack of intelligence that Don found school-life hard going. Don disliked being forced to learn about subjects which he felt could not be turned to practical use. Subjects which stirred his imagination – geography for instance – or subjects that enabled him to express himself physically, he loved and excelled at.

At eleven years of age, he left Lower Kersal Juniors and moved cautiously into the unfamiliar, larger world of the secondary school.

Broughton Modern School was a new red-brick barracks with all the latest educational equipment. Don was not enthusiastic at first; the place was large, most of the kids were strangers and he had to walk two miles to get there. Later he regarded getting there and back as far more worthwhile than being in school.

One feature of the school did interest him however – the
gymnasium. For the first time in his life, he found a place
where he was positively encouraged to behave according to his
natural instincts.

I couldn't wait for the gym lessons, but of course there were
only about three a week; it'd've suited me if there'd only been
three other lessons and we'd had all the rest of the time in the
gym. Funnily enough, the gym teacher was a woman, Yates,
her name was. She was a good gymnast herself and she really
encouraged me. Then she left and I was very disappointed
when her replacement turned out to be a chap who wasn't
interested in the gymnastic side of it; he was mad-keen on ball
games which held no interest for me. I started skipping his
lessons and after he'd been there about a year, he stopped me
one day in the corridor.

'What's your name?' he asked me.

'Whillans.'

'What form are you in?'

'2A,' I said.

He thought for a minute: '2A? Well, I take them and I've
never seen you.'

'No you haven't,' I said.

He appeared slightly puzzled by this and he asked me if I
was excused P.T. I told him that I didn't go to his lessons
because he didn't get any of the apparatus out. He was taken
aback and wasn't sure what to do. After a short pause he said
that he'd get the stuff out next time, so I replied that I'd go
along in that case. I went for a week or two but he showed no
interest so I just stopped going again and that was it. He never
bothered me again and I never bothered him.

Don did find an outlet for this enthusiasm, however. The
school ran several clubs, one of which was a Gymnastic Club
and there Don could measure his abilities against those of the
older boys. Speaking about Don several years later, the head-
master of the school, Mr Quinn, said that Don was the best
gymnast the school had ever had. The one regret in Don's life is

*that nobody told him that if he worked at two or three 'boring'
subjects, he could become a physical education teacher. But if
that had happened, the world might not have known Whillans
the climber.*

*During the early years of secondary school, Don's life out-
side the school gates carried on in much the same way as it had
before. The excursions of Don and the gang went a little
farther afield and without doubt their adventures moved steadily nearer the line which divides youthful exuberance from
juvenile delinquency. Most of the boys with whom Don asso-
ciated were older than he was and their attraction for him lay
in their desire to do things with a spice of danger in them.
Many of the escapades called for physical resource and courage, these Don enjoyed; others – the petty thievery and out-
right vandalism – Don avoided. It was during these early teen-
age years that the direction of Don's future life lay in the
balance. The war was still going strong and Don's father was
still away; Don was in need of mature masculine influence.*

I did have to depend on myself a lot because my mother was
so busy that I couldn't run to her at every situation which
arose. Maybe this having to make decisions when I was young
and sticking by them made me aggressive and stubborn which
a lot of people accuse me of being – and they're quite right too.
I can be so bloody stubborn that nothing'll shift me. I tend to
look at a lot of things on both sides and then suddenly I make
up my mind and I just won't budge. I was just the same when I
was young, I'd say to a kid – a big lad because I never fought
anybody my size, working on the principle that they were too
little to hit – 'Yeah, I'll fight you.' Then later on in the afternoon I'd wish I hadn't said it but I wouldn't back out. Once I'd
said it, it stood.

*It seems strange, knowing Don's dislike for organized
activity of any kind, that it was the most famous organization
of them all which took him off the streets and out of potential
trouble: he joined the Boy Scouts. Don, Bill Holland and one or*

*two other friends joined the 'Oates' Troop in Salford. The
scoutmaster was a middle-aged, dumpy little man called 'Pop'
Travis and he and Don hit it off straight away. The senior
members of the Troop made a big impression on Don.*

I used to look at the lads with all the little badges on their
arms. There was one of them who was a King's Scout and to
me that bloke was untouchable. I couldn't see how anybody
could be so clever as to get all those badges. I struggled like hell
for four years and I never got more than my Tenderfoot. I
don't know why, I should've waltzed the job. Four years and
never got past that scruffy thing.

*Just about this time, Don remembered how his father, years
before, had taken him for outings in the Peak District of
Derbyshire. For the first time, the magnet of the hills began to
draw him. With half a crown – a week's spending money – in
his pocket, Don began to visit Derbyshire each Sunday. The
return bus fare from Mosley Street Bus Station in Manchester
to Hayfield was exactly two and sixpence. Don would get off
the bus and walk. Every Sunday, in every kind of weather, he
walked. His routes had to begin and end in Hayfield because of
the bus and so he wandered in ever-widening circles, encom-
passing more and more of Derbyshire.*

I thought nothing of thirty miles a day when I'd been at it a
bit. I knew the moors like the back of my hand; I knew every
funny-shaped tuft of grass, I knew every stretch of peat, I
knew every grough, every feature in a radius of twenty miles
from Hayfield. I remember a particular instance on Kinder
Scout. It was blowing a blizzard, snow lay on the ground and it
was coming down thickly. I was walking up a gully, head
down, battling away, when I came across a bloke sitting on a
rock. I couldn't believe my eyes, he had shorts on. Shorts in
that weather! He was a scoutmaster and he'd got lost. He
looked at me – a little nipper – and I said: 'Where d'you want
to go?' So he told me and I said: 'Okay, follow me.' We set off

across Kinder. He must have been desperate, to follow a kid. Anyhow, I got him there. I'll bet he never told anybody what had happened.

Then someone at school formed a Ramblers' Club so I decided to join and give it a try. I didn't manage to stick it for long. They didn't walk, they went for afternoon strolls.

The teacher who ran the Ramblers' Club found it difficult to believe that Don covered so much ground on his lonely outings in the Peak District. Eventually, he admitted defeat when he realized that Don knew Derbyshire better than he did. The Ramblers' Club could not have been sorry to see this diminutive example of perpetual motion leave them to resume his solitary wanderings. It was on one of his Sunday expeditions that Don met a like-soul, a man who wanted nothing more than to be away from the smoke and noise of civilization. They formed a strange partnership.

I suppose he'd be in his forties. He was just an ordinary bloke to look at, nothing special. He told me he was an ex-Army officer, I remember. We just sort of met one Sunday and walked together. From then on, I used to meet him at Mosley Street and we'd be together all day. We used to go to places that had nice names – Ashbourne, Hartington, Bullithorne, Winberry Rocks. We never talked much except about the particular walk. I suppose this went on every week for nearly a couple of years and then one Sunday he said: 'I won't be coming next week, I'm getting married.' This was a big shock to me. I looked at him and said: 'When? Next Sunday?' And he said: 'No, Saturday.' So I said: 'Can you not come out Sunday then?' I didn't understand what all this was about, I couldn't imagine the partnership breaking up. He said he didn't think he could and so I asked him about the week after and he said that he probably wouldn't be able to make it. I only saw him once after that and that was a while later, when I was climbing. He was on the bus going back to the city. I said, 'Howdo', and he asked me if I was climbing now and I said I was. That fella pushed me pretty hard on those walks. There were many times when I'd really to work at the last eight or nine miles. Funnily enough, I never knew his name.

Just before I started these marathon hikes, I'd had my first taste of the Lake District when I went with the Scouts for a week's camp in Ennerdale. For me, this was a dream come true.

Coming home from Derbyshire on Sundays, I'd always looked at the older lads with ropes and rucksacks and nailed boots – I could forget a bloke's face but I never forgot his boots – and I'd thought: 'I'll bet they've been in the Lakes hundreds of times.'

During the long winter nights I'd get maps and spend hours looking at them. It was a great moment when I first got there. The hills were so big, everything seemed to be on a grand scale. I remember one day when most of the boys had gone off somewhere and there was just Bill Holland and myself left in the camp. I suggested that we nip off and go up one of the fells. We knew we'd get in bother if the rest got back before us and found that we'd left camp but, anyway, off we went. We set out for a nearby crag and we climbed the stream bed; I suppose we must've gone about 1,500 feet. We found a little bone dice right at the top of the stream and I couldn't fathom out how that'd got there because I was so sure that no other human being had ever been up there.

Don was now at school-leaving age; there was the problem of work to be considered. His father, Tom Willans, had held the same job in the same firm since starting work as a lad. He had, like Don has, certain tenets which he would stand by in the face of any opposition. One of his convictions was that once a man took a job, then that was his job for life; no chopping and changing, no aimless wanderings from firm to firm. He wanted Don to learn a trade but Don himself had not the faintest idea what he wanted to do.

I'd gathered that some jobs – architecture, accountancy, the law – were out of my reach. I didn't mind this; what I wanted, if I had to have a job, was something that wasn't tied to a desk or even to one place. I wanted something where I could use my hands and where I could get out into the air. My mother suggested being a joiner but I didn't fancy spending my life making window frames as my mother said they did, so I ruled that out right away. Then I went to see a plumbing firm – 'Plumbers and Heat Engineers', that's how they described themselves – and I got a job there.

Leaving school was no sad wrench for Don. He left and that was all there was to it. No doubt a lot of the staff were relieved to see him go, and no doubt the residents along Don's route from home to school breathed a sigh of relief when they noticed how peaceful things had suddenly become; but they weren't any more relieved than Don was. School was over.

2 | Early Climbs

I enjoyed the work although it was very dirty. We used to clean and repair boilers and I'd get black from head to foot. It was enormously hard work and I was always dog-tired at night. For years they couldn't wake me in a morning. I never realized until I left that firm, when I was about twenty, that the only reason I couldn't get up in the morning was that I was absolutely buggered. I used to work a lot with an old fella at the firm – he was about seventy – and so every time we got a really tough job, I had to pull all the stops out. They used to get these boilers, some of them very big, and there'd be only the two of us manhandling an eight-hundredweight section down a flight of stairs. It provided me with one hell of a training.

For 46½ hours a week and for 7½d an hour. The firm refused to allow Don time off to spend one day a week at a technical college and so he had to give up three nights each week to get any training at all. It does depend though on a definition of the word 'training'. If Don, on leaving school, had set out purposefully to develop muscle, stamina and persistence, he could not have found a better method of doing it. Years of hauling and heaving cast-iron pipes and boilers, of performing feats of physical strength far beyond the normal capabilities of a lad of his age and size, fitted him perfectly for the arduous climbing exploits that he was later to do.

The firm used to do really big jobs – central heating systems, hot and cold water supply right through new schools – and the only transport they had was an old hand-cart. Can you imagine pushing a bloody hand-cart from the middle of Manchester out to Sale loaded with stuff ? I remember once when another apprentice and myself – they had two apprentices sometimes but none of the others ever stayed long, I was the only one who never left and that was because of my dad and his ideas about changing jobs – anyway, me and this lad were pushing a great loaded hand-cart up Whitworth Street. We just got in the middle of a set of traffic lights when suddenly we heard a sound – like somebody running a stick along some railings. Before we'd chance to wonder what it was, the old hand-cart lurched over. Every single spoke in the wheel had come out. It dumped the whole lot of the junk right in the centre of the lights.

Don now had a new walking companion, a lad who was to accompany him through a vital stage in his development. The lad's name was Eric Worthington, who had attended the same schools and been in the same classes but had always remained on the periphery of Don's life. Eric was a tall, strongly-made boy with gentle ways and an amiable disposition. His dependability and steadiness were to stand Don in good stead over the next two years.

The meeting which began the partnership occurred by pure chance near the Snake Inn. Don, out on one of his solitary hikes, met Eric, who was with a mixed party from the local youth club. After a short conversation with Don, Eric deserted the youth club and the partnership began.

Every weekend they tramped the Derbyshire moors. Now that they were both working, the money situation had improved – Don had ten shillings a week to spend. They would leave the dusty city on Saturday afternoon, walk until it was dark, sleep wherever it was dry and then have the whole of Sunday free to continue their explorations.

Month after month, winter and summer alike, Don and Eric roamed over the green and grey Derbyshire countryside. Sometimes, passing Laddow Rocks and Yellowslacks, they would stop and watch foolhardy young men clinging for dear life on the gritstone outcrops.

We kept seeing these characters bedecked with ropes up on the edges. We'd look at them and I'd say : 'Well, this is bloody crazy. What if you fall off and hurt yourself? And anyway, you can see the view without going up them pieces of rock.' I wasn't with the idea of it at all. Then, right out of the blue, Eric said : 'Hey, why don't we have a go?' I wasn't keen at all but Eric was a good mate and if he wanted to have a go, then fair enough, I'd back him up. So I suggested that we'd better get a rope and do the thing properly. We had no idea what length or thickness we wanted. As far as I could see, a rope was a rope and it had to be reasonably thick so that you could get hold of it. I was very cautious, so we got a rope so thick and heavy that you could hardly pull the thing. You could've almost tied the Queen Mary up with it except that it was only 80 feet long.

Shining Clough, although not marked on the Ordnance Survey map, is quite an impressive outcrop of gritstone reaching a maximum height of about eighty-five feet. In parts it is extremely steep and many climbers consider it the finest edge in the Laddow area.

One fine, warm Sunday in April 1950, Don and Eric arrived at Shining Clough to do a climb. They knew nothing of climbing technique on different grades of climb and were ignorant of the fact that a number of routes had already been established on the rock. They had brought their rope, in front of them was a nice lump of rock, the sun was high and warm, everything was set.

I looked up a crack in the rock and I said to Eric : 'I wonder if anybody climbs up there?' It looked a bit frightening. I asked him if he wanted to give it a go and he said okay. As it was Eric who wanted to climb, I tied him on first and off he went. One thing worried me − I couldn't fathom out what use the rope was just tied around his waist. Anyhow, he got up onto a big ledge about halfway up. It seemed a hell of a way and he'd had a real struggle to get there. I thought : 'Well, this isn't much cop. There's no fun in this.' After he had got up, I went up after him and we both stood there on the ledge. I looked round and said: 'Where are we supposed to go from here?' I gave the wall a good going-over and saw some good holds but it looked overhanging to me. I was thinking that we couldn't chicken out of the first climb we'd ever done, so I thought I'd have a go. I set off up a slightly overhanging wall. The holds were good but they rattled a bit. I figured out that they were slotted together like a jigsaw, so I bashed on. I can remember getting to the top and thinking: 'Thank Christ for that.' That was the first climb I did and I never did another one quite like it. I said to Eric afterwards: 'Look, the next time we do one, one of us will go to the top and chuck the rope down and the other one'll tie on it. Then we'll do anything you want.'

This first climb by Don and Eric was, in fact, a route known as Atherton Brothers and is graded severe, which in those days was quite something. That same balmy afternoon, Don did several more climbs just for the sheer fun of it; already the bug was beginning to bite. Rock climbs are graded according to a standard scale of difficulty. Starting at Easy – a simple scramble – the grades are as follows: Moderate, Difficult, Very Difficult, Severe, Very Severe, Extremely Severe and Exceptionally Severe. Two qualifying adjectives, Mild and Hard, are also used in describing climbs of the Severe and Very Severe grades. The two top grades are fairly recent additions to the scale. The highest grade used when Don started climbing was Very Severe.

A few weeks later, Don and Eric were back at Shining Clough with another lad, Reg Gray. Reg had done a little climbing in the Lake District and was keen to have a go on gritstone.

We were walking along the bottom of the edge when Reg pointed to a crack in the rock.

'They'd climb things like that in the Lake District,' he said.

I looked at him and then I looked at this crack.

'Get away, would they hell as like. They can't climb things like that,' I said.

'Oh yes,' he said, 'that'd be Very Severe.'

'Aye, I don't doubt it,' I said sarcastically.

Two weeks later I came back and led the thing. It's called Phoenix.

A few weeks later, at Dovestones, Eric and Don met a group of climbers from Oldham. Don was impressed: these lads wore anoraks, their ropes were coiled neatly round their shoulders, their boots were heavily decorated with nails. Les Wright, Eric Flint, Jack Gill, Dick White, Fred Ashton, Stan Clough, Spike, Ted, Leo; few of these lads had ever seen a picture of an Alp, none had climbed one, yet they were part of the first wave of new climbers who were to revolutionize the sport in Great Britain. They accepted Don and Eric into the group, taught them some of the uses of the rope, introduced them to slings and belay techniques. Climbing with them in an exuberant spirit of competition, Don really began to discover his abilities as a climber. Before meeting the Oldham lads, Don's clashes with the rock had been more like exercises in gymnastics than genuine climbs; now, with a little technical knowledge in his head, Don started to serve his apprenticeship as a mountaineer.

In July, Don, Eric, and Leo set off for the Isle of Skye to experience the big hills for the first time.

We hitch-hiked up because we'd hardly any money even though this was our annual holiday. We'd read all about Skye and the gabbro rock that was supposed to be impossible to fall off. It didn't take us long to find out that a few tough climbs on gritstone were no preparation for long climbs in bad weather, or that hiking round Kinder Scout couldn't compare with being lost in a mist up on the Skye ridges. The first thing we did was a Very Difficult route on Sron na Ciche and it nearly put an end to us all. The climb finishes up in an open gully and we were just about in this when a tremendous cloudburst turned it into a veritable waterfall. We bashed on as quick as we could to the top. On the last pitch I got completely stuck. I unfastened myself from the rope and shouted down to Eric to try farther to my right. Then that silly bugger got himself stuck. This only left Leo who thought it was all a great joke. He came off his belay and climbed straight up through the torrent of water to the top. Then he dropped a rope to Eric and got him up and then did the same for me. It wasn't a very good start to the holiday and in fact it wasn't a good holiday for climbing. We climbed the Inaccessible Pinnacle which was a real disappointment because it was so easy. We were still very green, still impressed by names.

In Skye, Don learnt another vital technique of climbing: he learnt that there was an easier way of descending than climbing down.

We'd no idea about this job. We'd done a few very dodgy climbing descents before we caught on to the rappel bit. My first big rappel was off the top of the Inaccessible Pinnacle. There was a big, fat bloke sat on top when I got up and I said : 'Hey, how d'you get down off here?' And he said : 'Oh, you rappel down.' I looked round and I said : 'What off?' You didn't use pitons then, it was a big crime. He said : 'Off that block there.' I saw that there was a fair-sized block but there was no crack at the back of it. I said : 'What? Off that bloody thing? Is it safe?' He laughed and said : ' 'Course it's safe. I'll hold it on for you.' I wasn't too sure about this, it looked risky to me so I said : 'Have other people gone off this?' 'What,' he said, 'ten thousand people have rappelled off that.' Anyhow I took his word for it because I thought he had superior knowledge and I didn't want to appear a coward. I know now that people like that who think they're a bit of an authority on things can cause really nasty accidents.

The holiday in Skye helped Don to realize that if he was going to take mountains seriously, he still had an awful lot to learn. He and Eric returned to gritstone, having pushed back the horizon a little way.

There was a couple of local hard men from Oldham who were older than us. All the lads were a bit scared of them and you'd almost to ask their permission if you wanted to do a climb. Not long after we got back from Skye, I was up in the Lakes at Gimmer Crag and I saw Ted, one of the hard men, performing on the rock. Well, he put the fear of God in me. I thought he was going to fall off any minute he looked so shaky, but that only made me think that the climb was so hard; I didn't realize that it was because he was no bloody good. He came to me afterwards and I'd got this new nylon rope – they'd only just come out then.

'What've you bought that rubbish for?' he said, pointing at the rope.

I said: 'Well, it's a stronger rope and it doesn't absorb . . .'

'It's rubbish,' he said, 'I've had this rope for fourteen years – fourteen years.'

I know now what a load of tripe he was talking but I didn't then. About two weeks later, Eric and I were at Ravenstones, near Oldham. There's a pinnacle there called the Trinnacle, a strange-looking outcrop which seen from the front seems to have only two pinnacles split by a cleft, but in fact has a third which only appears when the outcrop is viewed from the rear. The two main pinnacles rise from a grassy slope to a height of about thirty feet and both were graded Severe. Who should be at the Trinnacle but Ted the hard man. As soon as he saw me he came across.

'Oh, it's you again is it? I suppose you think you can bloody well climb wi' that rope?'

I was a bit puzzled by this because I couldn't see what he was getting at at all.

'I don't think anything of the sort,' I said. 'A rope's a rope and that's it.'

He wasn't satisfied with this and he kept pushing it and then finally out it came.

'I'll see how bloody good you are,' he said, 'we'll have a race. You climb up the left face and I'll climb the right and we'll see who gets to the top first.'

Well, I couldn't see much point in this, but I thought: 'Bugger you, I'll not back down.' I asked him if we were going to use top ropes and he turned to his mate and laughed.

'Oh get that, he wants top ropes now – well, go on then if you're frightened of falling off,' he said.

So we started off on top ropes. About three-quarters of the way up, he fell off and his fourteen-year-old rope snapped like a carrot. He went rocketing down, hit the grass, and went bowling away down the hill. 'So much for your bloody fourteen-year-old rope,' I thought.

This incident gave me food for thought : if Ted's rope had gone on Gimmer a fortnight before, he wouldn't't've picked himself up in one piece as he did that afternoon. I thought he was a real climber until then; it made me realize that you couldn't judge climbers by the size of their mouths.

In September of 1950 Don fell ill. Sickness, dizziness and blackouts combined to make the doctor diagnose stomach ulcers. Don went into hospital where he was kept under observation. Examinations failed to verify the doctor's diagnosis and so Don went home thinking that he had been cured of a bad stomach. In reality, this was the first attack of what could have put an end to Don's climbing career – vertigo.

This short spell as an invalid did not deter Don from climbing; he was out on gritstone two days after coming out of hospital. He and Eric decided to spend Christmas in Snowdonia with the idea of doing a few climbs on snow and ice. They caught the 10.20 train from Manchester to Bangor on Friday, two days before Christmas Day.

This was the climbers' train. Dozens and dozens of young men, old men and boys, wearing a ragbag of clothing and carrying equipment and rucksacks of all shapes and sizes, journeyed through the night to arrive at Bangor at 2.30 in the morning. Parked in a siding at Bangor Station was a battered, dusty carriage; this was the early morning train to Bethesda, jumping-off place for the mountains. Joining the rush for places in the Bethesda carriage, Don thought he spotted a half-empty compartment.

I shouted to Eric who was charging about among the mob. Suddenly a big bloke leaned out of the window right over me.

'It's full up in here,' he said.

'What you talking about?' I replied, 'there's bags of room.'

He shoved his face down to mine. 'It's full up,' he said.

I thought: 'Hello, this looks like a good start to the holiday – a punch-up before we've even got there.' Just then, Eric grabbed hold of me and dragged me to a compartment with plenty of room in it. I spent the rest of the night on the luggage rack and I didn't wake up until we got to Bethesda. It was a long walk up to the Williams' Barn where we were going to be based, so Eric and I and a few others got a taxi. We passed two climbers walking up the road.

'Hey, that's Joe Brown and Slim Sorrell,' somebody said.

I looked through the back window of the taxi.

'Which one's Brown?' I asked.

'The little one.'

I remember feeling a bit tickled about this because the big one was the bloke I was going to thump the night before.

So there it was. On the road leading ultimately to Clogwyn du'r Arddu, Don had his first sight of Joe Brown. Neither of them could have dreamed that together they would form the greatest partnership in the history of British climbing.

On Sunday, 22 April 1951, Eric and Don were strolling leisurely along the top of the lower tier at the Roaches, a grit-stone edge six miles from Leek in Staffordshire. The day was hot and still; over the ridge on the grouse moor, skylarks rose from the wiry grass and sang their songs against the melting blue. It was much too hot for climbing.

Eric stopped suddenly and pulled at Don's arm.

'Hey, get that,' he said excitedly.

Don followed the line of Eric's pointing finger. His eyes opened wide with amazement. There, perched on the nose of a big buttress and some 70 feet above the ground, was a motionless figure. From this hair-raising stance, his rope dropped like a plumbline beneath him.

I couldn't believe this at first. The climber didn't seem to be in any trouble at all. He was inspecting a wide crack above him which went through two bulges. I knew he was doing something new so we decided to stick around and watch for a bit. There was a group of lads and girls sprawled about on the grass so we went down and sat near them. I didn't know it then but one of the girls was Audrey; I married her seven years later but I didn't take a bit of notice of her that day. I asked one of the lads who the climber was. 'Joe Brown,' he said, looking at me as if I was crazy. Now I'd been hearing about Brown on and off for ages, but I'd only ever seen him that once at Christmas. Young Fred Ashton, who climbed anywhere with anybody, had mentioned his name a few times. 'That bloody Brown,' he'd say with deep disgust, 'he did a thing last Sunday, nobody could follow him.'

From the foot of the buttress, I could weigh up how he had reached the tip of the overhang. He'd gone up by way of a crack running directly up to the bottom of the huge flake. Just then, his second began to climb and I saw that it was Slim Sorrell, Joe's right-hand man. Joe had reached the top of the climb and was on a good ledge. Slim went up and then started having trouble near the overhang. Actually he didn't look like he was trying very hard – he probably just wanted to sunbathe. He made a few half-hearted moves and then he shouted up to Joe.

'I'm going down, Joe,' he said and started to climb down.

When he'd got down, a couple of the lads asked him if it was hard and he said it was. I thought: 'I wouldn't mind having a try at that.' Before I could have second thoughts, I got to my feet and shouted up to Joe.

'Hey, can I have a go?'

'Aye, if you like,' came the reply.

I tied on and started off. I didn't take long to do the overhang and this made me sure that Slim hadn't been trying. One step to the left and I stood on the tip of the big overhang. I looked up the wide crack running through the two bulges. Joe's head appeared against the sky. I knew that he hadn't gone up the crack but found a way round it. We stared at each other.

'Are you coming up there?' he asked.

'Aye,' I replied.

It wasn't too hard and a few minutes later I was standing with him on the ledge. He looked at me curiously.

'How did you do it?' he asked.

'Fist jams,' I said. 'And it's a bit tough on th' hands.'

Thus ended the Valkyrie Direct Start, the first of many climbs to bear the Brown–Whillans stamp. Sitting on the warm grit, laughter and chatter floating up to them from the party below and with the distant view shimmering in the heat, they talked through the standard rituals of new friends.

I wouldn't've recognized him from my first sight of him from the taxi. He was slightly taller than me but of a very similar build. He had long, black hair which he pushed back all the time and his face was almost oriental – flattish and oval with wide-set grey-brown eyes which slanted slightly. He had a mouth packed with big, white teeth and he grinned a hell of a lot. While he smoked a fag, I looked at his hands and noticed the wide palms and thick fingers covered with hard skin and deep cracks – that's what comes with mucking about with cement and plaster. He was definitely not a bank clerk.

Joe Brown is a legend in his own time: the idol of thousands of young enthusiasts and one of the few climbers known by name to the public. But the Joe Brown of 1951 was a far cry from the television star and successful businessman that he was later to become. When this encounter with Don took place, Joe had just completed his National Service. Before serving his two years in the army, Joe had gathered several years' climbing experience in Derbyshire and Wales; when Don met him he was already – although unknown to himself – in the van of British climbing. He made the most difficult climbs look ridiculously easy and time and again, on gritstone and in Wales, it was the same story: 'The rest of the party were unable to follow.' This was not because Joe's climbing companions were hopeless climbers – the opposite was true – but because Joe himself was so brilliant.

Joe climbed because his instincts told him that this was what he was meant to do. From the very beginning he possessed a powerful affinity with the rock; Joe on a climb was a man completely in his natural element. Like Don, Joe learnt slowly and thoroughly; never stretching himself beyond the limits of his capabilities but always expanding these limits. He climbed with the same enthusiasm which was to become the raison d'être *of the future Rock and Ice Club.*

We sat on the ledge, chatting, while Joe smoked incessantly. I asked him about Cloggy and he said he thought I'd find the climbs pretty easy. I was a bit doubtful about this myself but anyhow that's what he thought. Eric and I and a few of the lads were going down to have a look at Cloggy that Whitsuntide. After we'd been sitting there for a while we got up and wandered over to the upper tier, the main crag at the Roaches. Joe pointed to a huge overhang, about 70 feet up, which runs most of the way across the face. Right in the middle of it, there was a green-streaked crack – a bit indefinite but a crack all the same.

'Ever thought of having a try at that?' he asked me.

'I've thought of it but that's as far as I've got,' I said.

We grinned at each other. I think we'd finished weighing each other up by then. We did that thing later; Joe christened it the Sloth because I spent so long hanging upside down on it.

A month later, Don was at the foot of Cloggy – Clogwyn du'r Arddu. Don has never been a romantic as far as mountains are concerned but Cloggy always has a strange effect on climbers and Don fell under the spell from the first.

This most famous cliff lies about one mile from the summit of Snowdon itself. It stands, gaunt and formidable, frowning over the dark waters of Llyn du'r Arddu which lap fretfully on the rocks at its feet. Familiarity brings tolerance but never contempt to Cloggy. Even on a mellow summer day, the sun does nothing to soften the fierce aspect of the slabs and buttresses nor does it ease the frightening angles of the cracks,

clefts and chimneys. Cloggy remains the most ominous sight in
Snowdonia.

When Don first set eyes on Cloggy, it was late evening on
Whit Saturday.

Eric and I had decided to hitch it separately – we thought we
stood more chance like that. We arranged to meet at the foot
of Cloggy and I had half of the gear – the tent and so on, and
he had the other half, which included the food. We weren't all
that well organized. Eventually I got to Llanberis and I set off
up the Snowdon track. I stopped at the Halfway House and had
a cup of tea. There was a few lads in there, talking about what
they'd just done. They'd climbed Great Slab on the West Buttress. I was impressed with this because I'd heard of this climb
and I knew it was pretty hard. One of these lads was really
quite small and even younger than I was. I reckoned that if he
could climb on Cloggy, then so could I. Anyhow, they pushed
off and I thought I'd better get going as well, because time was
getting on and I didn't fancy wandering about in darkness. I
went on up the track and then on to Maer du'r Arddu and I
stopped there ages just looking across at Cloggy. It was a forbidding sight and one that I'll never forget. Everything was still
and quiet, the wind had dropped, the sky was in that middle
stage between light and dark. Cloggy stood there, huge and
solid. This was it. I don't remember exactly what I thought as I
looked at it, but I know I was impressed – and excited Eric
eventually arrived and we pitched the tent under the shadow
of the great cliff, gazing at the wet, uninviting rock. We had no
guide book, all we had to go on was a couple of photographs
that I could remember seeing. We stopped at the bottom of the
East Buttress and I looked at a crack.

'Hey,' I said to Eric, 'that's in Kirkus's book. That's Curving
Crack. Let's do that.'

I uncoiled the rope and got started up the crack. I laybacked
most of the way up the first pitch and then brought Eric up. He
had to jam, I remember. Anyway, we were standing on a good
ledge on top of the pillar. I wondered where we went from

there, because I couldn't see any hope up the wall. I decided to swing round the corner and see what was there. I swung round and got into a vee-chimney running right up the face; I knew that that must be the route. The rest of the climb wasn't too difficult – I'd done things much harder technically – but even though it was a fine day, the rock was a bit greasy and there was a hell of a lot of grass about. Nevertheless, I'd done a famous climb on a famous cliff and I was pleased about it.

We climbed down via the East Terrace and enjoyed a deserved rest. As we were lounging about, talking happily, three more of the boys arrived – Eric Flint, Jack Gill and Stan Clough. We told them what we had done and, full of enthusiasm, decided to try something else.

We walked over to a crack which was absolutely dripping with slime, moss and all kinds of stuff.

'Oh, this is the Direct Start, let's have a go at this, it's harder than the ordinary start.' Stan said.

So I set off. I was saturated before I got to the top. I'd heard a lot about the Faith and Friction slab and one of the other main features of the climb, the Overhang. When I got to the Faith and Friction, I thought I'd reached the end of the earth. It was quiet on Cloggy, there was only us on it and I'd lost sight of the other lads below me. It was quite an impressive moment. I finally made my move up the slab and it was a bit scary but really enjoyable. That was actually the crux of the climb for me because I've never had too much trouble with overhangs and this one on Cloggy didn't bother me at all. The thing was, I'd led another route.

After another night at the foot of Cloggy, Don and Eric made their way back to Llanberis to start the journey home, for Don was due in at work the following morning. In the Llanberis Pass, behind the Cromlech Stone, they saw two figures sprawled out in the sun. Don recognized one of the two as Vin Ridgway.

Vin was one of the real characters who was knocking about at that time. He was an ex-paratrooper and when he worked he was a steel erector. He had a big, flowing moustache and very white, even teeth and an infectious grin. In the climbing world in general Vin had a bit of a dubious reputation: he used pitons. There was a kind of gentleman's agreement in climbing then that pitons were strictly for the continentals. If you put a piton in a climb, it was the equivalent of shooting a fox. But Vin was no gentleman so he didn't recognize any agreement. Vin walked around quite openly with enough ironmongery on him to sink a ship. When we saw him that day, he was belting holes in the turf with a piton hammer – this only confirmed the suspicions to me. I'd heard tales of him doing a climb called Ivy Sepulchre on Dinas Cromlech and spending hours sitting in slings. They said later that when he did Narrow Slab on Cloggy he used six pitons and I wouldn't have put it past him either. Vin formed the Cromlech Club but he soon fell out with them because they were too strait-laced for him. Sadly, Vin came to a weird end: he fell out of the loft in his own home and broke his neck.

Sooner or later, every serious climber sees, or takes part in, tragedy on the mountains.

To the layman, the attitude of climbers towards death can seem callous and almost indifferent; they waste few words in mourning and they make no eulogies. The fraternity of climbers is large but closely knit; the news of a brother-climber's death is automatically received with sadness, but then come the questions: how? why? If the cause of the death was an act of hostility by nature, the news is greeted with characteristic stoicism; if the dead climber virtually committed suicide through his own carelessness or bad judgement, the news will receive only a cold-eyed shrug. But in either case, the climbing world will pay its only tribute – it will go on climbing.

This is not to say that climbers are indifferent to injury and death, for most of them will risk their own lives to rescue someone in distress on the mountains. It is just that climbers learn to live with the idea of sudden death. Their philosophy

towards death can be summed up in a few short words: moun-
tains give, mountains take.

Don's first taste of tragedy on a mountain was not long in
coming. In July of 1951, Eric and he decided to spend their
annual holiday in Glencoe, the centre of Scottish rock climb-
ing. Remembering their miserable visit to Skye, they reckoned
that the weather could not possibly be against them for two
years in succession. They were wrong: out of the fourteen
days they spent in Glencoe, only two were fine.

After a week of watching the rain and mist sweeping
Buachaille Etive Mor, they lost patience and decided to climb
in spite of the wretched conditions. The route they chose was
on the Rannoch Wall, a climb called Agag's Groove, graded
Very Difficult.

We got soaked through ploughing across the heather to the
foot of the Wall. Water was cascading down the rock which
looked really uninviting. The Groove was obvious, it was well
scratched and there was a little stream running down the back
of it. I went up all right and reached the crux of the climb. I
was standing, working out my moves, when suddenly, without
any good reason, I became very apprehensive. The mist had
thickened and I could hear the thunder rumbling away over
Rannoch Moor. This may have helped, I don't know, but I was
certainly scared and I shouted to Eric to watch the rope. He
seemed a bit surprised at this and asked me if it was hard. I
replied that the rock was greasy but the holds were big; I didn't
mention my feeling of fear. I wanted nothing more than to get
off the Wall.

I went like a bat out of hell up the rest of the climb and I
began to feel a bit better by the time we were both at the top
and sheltering from the rain under an overhang. We'd heard
voices from below us when we were on the final pitch and it
wasn't long before a lad joined us on the top. He was a Scottish
student and he said that he'd done the climb four or five times
before. I noticed his boots and stared in disbelief; they were
barely hanging on his feet, full of holes and gashes. We talked

until his second arrived and then they set off down the track along Curved Ridge.

'Hey, come on,' grumbled Eric, 'there's no point in stopping here. We can follow them down.'

I was still feeling jittery and I couldn't fathom out why but I reckoned that we were out of danger, we'd only to walk down the track. We started off in the thick mist.

'What was that?' Eric stopped dead.

We both listened, straining our ears. Then a voice floated up to us.

'Help.'

We looked at each other. I could hardly swallow and Eric had gone white.

'Come on,' I said, 'it's them lads.'

We scrambled down the track helter-skelter and reached the two lads on a kind of ledge. The one with the tatty boots was lying on the ground moaning. The other lad looked shattered; he pointed up about 50 feet to where the track skirted sharply round a small outcrop.

'He slipped off there,' he said. 'We were running down.'

I looked at the student's boots again. I don't suppose he would have saved himself even with good boots on, but even so he might have had a chance. It was just one of those daft accidents that should never have happened. A steep path is not made for running down. The lad was in a bad way, that was for sure, there was blood coming out of his ears. I left Eric with the unlucky pair and went off as fast as I could to get a rescue party. We were just setting off back when Eric arrived with the news that we were too late, the lad had died.

Fear is a feeling with which most climbers are familiar. Throughout the years, Don can recall a series of situations on a wide variety of climbs when fear has either frozen him into temporary inactivity or caused him to move as if his life was hanging by a thread. But there have been other instances of a different kind; times when apprehension and a feeling of dread have become so strong in him that he has refused to move until the sensations have passed away. This incident on the Rannoch Wall was the first.

It fined up for a couple of days during the second week and myself and a lad called Robert did the hardest thing I'd done in Scotland up to that time. There's a route on the Buachaille called the Gallows and then it had only been climbed once and that was by the Scottish climber, John Cunningham. It had never been repeated because, according to the story, Cunningham's second had pulled a vital hold off.

This Robert character – who was an extraordinary bloke, he practically lived on lentils – and I set off to do it on a great day. It was fine and warm and the rock was dry. I wasn't too bothered if Robert could not follow me on the climb, because it was only very short – one pitch in fact.

I was so pleased to be on good, dry rock that even the technical difficulties of the route did not seem to be too bad. As it turned out – maybe he'd eaten too many lentils – Robert couldn't manage the traverse to start the climb, so I did it on my own. As I was scrambling down, I noticed some lads shouting to me from the bottom of the mountainside. We went down to see what the fuss was about.

'Do you know what you've just done?' one of them asked me.

'Yeah,' I replied, 'the Gallows.'

He looked at his companions and then back at me.

'Did you not find it – a bit hard?' he asked.

'Fairly hard – not too bad,' I replied, faintly puzzled by his attitude.

'Come on down and have some tea,' another one of the lads said.

This was my first meeting with the Creagh Dhu Club from Glasgow. They had a big reputation then; they were really hard, those boys. They had a battered old hut at the foot of the Buachaille which they called 'Jacksonville'. We went down with them and drank some of their tea. They've always been good mates of mine since then.

The fortnight in Glencoe was the last time that Don and Eric climbed together, for Eric had decided to join the Royal Air Force.

The break-up of one partnership heralded the start of another. Through the next fifteen years of Don's life, the name of his new partner and friend runs like a thread – Joe Brown.

3 | The Rock and Ice Club

I met Fred Ashton in Albert Square – some time in August, I think it was. We got talking and he asked me why I didn't go down to Levenshulme Skating Rink on Wednesday nights. I didn't know anything about this, but apparently Joe and some of the other lads had a meet there to discuss what they were going to do the following weekend. So on the next Wednesday night I trotted off to Levenshulme. I really used to enjoy myself there. It wasn't quite the tame sort of thing you might expect. We used to get on the rink and form a big whip – blokes flew off in all directions. Eventually it got too rough for the management – we were smashing the place up bit by bit and all the people who wanted to learn to skate weren't getting any chance at all, so we moved across the road to the Palais. Wednesday night there was called 'bob' night – it only cost a shilling to go in but in spite of that, it got to be a bit of a bind. There was only a couple of the lads ever danced but we all had to get reasonably dressed up, ties and things, to get in. So we packed that place in. We finally ended up in the Y.M.C.A. in the centre of town – none of us were members of course.

Socializing at Levenshulme Skating Rink, the Palais and the Y.M.C.A. was a far cry from Geoffrey Winthrop Young's elegant evenings at Pen-y-Pass. A new élite of the climbing world, with very different backgrounds, was emerging.

The group was held together at first simply by an abundance of enthusiasm and talent. Individually, the members were firm friends; rivalry among them was rare. They climbed together because they liked climbing together; they spurred each other on to ever harder and more challenging feats. The fantastically

high standards they set each other ensured that the group remained exclusive.

On the 26 September 1951, the loose structure of the group
crystallized and the Rock and Ice Club came into being. The
original members were: Nat Allen, Doug Belshaw, Joe Brown,
Don Chapman, Don Cowan, Jack Gill, Pete Greenall, Ray
Greenall, Ron Moseley, Merrick (Slim) Sorrell, Dick White and
Don Whillans.

Nat Allen from Derby, then as now, was a great climber
whose selflessness and utter reliability in all situations made
him the solid backbone of the Rock and Ice. It was Nat who
insisted on recording the exciting new routes put out by Joe
and Don; it was Nat who fostered the community spirit among
the Rock and Ice members and helped keep rivalry and com-
petitiveness down to a minimum.

Nat's never had the credit he deserves. I've done all sorts of
things with him, in all sorts of conditions, and he's never failed.
He could get a laugh out of a bloody camel, that fella – and
believe me, if you don't know what it's like to laugh till your
ribs ache when you're piss-wet through, half-frozen, hungry
and dog-tired, you haven't lived.

Doug Belshaw was a quiet, rather shy man who climbed
extremely well when in the mood. Likeable and easy going,
Doug was a counter balance to the forceful Ron Moseley.

Moseley, who has a list of first ascents rivalling those of Don
and Joe, was perhaps the dominating force in the Rock and Ice
He was the keenest competitor in the Club, and his persistence
in attacking a particular climb is legendary. His ascent of the
famous Kilnsey Main Overhang was an effort of Homeric pro-
portion which dragged on for weeks and almost bored his
variety of seconds to death.

The Greenall brothers, Pete and Ray, were opposites in tem-
perament. Pete was a happy-go-lucky, hit-or-miss type. He
climbed well when he wanted to but was never as dedicated to
the sport as was his elder brother. Ray, now an instructor at
Plas-y-Brenin, was even then the ideal teacher.

Before Don came along, Joe Brown's most consistent partner was Slim Sorrell, a tall, powerful man who, after a lengthy period in the police force, is now on the permanent staff at the Ullswater Outward Bound School. Slim was a hard, uncompromising sort of man and has always been a climber of the top quality.

Jack Gill, Pete and Dick White were all climbers of above average ability who were perhaps a little unlucky in having to climb in the shadows of Joe and Don. The remaining two original members were the other Dons – Cowan and Chapman. Cowan, careful and skilled, had stretched his climbing experience beyond British hills and was a regular visitor to the Alps. Don Chapman was another first-class climber; a man of few words who typified the Rock and Ice approach.

The constitution of the Club was simple and straightforward; the meetings were almost completely informal and paper work was kept to a minimum. To most of its members, the Rock and Ice existed in name only; the climbing and socializing went on exactly as before.

*   *   *

High above the Llanberis Pass, Dinas Cromlech glowers across at Crib Goch. Long ago, the sculptor-god who used the rocks of Snowdonia for his experimental work drove a chisel with a blade shaped like angle iron into Dinas Cromlech. The result was the most eye-catching rock feature in Wales – Cenotaph Corner. The Corner rises vertically for 120 feet and its containing walls are smooth and sheer. From immediately below, Cenotaph Corner is an awe-inspiring sight.

Joe had made one attempt on the Corner itself earlier in the year. The attempt had nearly ended in disaster when Joe, almost at the top, had dropped his peg hammer. Joe's second, Wilf White, was hit a glancing blow on the head by the hammer and Joe had had to climb back down to see what damage had been done.

Joe suggested the crack on the right wall of the Corner. I didn't understand why he wanted to do the crack when the

Corner itself hadn't been done, especially as he'd already almost climbed the Corner not long before. It seemed to me to be
doing things the wrong way round. Anyway, I was game because it looked a hell of a route to me. Peter Harding was
supposed to have had a look at it and had his doubts. The first
time we tried it, we just did the first pitch and left it because it
started to rain cats and dogs. But that first pitch was scary
enough. Joe led it and he had a really hard time. Eventually, he
tied on to a holly tree and I climbed up to him.

'About seventy foot I reckon,' he said.

'Aye.' I wasn't really listening, I was weighing up the chances
on the second pitch. That was obviously going to be the crux.

We rappelled off the holly tree and on the way down I
pulled a loose block out from just above a small overhang
where Joe had had his struggle. That'd make it easier for the
next time.

The second attempt was much different. It was a great day
and what's more we had a photographer with us – Ray
Greenall, who was nursing a burnt hand which he'd got from
holding me when I'd fallen off Peapod at Curbar in Derbyshire.

Joe got up the first pitch without much trouble this time and
then it was my turn. The second pitch was just a crack up a
vertical, smooth wall. I started off up this and Joe kept saying:
'Get some more runners on, get some more runners on.' He was
stood in slings tied on to the holly tree. I got a few on and
there were holds on the wall as well as in the crack; not too
solid but as long as I'd got a good jam, I didn't mind standing
on them. Inch by inch, I got to the crux move where the holds
on the wall seemed to disappear. I had a nose around for a
while, reaching up and trying out possible holds. I saw one
which was a sort of pocket. It looked really good, so I reached
up and grabbed it. It turned out to be full of razor-sharp little
flakes which cut my fingers pretty badly but I knew that this
was the key. After a time, I launched up and made my move
and that was that. We knew we'd virtually cracked it because
Joe had seen the last pitch from the Corner and he knew it'd
go.

It was a terrific climb, and I really enjoyed it. Technically I don't think it was of the top quality but it was certainly exposed and scary. We called it Cemetery Gates after a bus we saw in Chester. What with that, Ivy Sepulchre and Cenotaph Corner, if you planted some poppies on Dinas Cromlech, it'd be like a garden of remembrance.

Two weeks later, the whole gang was in Wales preparing for a mass assault on Cloggy. Just off the Llanberis – Snowdon track, there is a derelict, battered, stone farm-house and barn which bears the name of Bryn Cork. In 1951, in spite of the holes in the roof and the lack of doors and windows, this became the weekend residence of the Rock and Ice.

Some of the happiest moments of my life were at Bryn Cork. I used to love waking up in the morning; the sun streaming through the holes in the roof, the sound of church bells floating up from Llanberis. I used to get out of my sleeping bag and pick my way between snoring bodies. I'd sit outside and just drink in the air and the view. Then there'd be the sounds and smells of frying sausage and bacon and us sitting there, laughing and talking, drinking tea and knowing that within an hour we'd be on Cloggy. Sometimes Nat didn't arrive till early Sunday morning. He'd've come on the train to Caernarvon, arrived there in the middle of the night and then walked from Caernarvon to Bryn Cork. He'd come in quietly, creep over to Joe, who was always a sound sleeper, and grab him. 'Now then, youth,' he'd say. Joe had an old sleeping bag with holes all over it. He'd get out of it looking just like a half-plucked chicken, feathers and down all over him. And then there was Slim who was always one of the early risers. He'd come over to you and grab a handful of your cheek and hiss in your ear, 'C'mon, get out.' They were great times, those.

That particular weekend, a vendetta was due to take place: Joe, this time with Don, was going to resume his battle with a climb which had the rare distinction of being one from which Joe had fallen. The route is now known by the beautiful name of Vember – in honour of Vember Williams, daughter of Mrs

Williams, who owned the Halfway House on the Snowdon track.

Joe's first attempt at Vember had taken place in foul weather; the second attempt had perfect conditions.

Joe was going to lead all the way because, really, it was his climb. We got up the first pitch okay and I got myself solidly belayed on a tiny ledge. I'd heard enough about how Joe had come off the last time, and I was making sure that if he capurtled off this time, I wasn't going with him. Joe set off up the crack and reached the point where he'd fallen before. Then he seemed to be having some bother. I gave him time and then I called up to him.

'What's it like?'

There was a long pause and then: 'Oh, it's all right.'

'Is it dry?'

'Yeah, it's dry, it's okay.'

But I got the impression that it was really pretty hard. Anyway he kept moving up a bit at a time. Eventually I heard him give a little grunt.

'I'm about three foot off the ledge now,' he called.

I didn't say anything because I could see he was definitely gripped up, which was unusual for Joe. Slowly, he made the moves up to the ledge. When he'd got there, he turned round and called down, his voice shaking.

'Well, I'm up but I thought I was off there.'

Afterwards, he said that he'd had psychological trouble when he'd reached the place where he'd fallen off before. You see, he'd never really fallen off anything else. I think he thought at the time that it was the hardest climb he'd ever done. I'd been watching him very carefully, and I thought that if it was as hard as he had made it look then I was going to have to climb well to get up it at all. So I just forgot about everything except the rock in front and that was it; I found it reasonable.

Joe was a bit surprised at this.

'D'you think you could lead it?' he asked me.

'Aye.'

I suppose I'd no psychological problems with it, that was the difference.

Don and Joe then walked round Llyn du'r Arddu and lay in the sunshine watching the crag and listening to Slim singing as he attacked Narrow Slab.

'You know,' said Joe, wrinkling his eyes up from the drifting smoke of his cigarette, 'I'd sooner just sit looking at Cloggy than climb on a lot of the other crags.'

In later years, Joe was to climb successfully both in the Alps and the Himalayas: he was to partner Don on their amazing series of Alpine ascents; he was to be on the first ascent of the magnificent Mustagh Tower in the Karakoram range and the redoubtable Kanchenjunga. But Joe was at his best in the mountains of Wales and, in particular, on Cloggy. Nothing in Snowdonia could defeat him for long and 1951 marked the beginning of the most remarkable succession of climbs in the history of British climbing. The ascents of Cemetery Gates and Vember were confirmation that in Don, Joe had found the perfect partner – capable of doing anything that Joe himself could do and even, when it was necessary, of doing that little extra. It is futile to argue about which of the two was – or is – the better climber; both were so much superior to anyone else that no one is in a position to pass an opinion.

Christmas came round and the Rock and Ice decided to spend it in Bryn Cork.

There was one room in the farm-house which was only small but really good. You could have a nice fire in it and be dead cosy. The walls didn't reach the roof, but the fire made up for that. This Christmas, though, dozens of people arrived so we had to go into the barn where we lit a big, roaring fire. It didn't stop raining and sleeting the whole time we were there and everything was awash. There were great holes in the roof and water streamed in. Some bloke'd spend hours drying his gear in front of the fire, then he'd hang it up on a line stretched from wall to wall and it'd get soaked through again in thirty seconds flat.

That year, I think everybody had something burnt because the only dry place was near the fire. The rest of the place was just a quagmire – sleeping bags inches thick with mud, pieces of clothing trampled into a black mess. None of the lads drank then but we all gave serious thought to getting out and going down to the pub even though it was a couple of miles away and we'd have got yet another soaking. It was too bad to climb, so all we could do was just go out and do a few walks.

After one of these walks we came back without a dry stitch between us. I put my boots down near the fire and Ray Greenall – who always looked after the fire – built it up into a great bonfire. Suddenly I remembered my boots. I looked and there they were – just the tops of them sticking out of the blaze. I whipped them out but I was too late. The toes had gone completely and the uppers were just sort of gluey. Well, we'd burnt holes in anoraks, scarves and shirts before, but this brought the house down.

By the time Boxing Day arrived, we were all sick and fed up of messing about and Joe and I decided to have a walk up to Cloggy. It was still howling a gale and sleet was slashing down. Joe had an idea that he wanted to have a look at a thing called the Black Cleft. It was never on from the start because the Black Cleft is a natural sluice – it takes about three weeks of fine weather for it to begin to dry up. Trudging up to Cloggy was a nightmare; every time I put my feet down, mud and slush squelched in through the non-existent toes of my boots and out again at the back. When we got into the snowline it was even worse, because my toes were just sticking out. There was another thing too: at some point, I'd ripped my pants from top to bottom on the inside leg.

We got to the foot of the Cleft and looked up. Water was just pouring down. I started up and got about ten feet up the crack and then I'd had enough. It wasn't much fun jamming my bare toes into hard, cold, wet rock and in any case water was flushing down my sleeves and running out the bottom of one trouser leg and out of the tear at the top of the other leg. Talk about brass monkeys. Joe had had enough by this time too, his nose was like a road-mender's lamp and all his fags were damp. So we set off back to Bryn Cork. And that was the end of 1951. It went out like a wet firework.

One of the visitors to Bryn Cork that Christmas was a slim, fair-haired girl called Audrey Whittall. Don had noticed her before on occasional weekends in Derbyshire, and he remembered that she had been in the audience which had watched the ascent of Vember. He had been introduced to her and her companions – Don Roscoe, Eric Price and Alan Taylor – after the climb. She seemed to him to possess all the attributes necessary to make a climber's girl; she was attractive, she had a strong sense of humour, she obviously didn't mind living rough and she was no mean climber herself.

There were, however, several problems. Firstly, some of the lads were talking of having a fortnight in the Alps in the summer and Don was determined to go with them. This meant saving every penny even to the extent of sacrificing the regular weekends in Wales. Secondly, he was attending night-school classes three nights each week which severely limited the time available for social life. Thirdly, Audrey was already courting.

Minor drawbacks such as these did not hold Don back for long; by the month of May he had saved almost enough to get him to the Alps and back, decided to discontinue night-school and had taken Audrey to the cinema and up Longland's on Cloggy.

I was getting a bit fed up of listening, every Wednesday night, to what the lads'd been doing on Cloggy the weekend before. So finally, I shoved the Alps to the back of my mind and went down there to join in the fun. Joe collared me straight away and we went to have another look at the Black Cleft. This time, the weather was great but the Cleft was still pouring with water. It was an epic climb.

Looking up the Cleft, you could see great clumps of what looked like watercress growing out of all the crannies and the rock was just shining green with slime right the way up. All in all, it wasn't very appetizing. However, there was one consolation – I had toes in my boots this time. It might have been better if I hadn't had because I had on a new pair of vibrams, which are just about the worst thing you can have on your feet on wet, greasy rock.

I fought my way up the first pitch, chucking stuff down by the bucketful. I reached one place where I couldn't see any holds at all on the wall so I had to dig the crack out. What made it awkward was that there was only one place where I could get a jam in.

I was hanging from this jam for well over an hour with cold water running over my hand. For about a month after that, I could stick a pin into my thumb – it was completely dead. I was digging away in the grass and weed – just like the Hanging Gardens of Babylon it was – for ages and ages. Finally I got about eighty feet up and decided I'd had enough and it was about time Joe had a go. I belayed on a very tiny ledge and he came up.

I was shivering and soaked through, it was a bloody miserable place that. Joe was wearing nails which were better than my vibrams but still clumsy enough. His pitch was exactly the same as mine had been – packed with vegetation. The trouble was, you couldn't pull this stuff straight out; it was so full of water and mud that it just fell apart. Half of it he was throwing clear but the other half was landing on top of me. After about half an hour of this, I was being pushed off my stance with all the stuff piling up between me and the rock.

Up above, Joe had got into a chimney and he seemed to be making good progress up it. I saw him step to the left and then he was out on a stance that he'd used on another route called the Boulder which runs into the Black Cleft. I was glad to see him get there because after my long slog up the first pitch and then having to stand there being pelted with all the muck and everything, I was just about frozen. He shouted for me to come up and I fairly whipped up the pitch – it was difficult but I was so relieved to get moving again that I didn't take too much notice of it.

When I got to Joe, he was worrying about the next pitch, which had been a struggle when he did it on the Boulder route. It had been dry then but now it was running with water. He knew that I'd have a real struggle to get up it in my vibrams so he wanted to lead it.

'Have I to go on then?' he asked.

'Why?' I was standing there, shivering.

'Well, I know how I did it last time and I've got nails on.'

I looked at him and nodded, 'Get stuffed.'

I was really fed up with the climb and I wasn't going to stand about on another ledge while he fooled about and got off before me. So I shot off up it and got to the overhang which had been the problem before. I was standing there, weighing up the moves.

'You climb it facing left,' I heard Joe say from below.

I had another look. 'You what?'

'Left.'

'That's a bit of an arse-about-face way of doing it, isn't it?' I called back to him.

He shrugged. 'Please yourself.'

I faced right and I was up in a flash. Apparently he'd had a desperate struggle there before – tearing the hood off his anorak in the process.

So that was the Black Cleft. Joe had a strange attitude to that climb: he didn't think it was really hard; he used to say that given dry conditions it'd be a piece of cake. He repeated it again later with Ron Moseley in desperate conditions and wearing a Pakamac. He almost drowned at the overhang because of the torrent pouring over it. When they'd finished the climb, I grinned at Joe.

'Taking all in, that bloody thing's hard, mate,' I said. 'You can say what you want.'

The month of June 1952 was remarkable for two reasons: the weather was beautiful, and six new routes went up on Cloggy. Joe was involved in five of the new climbs, Don in two. But straight out of the blue, the Rock and Ice's almost propri-

*etary right to put out all the new routes on Cloggy was inter-
rupted by the singular appearance of a climber from Cambridge University Mountaineering Club, John Streetly. Streetly
took the opportunity of the absence of Don and company from
Cloggy to put out a new route called Bloody Slab.*

This was one of the biggest bombshells I can remember. I
was walking down Regent Road in Salford with Sher Wiseman
who'd been to Wales the previous weekend, and he casually
mentioned that a bloke had done the Red Slab on Cloggy. I
stopped dead in my tracks.

'He what?' I said to him. 'Who?'

'Oh, some bloke from Cambridge.'

I thought: 'Bloody hell, where's he come from?' There
wasn't anybody around doing things like that. I hadn't a lot of
interest in the Red Slab myself, it'd been Joe's – he'd talked
about it on and off for ages. Peculiar really, because he'd had
doubts about whether it'd go and yet he never did anything
about it; usually he didn't talk about things, he just went and
did them. I suppose one reason could've been the White Slab
which was the really big thing then – he'd been bashing at that
for a very long time.

'Oh, aye?' I said. 'What's his name?'

'I think it's Streetly or something,' he said. 'He's over here on
holiday.'

I thought: 'Well, this fella's either a real tearaway or else it
was a piece of cake.'

'Yeah, he did the Black Cleft and Cemetery Gates and a
couple of others as well,' said Sher.

'Oh, well,' I said, 'in that case I don't believe it.'

He was quite hurt. 'There's other buggers climbing besides
you, you know,' he said.

'Aye, I know,' I said, 'but there's not so many climbing like
that.'

As it turned out, Streetly *was* one of them like that. I did the
third ascent of the Bloody Slab, as Streetly called it, a year later
and it was bloody hard. John Streetly was a brilliant climber.

4 | Chamonix

Don's determination to go to the Alps reasserted itself as the time for his annual holiday approached. He confined his climbing to the local edges, regretfully leaving Joe to continue his devastating progress in Snowdonia with a series of new partners. The weekly meets in the Y.M.C.A. were agony for Don; he would listen in envious silence as the lads related the previous weekend's achievements. It seemed to Don that in exchange for one brief fortnight in the Alps, he was sacrificing all the major problems in Wales. One particularly bitter pill to swallow was handed to him by Ray Greenall.

'Guess what the lad did last weekend,' said Ray, grinning over his coffee.

'Who?' asked Don, knowing full-well what the answer would be.

'Joe,' replied Ray.

'Go on, what?'

'Cenotaph Corner,' said Ray, 'and he only used two pegs did the lad.'

'It'd better be worth it in th'Alps,' was Don's only comment.

Although the original plan had been for all the lads to take the trip to the Alps, only Don, Nat, Don Chapman and Don Cowan actually made it. From Don's point of view, this small party was ideal. Nat had four seasons of Alpine experience behind him and in the Alps, as everywhere else, he was the ideal companion – skilled, knowledgeable and cheerful. Don Chapman, two years older than Don, was strong and enthusiastic but relatively inexperienced in Alpine conditions. The

doyen of the party was Don Cowan from Sheweld. Cowan,
even in 1952, had had half-a-dozen seasons in the Alps; he knew
all the wrinkles and his thoroughness in planning and execut-
ing climbs made him a model leader. Cowan's wary approach
to life in general, and climbing in particular, resulted in his
refusal to recognize his own ability as a climber and yet there
have been very few more accomplished British Alpinists. The
advantages for Don in having his first Alpine experiences in
such company were enormous: he learnt more from this one
short visit than most climbers learn in several seasons.

Because Don Cowan worked on the railways and could get
cheap travel, we went by train – the first and last time for me.
I couldn't stand all the pushing and shoving and charging about
from one station to another. I was a bit disappointed by my
first sight of France, I think I expected to see Mont Blanc from
the boat. But as we neared Chamonix I began to regain my
enthusiasm. I was very impressed when, eventually, I did see
Mont Blanc; there seemed to be an incredible amount of snow
on it and I was surprised at the size of the glaciers flowing
from the summit. I began to get an idea of the sheer size of the
Alps.

'Hey, you could lose Cloggy down one of the cracks in that
thing,' I said, pointing at Mont Blanc.

Nat laughed. 'You ain't seen nothing yet, youth,' he said.

The granite spires of the Chamonix Aiguilles came into view.
I couldn't wait to get at them, but of course, I didn't know how
to begin.

We were staying at the Chalet Violay in Chamonix, where
for two bob a night you shared a communal bed of straw, a
primitive toilet and shower and the use of large tables on
which you cooked your own food on your own Primus. All the
British climbers used to stay there; it was like an old boys'
reunion when Don Cowan and Nat walked in.

I had one or two weird ideas about what I wanted to climb.
My first objective was the famous Walker Spur on the Grandes
Jorasses.

Don Cowan came into the bedroom where I was unpacking my gear.

'MacNaught Davis has done the traverse of the Aiguille du Diable,' he said, his eyes shining with British pride.

'Is it hard?' I asked.

'What? I'll say – and long,' he replied.

'Anything like the Walker?' I asked.

Don looked at Nat who pursed his lips and frowned.

'No, nowt like that,' said Nat and shook his head at my ignorance.

I was beginning to get the message. Apparently there were routes you talked about doing – like the Aiguille du Diable – and routes you didn't mention – like the Walker.

'Listen, youth,' said Nat, 'I was in the Requin Hut on the Mer de Glace when Heckmair was caught in a storm on the Walker. I don't know what it was like up there, but I do know that the snow was getting through two sets of shutters into the Hut.'

I shut up. I'd done some hard rock climbing with these lads and if the very mention of a climb filled them with horror then it was obvious that things couldn't be taken lightly.

'Come on, let's go and get some grub and get you fixed up with some boots,' Nat said, bringing the discussion to an end.

I needed some boots and crampons so we went to our Mecca – Snell's Sports shop. Snell Junior was serving in the shop and we exchanged a greeting which was to become very familiar over the years.

'How long you stay in Chamonix?' he asked in his slow English.

He always had a soft spot for the poverty-stricken British climbers and he never did them down. Even so, when we left the shop, my worldly wealth had been reduced from twenty pounds to nine.

Don Cowan bought the grub in double-quick time. I was willing to leave the shopping to the others because I couldn't speak a word of French and anyway, as dozens of climbers would agree, I'm bone-idle when it comes to things like that.

Later in the holiday, I wished that I had helped in buying the food because Nat and Don had a mania for spaghetti which in those days I couldn't stand.

Our first climb was going to be the Ryan-Lockmatter Route on the Aiguille du Plan, which had the reputation of being a good rock climb of a reasonably easy standard. The lads decided to improve their fitness by walking up to the Montenvers Hotel which stands some 3000 feet above Chamonix. From there we would go on to the Envers des Aiguilles Hut just below the Envers de Blaitière Glacier.

I'd heard all about this long slog up through the tall pine trees to Montenvers and I wasn't at all keen to do it – especially in my new boots. We left the Biolay in blazing sunshine, loaded down with spaghetti. The pine woods effectively mask the scenery practically all the way up to Montenvers and I spent the whole trek cursing Don, Chapman, Nat, the Alps, my new boots and wishing like hell that I was back on Cloggy, sitting soaked to the skin while Joe battled on above me. The weather worsened as we neared Montenvers and a sudden shower of rain sent us scurrying to a woodcutter's hut which Nat and Don knew from previous experience. The rain settled in and we spent a cold night without blankets in the hut.

The following morning the weather had cleared and the sun was shining out of a cloudless sky. We pressed on up to the Hotel. Loads of tourists poured out of the railway station at Montenvers and flocked like sheep down to the ice caves in the glacier. I remember standing against the wall outside the station, mouth and eyes wide open.

'What the bloody hell is that?' I managed at last.

A tremendous, black, snow-plastered wall towered above the surrounding peaks, completely dwarfing them.

'What?' said Cowan, trying to appear disinterested.

I pointed, unable to say anything else.

'Oh that,' said Don, 'that's the Grandes Jorasses.'

'Is it?' I swallowed.

'Yeah. See the highest bit?'

I nodded.

'That's Pointe Walker. Follow it down vertically and you've got the Walker Spur,' Don said casually.

'Christ,' I muttered.

We stayed for ages, looking across first at the slender orange and brown spire of the Dru and then at the great bulk of the Grandes Jorasses. Then I had one of those moments when suddenly everything becomes clear to you. I knew that from that moment on I was going to dedicate my life to climbing the hardest and most inaccessible mountains in the world; Derbyshire, the Lakes, Snowdonia, Scotland, suddenly assumed their true perspective. I looked across at the Grandes Jorasses and I saw the Himalayas and the Andes.

'Hey, come on!'

Cowan was shoving me in the back. I turned and followed him down the path to the glacier. My life had just been settled.

This first visit to the Alps was a great success. Don Cowan and Nat Allen proved to be the sort of expert teachers all Alpine novices should have; never allowing Don to attempt too much, insisting that he climbed below his limits yet introducing him to as many of the varied Alpine techniques and conditions as their limited time allowed. Towards the end of the holiday, a strange and touching encounter took place.

Don Cowan and I had decided to have a go at the Route Major on the Italian side of Mont Blanc. This route, the first ascent of which had been made by F. S. Smythe and T. Graham Brown in 1928, was one of Cowan's greatest ambitions. It's a classic mixed route, one of the best in the Alps, and I was looking forward to it. We slogged up to the Col de la Fourche bivouac hut which was perched in a really dodgy position on the Frontier ridge. The door in the hut opens outwards and if somebody opened it as you were standing on the doorstep admiring the view, you'd find yourself in bits and pieces 500 feet below on the glacier. The hut hadn't been finished then but it was very cosy. Unfortunately, the weather turned bad when we got to the hut and it started snowing; it looked like our long trudge had been for nothing.

As we were brewing up, we heard voices outside the hut and then the door opened and in came a young Italian guide with an old man. We were surprised to see such an old bloke up there and we were just going to make some sort of comment when he spoke – in English.

'Nice weather we're having,' he said with a grin.

We nodded and grinned back.

'This is Mister T. Graham Brown,' the Italian said, proud as Punch.

We looked at the pair of them in amazement. The old chap nodded.

'Yes, I'm afraid it is,' he said.

'Mister Brown is seventy today,' explained the Italian. 'We have come to do the Old Brenva route to celebrate. Last week we did the Matterhorn.'

Hell, I thought, going to the highest point in Europe at seventy, there's hope for me yet.

It snowed heavily during the night and both pairs abandoned their plans and descended but it had been a worthwhile night in the Col de la Fourche hut: a meeting of the past and the future of British climbing. Graham Brown, the old tiger, still with a few teeth left and Don, the young tiger, busily cutting his fangs.

5 | The Girdle Traverse

His first visit to the Alps convinced Don that if he wanted to become a 'big hill' man, he first had to improve his technique in the use of artificial aids. He persuaded some of the lads to climb in Dovedale in Derbyshire and Gordale and Malham in Yorkshire where the limestone had always been regarded as bad rock.

We started putting up new routes in Dovedale and on Gordale Scar. We used stacks of pegs, we knocked pegs in just for the sake of knocking them in. People since then have gone along and done those climbs practically free. I don't know whether they thought we'd needed to use the bloody pegs or not but as far as we were concerned, it was the fun of knocking them in and trusting yourself to them, that's all. From then on, we nearly always went on limestone in the winter. We'd find a nice sheltered overhang – often with a cave – and there we'd knock pegs in to our hearts' content while the snow and wind howled past and the lads sat in the cave brewing up, smoking and holding the rope. I don't think any of us got really competent at artificial climbing this way but at least the practice got us over the psychological barrier of not using pitons on British rock. Very few of the climbs we did on limestone were ever recorded. When the guide books came out for places like Stoney Middleton, I noticed several first ascents of routes that we'd done years before.

The Rock and Ice held their first annual dinner at the Pen-y-Gwryd in October 1952 when their guest speaker was Scotty Dwyer, one of the few professional guides then operating in

England and Wales. The occasion was rather spoilt for Don by
an unfortunate accident which occurred while returning to
Llanberis from the Pen-y-Gwryd.

I'd just got my first motor-bike. I couldn't afford to have one
really but I was missing out on so much by not getting to
Wales every weekend. After a lot of argument and persuasion,
I finally got my father to put up the money to buy me a bike –
it was a 350 Royal Enfield and it cost him about £120. I started
to pay him back week by week. It took so long to repay that
I'd got through half a dozen bikes before I'd paid it all back.

I hadn't got a pillion on the bike so Audrey used to sit on the
mudguard. When we came out from the Pen-y-Gwryd it was
raining heavily. We were going up towards the top of the Pass
and we got to a place nicknamed the 'Magnetic Wall'. God
knows how many blokes had piled into it. Right on the bend,
my goggles got so rained up I couldn't see a thing. I lifted my
hand to push them up on to my forehead and before I knew
where I was, I was into the wall. I clattered along it, bumping
round the bend. I bounced off the wall three times in all. The
first time, Audrey flew up into the air but somehow held on;
the second time she damn near pulled me off and the third time
she catapulted off into the darkness somewhere. Everything
that stuck out on the left side of the bike was wiped off and the
front wheel was like an egg. My left leg was a bit shredded as
well. I finally stopped the bike and staggered off to look for
Audrey. The headlight of another bike coming after us picked
out a bundle in the middle of the road – it was Audrey. The
bike stopped and I saw that it was Scotty Dwyer on his combination. Audrey was sitting there, a gaping hole in her knee and
tears streaming down her face. What a mess, I thought, I
crunch my bike and Audrey in one go. Anyhow, Scotty whipped
her off to Bangor Hospital and I left my bike against the wall
and got a lift with Don Cowan down to Llanberis. We went
back for the bike the following day and I managed to ride it
back home, God knows how. I didn't dare go round to Audrey's
place for a while after that. Her dad was never very keen on

me anyway and I reckoned he must've taken a pretty dim view of my smashing his daughter against a wall.

The end of the year saw one of the most sensational climbs ever done on gritstone. It was confirmation that a new generation was lifting the standard of rock climbing to an undreamed-of level. The venue was the Roaches where the partnership between Don and Joe had begun.

We were lying in the barn where we used to sleep. Great place that, situated nicely between the Roaches and Hen Cloud, it cost a tanner a night or something. They kept cows in the bottom half of the barn and we slept in the top so it was always nice and warm. We'd been out on the crags once that day but it'd started snowing and we'd come back to the barn.

'Hey, how about having a go at the big overhang?' Joe Brown said suddenly.

I looked at him like he was daft.

'What now? In this?' The snow was drifting down quite thickly.

'Why not? It'll be dry under the overhang,' he said.

I thought about it for a bit while he lay there waiting. I knew very well that it would be dry under the overhang but that didn't seem to me to be a very good reason for trying a climb like that'd be.

'All right then,' I said, thinking that he must be crackers.

There was a whole mob of people around and as soon as they found out what we were going to do, they followed us up to the crag.

We tossed up for who was going to lead and I won, much to Joe's disappointment. He led off up the Pedestal route and took a stance on top of the Pedestal, sixty feet up and about fifteen feet below the overhang. I followed him up and stood there blowing on my fingers.

'Big, isn't it?' said Joe grinning.

It looked about twelve feet across the overhang. We both inspected it.

'If I come off that I'll dinge myself a bit,' I remarked.

'Unless you land on your head,' Joe said.

'Aye. Well. First thing is to try and get a runner round that block under the roof. We want a long full weight sling.'

After a bit of moaning and groaning from Joe, I stepped up from his shoulder and pulled up to the block beneath the over-hang.

'Is it all right?' Joe asked.

'Aye, perfect. Hold an elephant will this,' I replied as I got the sling round the block.

Really good protection, I thought. If I fell off I'd get a nasty bang but at least I wouldn't hit the deck. Stuck to the ceiling was a long flake and this was the only chance. What I intended doing was easing myself into the gap between the flake and the ceiling and then gradually pushing myself farther out from the wall, wriggling out of the flake until I could reach a crack which split the overhang about halfway under it. Once there, I could jam the crack and then work out over the lip of the overhang.

Slowly, because I wasn't too sure that the flake was all that sound, I eased myself into it.

'Is it all right?' Joe asked again, a bit anxious.

'I hope so,' I muttered, knowing that in a few more seconds I'd be lying full length along it, facing the roof.

Very gingerly I worked my way inside and along it. The crowd below were enjoying the spectacle and I could hear them asking each other what was I going to do next, which I thought was a pretty good question. I reached to the crack and got a good hand jam in. By this time I was committed. I jammed my way along the crack until only the heel of my foot remained in the flake. I stopped there and had a think. I knew that I hadn't used much strength so far and I also knew that I couldn't get back. Right. I reached out over the lip of the over-hang for a hold above it and my foot came off the flake. I was hanging free from the tip of the overhang. I quickly pulled up, jammed a foot in the crack, whipped a runner on in case any-thing unaccountable happened, and pulled over the overhang. I was up.

Joe managed it easily enough and we were both very pleased about it. In fact, it had turned out to be nowhere near as difficult as we'd anticipated. The Sloth is not the hardest thing on gritstone by a long way, but I should think it's the most hair-raising.

At Christmas, the Rock and Ice invaded Scotland and climbed in Glencoe – invaluable experience for Don of hard, wintry conditions. The trip was a success and at Easter the following year, the Club returned to Scotland, this time to Ben Nevis. The weather was still almost Arctic, plumes of snow being whipped up off the ridges in true Himalayan fashion, and the ground frozen solid from the pre-Christmas frosts.

There was one climb I wanted to do – the Ordinary Route on the North East Buttress which has this nose of rock on it called the 'Mantrap'. It's a very easy route in good conditions but I reckoned it'd be a good climb with loads of snow and ice on it. The local experts in the Scottish Mountaineering Club Hut laughed their sides out when they heard what we were going to do; they said we didn't stand a chance. Anyhow, there was Don Cowan, Joe and me and we thought we could manage it.

The weather was absolutely desperate, it was blowing a blizzard. At one point – it might have been this 'Mantrap' thing – I had to stand on Cowan's shoulders to get up. I was standing there, belayed, on the ridge when the wind got hold of me and lifted me right off my feet and dropped me on the other side of the ridge. Talk about battling against the elements. Anyway we did the climb.

There's a thing about Nevis, they call it the 'Nevis Ghost'. Ben Nevis is one of the few mountains in Britain where you really feel that you're on something serious and in winter there's always this other feeling, the 'Ghost'. It's oppressive, there's a sense of danger, you never feel happy or relaxed; you feel a kind of threat, as if at any moment the mountain's going to get you. It's almost an Eiger-feeling, just as if you're not wanted about the place. There's a hell of a lot of accidents on the Ben in winter. People who don't know what they're doing should keep well away from it.

Earlier in the year, Don had received a letter from a London climber called Ted Wrangham, inviting him to join a new climbing organization to be called the Alpine Climbing Group.

The formation of the A.C.G. was a landmark in the history of British climbing; it broke down the real class barriers that existed in the climbing world, and demonstrated to the continental climbing fraternity that the new wave of British Alpinists was to be taken seriously.

The A.C.G. grew out of the dissatisfaction felt by many of the young climbers for the long-established Alpine Club.

It seemed impossible for young climbers to get in that club. Personally, I wasn't bothered about joining the bath-chair set but there seemed to be a lot of ill-feeling among climbers about the Alpine Club and its rules and standards. I gathered that it was something to do with money, education and background stuff, which as far as I was concerned had nothing at all to do with climbing. I heard about the 'old school tie' and frankly I didn't know what they were talking about.

Some of the younger lads who had been doing unguided climbs in the Alps over the past few years thought up the idea of this Alpine Climbing Group. Most of them were university types, but they weren't standard issue – Bob Downes, Geoff Sutton, Hamish Nicol, George Band, Ian McNaught Davis and so on. When I received my invitation to join, I couldn't understand it. I mean I'd only had one short fortnight in the Alps which hardly qualified me as an experienced Alpinist. I wrote back to Ted Wrangham pointing this out, but all I got in reply was another invitation, this time to the inaugural dinner at the Pen-y-Gwryd. Don Cowan and Nat had also been asked to join so the Rock and Ice were well represented.

The dinner was a splendid affair and Don, Nat and I put out a new route – Erosion Groove – on Carreg Wasted, one of the Three Cliffs. All the other lads enjoyed themselves falling off it, with holds breaking off and loads of muck all over it.

Much to my surprise, I found myself elected on to the committee of the A.C.G., even though I wasn't clear just what the whole thing was about. There was some talk of translating foreign guide books which I was very much in favour of. This was the first time I'd got together with these university wallahs. I'd never had much time for them before, and Joe and I had had some good laughs at their expense.

I remember one weekend when we were at the Roaches and a whole coach-load of blokes arrived from Oxford University Mountaineering Club. You should have seen them. They were capurtling off all over the place. We were just walking along the foot of the crags when one of these lads crunched down just in front of us. I turned to Joe.

'Bloody hell, Joe,' I said, 'I wonder how many they write off every weekend?'

And there was the time on Cloggy when Joe was trying the Left Edge of the Boulder and this character came walking down the East Terrace and shouted to him.

'I say, are you Brown?' he called.

Joe turned and looked at the fella. 'Yeah,' he said.

'Oh good,' the bloke said. 'Tell me, is it true that you bivouac in étriers?'

I mean, apart from it being a bloody stupid question, you just didn't go around shouting at blokes you didn't know.

I could see that most of the lads at that first dinner were okay. They spoke differently than I did, fair enough, they were much better educated but at least they seemed like genuine lads. They certainly had the right ideas and the courage to carry them out. I was just a nineteen-year-old monkey from the city then, they could easily have ignored me but they didn't. The climbing was the thing that mattered.

The months of May and June 1953 were productive on Cloggy. Joe and Pete White added Gargoyle on the Pinnacle, Joe and Don did East Gully Wall, Don and Nat put out East Gully Groove and Joe, Don and Nat made the magnificent Girdle Traverse of the East Buttress.

We'd talked on and off about the possibility of a Girdle and finally we got around to doing it. Joe was going to lead, Nat would be the middle man and I'd be the third man. I wasn't too thrilled at the prospect of being last on the rope as it could be extremely difficult, particularly if there were any long, downward traverses.

We'd weighed up the problems as far as we could and we'd come to the conclusion that the big obstacle to the complete traverse was the large, blank wall between Diglyph and Vember. There appeared to be a faint break with the odd grass ledge, but this faded out halfway across the wall. We slept on the problem at the foot of the cliff and wakened the following morning to a beautiful day. We had the usual greasy breakfast of sausages and bacon and then plodded slowly over the scree to the foot of Sunset Crack.

'Go on then, get up it,' Joe said, arriving out of breath.

'I'm tired,' I was overcome with yawning.

'You're idle.'

'I'm tired.'

'Hey, are we going or not?' Nat chipped in.

I led off up Sunset Crack and took a stance after two pitches. The Girdle started from there. After a bit of messing about, Joe began the traverse with some delicate moves to a small overhang. This was the beginning of the pendulum pitch of Lithrig; the last few feet across to the ledge Joe negotiated by a kind of crab-like movement across the blank wall while suspended from above by a sling he had on a rock spike. That pitch was quite difficult but no worse than we'd expected. We had no trouble getting on to Pigott's Climb or from there to the groove on Diglyph. When I reached Joe and Nat, they were giving the steep, grey slab between them and Vember a good going over.

'I dunno,' Joe was scratching his chin and gazing blankly at the wall.

'Now Joe,' said Nat, 'it must go – at least until that grass runs out.'

'Aye, and what happens then?' Joe asked nobody in particular.

'Get out there and find out,' I said with great relish.

'Runners won't be much good on there,' said Nat, joining in the fun.

'I probably won't get any on anyway,' grumbled Joe.

'No.'

'Hard luck.'

Joe got the idea and set off, descending the grassy ledges. First lowering himself gently, then inspecting each piece of grass to see if there was a good rock ledge under it.

I didn't much care for all this downward movement but I realized that there wasn't much I could do about it. I stared out away over Llyn du'r Arddu and enjoyed the view.

'How's it going, youth?' Nat called out to Joe.

Joe had stopped going downwards and he'd made a short traverse which had fetched him up in a shallow, vertical depression.

'Eh?' Joe wasn't feeling very talkative so we let him go on in silence.

About 35 feet above his head was a grass ledge. The problem was, would the line of holds continue as far as that? If they did. Joe would get a good stance at a point almost horizontally across from where Nat and I were standing.

Slowly and carefully, he moved up, inspecting each hold and surveying his next move. He really was great to watch on a climb like this. It was impossible to imagine anybody being able to do it better. Now he was six feet off the big ledge; Nat and me were both beginning to feel the suspense. Surely he'd do it now, surely he would, he must. He seemed to stand for ages and then with a swift, almost nonchalant movement, he stepped up, straightened out and grasped the ledge. He'd done it.

'I say, jolly good show,' called out Nat in his best lace-curtains voice.

Joe grinned across at us. 'Come on then, sonny,' he shouted.

Soon we were all together again on the spacious ledge, pondering the next move. There was no question of climbing the next section, what we had to do was arrange an abseil down to the stance on Vember.

'Who's going first?' asked Joe.

'Whose sling are we using?' I asked, looking at Nat.

'By the bugger here,' he replied, hanging me one of his old line slings.

I climbed up to the right to a large flake and fixed the sling round it.

'I'll have a brew ready for you,' remarked Nat as he disappeared over the ledge.

We watched the taut sling anxiously as Nat swung gaily about. After what seemed ages, he shouted up from below to say that he was on the stance. Well, Nat was the heaviest of us and the sling had held okay. Joe followed quickly and then, with eyes riveted on the old sling, I slid off down the rope without a jar or a jerk.

At the top of the chimney pitch on Curving Crack, Nat and Joe were discussing a climbing descent down to the top of the Pedestal on Pedestal Crack when I joined them.

'Aye, you know what you can do with that an' all,' was my contribution.

'He's tired,' said Nat.

'And alive,' I added.

We abseiled down to the Pedestal and then decided to climb the Corner direct instead of attempting to cross the wall. By this time we'd been on the Girdle over five hours and we were in a hurry to finish it off. Joe did what was the second ascent of the Corner in fifteen minutes flat.

'Oh well, here goes,' said Nat.

He moved over to the foot of the Corner.

'Right,' he called in a tone which obviously indicated that something had to be done before he could start to climb.

Joe's head poked over the top.

'Right what?' asked Joe in a puzzled voice.

Nat sighed heavily. 'Pull, you silly bugger,' he yelled.

Joe's grinning face disappeared. Nat turned to me.

'I'll tell you something, youth,' he said heavily. 'I tore my toes to pieces when we put this out.'

'Oh aye.'

'Aye. No skin, just tatters.'

'Hey Nat, are you coming up or what?' Joe called out from above.

Nat shook his head. 'Just listen to that,' he said.

I watched as, still grumbling, Nat set off up the rock. I remembered that on the first ascent of the Corner, Joe and Nat had climbed in stockinged feet as it had been pouring with rain. Still, he'd got it good today.

Half an hour later, I pulled over the top right into a mound of stinking, rotting socks, left there by Joe and Nat as a memorial to their first ascent.

'We built a cairn for you for chance you lost your way,' said Nat.

6 | The Alpine Climbing Group

On 29 May 1953, Edmund Hillary and Tensing stood on the summit of Everest and the highest mountain in the world had at last been climbed. The pursuit of height was over; quality and difficulty were to become the new criteria in the mountaineering world.

On a more modest scale, Don and Don Cowan persuaded Joe to abandon Cloggy for a fortnight and join them in the Alps. Don's experience of rail travel the previous year made him determined to get to Chamonix under his own steam, and so, with Audrey on an improvised pillion seat, he set off in high spirits on the repaired bike.

In spite of bad road surfaces, heavy rain, and occasional excursions on to the wrong side of the road, the pair arrived safely in Chamonix. Audrey had suffered agony on the pillion seat and had created quite a stir on the last stages of the journey by sitting on all available padding and towering some two feet above Don.

Don Cowan with Joe on his pillion seat arrived at the Biolay shortly after Don and Audrey. They were both soaked to the skin.

'Wet, isn't it?' Don said by way of a greeting.

'It is where we've been,' replied a disgruntled Joe. Don was puzzled. 'Why, where've you been?' he asked.

'In the bloody river,' said Joe.

'Braked on a bend down the valley and shot over a bank into it, bike an' all,' explained the bedraggled Cowan.

After a warm-up climb of Grade VI on the West Face of the Pointe Albert, the party attacked the East Ridge of the Croco-

dile on which Joe broke the shaft of his ice-axe and a 250-foot
rope jammed and had to be cut into four pieces.

Because of all the delay with the rope getting stuck, we were
late getting to the top and it was dark when we began the
descent. Before we'd gone very far, it got pitch black and we
were climbing down by torchlight. By the time we got to the
bergschrund we'd been on the go for twenty-one hours. Without a word, Joe banged his broken axe shaft into the frozen
snow and not bothering to ask what was below, rappelled off
over the edge. Cowan shrugged and went after him. I slid
down the rope and found Joe standing on the lower lip of the
bergschrund, Don having already led off down again.

'Okay, fella,' I heard Don call from below.

'Go on, Joe,' I said.

Joe made no sound, so I leaned over and shouted in his ear.
His head jerked up.

'Eh? What's up?' The bugger had been fast asleep.

'Get going, Don's ready,' I said.

He yawned and crunched away down the slope.

We weren't in any real danger by then. We were descending
a basin which went down in a smooth sweep for about 400 feet
to the glacier, but it was frozen hard and we had to be a bit
careful.

The next time I reached Joe, he was having another little
nod. I wakened him up with a prod in the back.

'Hey, I'm knackered,' he said. 'Does Cowan never sleep or
summat?'

Conditions affect people in different ways. Joe never seemed
to be troubled by damp or cold but hot sun or lack of sleep
soon had its effect on him. And he could sleep standing on a
needle if he was tired enough.

We continued on down the snow slope. I hadn't gone very
far when I legged myself up, getting my crampons entangled
with my torn trousers. I fell head first down the slope. Joe was
having another doze when I hit him in the small of the back
with my head and we both whirled off together. I thought

about poor Don who wouldn't have the faintest idea what was going on until we hurtled past him. Suddenly the rope tightened and I came to a sliding stop. 'Good old Don,' I thought and sighed with relief. Before I'd time to pick myself up, Joe landed like a ton of bricks on top of me, planting one cramponed foot firmly on my backside and the other on my thigh.

'Have you finished?' panted Joe, pulling himself to his feet.

'I'm like a bloody pin-cushion,' I moaned, gingerly feeling my punctured behind.

'Are you two thinking of joining a circus or something?' inquired Cowan, who had heroically held us both at some cost to his hands.

Eventually we reached the hut and, in spite of a shortage of blankets, we slept for fourteen hours solid.

On returning to Chamonix, they were greeted by two of the members of the Alpine Climbing Group – Geoff Sutton and Bob Downes. This was the first time Don had met the quiet, swarthy Downes who was then a student at Cambridge University.

Sutton joined the Rock and Ice party and the four decided to have a look at the West Face of the Blaitière, which at that time was the only climb in the guide book with a rock pitch graded VIb. The West Face triumphed this time, but Don and Joe swore to return the following year. If the party had succeeded in climbing it it would have been an outstanding first ascent, for since the original route had been climbed, an immense rock-fall on the Face had wiped out most of the line of the climb.

An incident occurred on this first attempt which sustained the comic trend of the holiday.

Right at the beginning of the climb, Joe was up a wide crack which had a difficult bulge in it about forty feet up. He was messing about for a while and then with sudden decision he took off his Jaeger woolly hat and lowered it down to us.

We were a bit puzzled. 'D'you want a butty sending up?' I asked.

He shook his head and in a very solemn voice said, 'Put a big chockstone in it.'

'In your hat?' I asked in surprise, knowing how fond he was of it.

He nodded. 'In my hat,' he said.

I did as I was asked and stuffed a big rock in it. Joe tried to haul it up but the hat was stubborn, it just stretched and stretched. It was the first time it had let him down. It was a dead versatile hat, but it had a mind of its own. It didn't mind being used as a pair of swimming trunks but it objected to being a bucket.

1954 *looked like being a bad year all round for Don if for no other reason than that he was due to finish his apprenticeship as a plumber, and would then automatically be called upon to serve two years in the forces as a National Serviceman.*

'They'll shake you up all right,' said Ron Moseley, with great relish.

'You can come and whitewash our coal-place for a bit of practice if you want,' offered Joe.

All the lads had either already completed their two years or had somehow scraped out of it and they seemed to derive pleasure from the prospect of Don tangling with the military authorities.

As if to rub salt in the wound, Joe, Ron and Ray Greenall announced that they were going to spend the whole summer in the Alps.

'I might not pass my medical,' said Don with a sinking heart and then listened in misery as the Y.M.C.A. lounge echoed with shouts of mocking laughter.

In April, Don reported to the Medical Board, had his examinations and filled in the requisite forms.

A weird-looking bod with long, greasy hair, a shortie over-coat and brothel-creepers had attached himself to me during the waits between examinations. When we came to filling in a form, he'd give me advice. I was getting a bit browned-off with him towards the end. I was looking at this question about past illnesses and he whispered in my ear.

'Don't put anything in there or they won't take you,' he hissed.

'Don't let them hear you say that or they won't take you,' I snarled back and promptly wrote in everything I'd ever had in my life with my 'stomach ulcer' in pride of place.

I never thought about it afterwards. I was just resigned to wasting two valuable years, and then one morning I got this letter from the Ministry of Labour and National Service. I couldn't believe my eyes, it said that I was Grade Three, unfit for military service. I walked into the Y.M.C.A. that night and casually remarked that I'd got my grade card.

'Oh-oh, this is it then,' taunted Moseley. 'Acting unpaid, un-washed, unwanted Private Whillans.'

I let the rest of the lads have a good guffaw and then I dropped the bombshell.

'I'm Grade Three, they're not taking me,' I said.

Talk about staring eyes and open mouths. Moseley went bright red and started spluttering.

'You what? What? You skiving get.'

'You jammy bugger.'

'You? Not fit? Let's have a look.'

I smiled quietly. 'Now, who's going to the Alps?' I asked.

'Bloody hell,' said Moseley with deep disgust.

7 | Ben Nevis

At Easter, the Rock and Ice took a trip to Ben Nevis. Ron and Joe had made a small bivouac tent which they intended using in the Alps during the summer. Much to the amusement of the rest of the lads, Ron insisted that Joe and he test the tent out under the most severe conditions available, and so on an absolutely filthy day the intrepid pair staggered off through the wind and snow to bivouac at the foot of Point Five Gully. The memorable night which followed convinced Joe that if he was going to die, it might as well be in the grand manner and so he abandoned Moseley and joined Don on the massive Carn Dearg buttress.

I'd got really wrapped up in finding a route up the huge open-book corner which started about 150 feet up the crag. I knew that half a dozen of the top Scottish climbers – Tom Patey, Dan Stewart and so on – had tried unsuccessfully before me but I was very determined to make it go. I'd been at it a couple of days with Nat seconding when Joe came over. He provided just what was needed.

'How's it going then?' he called out to me.

'Oh, not so good,' I replied.

'Let's come up and have a look.'

I brought him up and we surveyed the great mass of rock.

'I think we'd better have a fresh start,' he said after a while.

'All right,' I agreed, without much enthusiasm.

'I'll just have a look on the right,' he said, and began to traverse across a long crack which started almost from the ground and ran directly to a massive overhang.

'Hey, there's somebody been before us,' he called in surprise, having reached a ledge with a good belayed stance. 'There's an old sling hanging here.'

'John Cunningham or somebody I should think,' I replied.

Cunningham was known to me by reputation. He was probably the best of the Scottish climbers and I reckoned if anybody had got that far up, it could only have been him.

I climbed across to Joe and we stood together on a blunt pinnacle backed by a vertical wall which led up to the overhang rearing out all of fourteen feet above our heads. Down below I saw Nat scratching his head, no doubt wondering where the hell we were going to go from there.

'You're not thinking of going over the overhang, are you?' I asked, a bit sarcastic.

'Might as well have a go now we're here,' said Joe not very convincingly.

Just under the main overhang was a smaller one some ten feet up the crack. He put a couple of chockstones with slings in the crack and used the slings to pull up over the small overhang to the base of the main roof.

'Right,' he said. 'Now what?'

'Well, if you can get out about eight feet,' I said, 'there's a big chockstone there. Get a sling round it and you could sit there all day. I don't know how you're going to manage it though.'

'No, I don't either,' Joe retorted.

Anyway, he kept moving out and moving out until he got within touching distance of the chockstone. He was in a breathtaking position, as I stood looking up and out at him. Slowly he reached for the chockstone and grasped it. I held my breath, hoping it would hold. Quickly, he got a sling round it.

'Hey, we've cracked this thing,' I shouted. 'You've done it.'

'I'm coming back, I was nearly off there,' Joe said shakily.

'You've done it, man,' I said, surprised at his wanting to climb down. Carefully, he climbed back, removing all the slings until he stood on the pinnacle again.

'It's too strenuous,' he said, shaking his head.

'Well, it must go now,' I reasoned.

'I don't think it will,' Joe replied. 'Anyway, it's getting dark.'

'We'll come back and have another go tomorrow then,' I said and Joe agreed. We roped off in the gloom and joined an anxious Nat at the foot of the crag.

'All right is it?' he asked.

'We'll let you know tomorrow,' I replied.

We had a discussion as to the best method of attacking the overhang, which Joe said was too strenuous for one man to do in one go. Eventually we agreed that one of us should climb and fix the slings which would enable the other to save his strength for whatever lay beyond the chockstone.

The following morning, I led direct from the ground to the stance beneath the overhang. I'd volunteered to do the sling-fixing in view of Joe's great effort of the day before. I used shoulders, knees, elbows – everything possible to conserve my finger and arm strength – and when I got to the chockstone I felt quite fresh.

'How're you feeling?' Joe called up.

'All right,' I replied. 'I've bags of strength left.'

'Well – you go on then, might as well,' Joe said.

I didn't know what to do really. After all, it was Joe's pitch. Anyway, I asked him again and he said it was okay so I started off. I moved out and round the edge of the overhang. Straight away I knew why Joe had said it wouldn't go. The only holds were small, slanting grooves leaning awkwardly to the left. I got my right leg jammed in the crack, foot tapping against the chockstone and levered myself so that I could see the rock above. Stretching my right hand, I gripped the top of a V-shaped block. I was just preparing to put my full weight on it, when I felt it move. Like lightning, I jammed my leg even farther into the crack. Carefully, I tested the block again. It was either that or nothing. I decided it probably wouldn't pull out any farther and before I could have second thoughts, I put my weight on it. A couple of moves to the left on the sloping holds and the pitch was finished.

'Bloody marvellous,' I heard Joe shout from below.

I sighed with relief and satisfaction. I think that was the most sensational pitch I'd ever done. Joe came up with a grin wide enough to split his face. As we stepped to the foot of the next pitch, we heard a great shout from across at the Hut.

'English bastards!'

Some of the S.M.C. had been watching and they were upset because we'd nabbed one of their plums. Very fittingly, we called the climb 'Sassenach'.

The plans for a night of celebration were interrupted when, just as darkness closed in, a breathless climber rushed into the camp with the news that a girl had fallen from the Great Tower on Tower Ridge and was hanging on the rope. Don and Joe lost no time in discussing whether or not the girl could possibly be still alive. Grabbing a minimum of gear, they set out for the summit of Ben Nevis at breakneck speed.

The Great Tower is only 400 feet from the summit of Nevis and therefore the logical way of getting to the girl was to reach the summit and then descend to the Tower. Don, usually a slow mover, drove himself to the limit following Joe up the long, sloping track. As the pair pounded up towards Tower Ridge, the moon broke through cloud and bathed the frozen summit plateau in cold, silver light, but the steep, jagged west face remained in black shadow. A solitary figure stood on the edge above the Great Tower.

It was bitingly cold on the summit and everything was either jet-black or glaring white. This bloke was one of the girl's party – he said she was called Betty Emery – and he told us where to start the descent and he lent us an extra rope.

'I'll go, eh?' said Joe and I belayed him well back from the ledge.

'Can you see anything?' I called out as he started down the rope.

'No, it's as black as a bag,' he shouted back.

It really was dark, I'd lost sight of Joe almost before he'd gone over the edge. The full length of the rope ran out and I shouted to Joe to take a belay. When he was ready, I began the climb down into a black nothing. I fumbled around for holds and steps until, gradually, my eyes became accustomed to the gloom and I could make out the figure of Joe against the snow below me. Another rope length down and we reached the Tower Gap which is a notch separating the Great Tower from the slope. The normal route of Tower Ridge traverses the side of the Great Tower and apparently Betty Emery had fallen while doing the traverse.

'Hell, I'm cold,' I said to Joe. The sweat worked up on the slog to the summit was freezing on me.

'The rock's covered with verglas,' Joe said as if he was telling me that he'd just put the kettle on.

'Put a load of pegs in then or I'll be off an' all,' I said, handing him the collection of pitons I'd brought.

'She'll have had it, you know,' said Joe flatly.

'Aye,' I nodded. 'No chance.'

Joe carried on down and I heard the reassuring clunk of his hammer every two or three minutes. It was very eerie standing there in the darkness with the sound of the hammering echoing round the icy rock.

'Okay, Don.'

I heard Joe's muffled voice from below and I climbed slowly and carefully down to him.

'All right?'

'Aye. Thanks for putting the pegs in,' I replied.

'Should find the rope on this next pitch,' Joe said as we changed belays.

He continued the traverse down and round the side of the Tower and within a few minutes, he shouted up to me.

'It's here, Don. Come on down.'

He was on a small ledge and tied over a smooth bollard was an icy rope.

'We'd better give a shout just for chance,' I said, though I knew full well that it was hopeless.

'Betty?' We both shouted down into the echoing darkness and strained our ears hoping against hope to hear some sort of sound but there was nothing.

A cold breeze had got up and it was getting to be very unpleasant.

'That must be the lads,' Joe said and I saw bobbing lights hundreds of feet below.

'I wish they'd hurry up,' I said.

'Well, are we giving it a pull then?' asked Joe after a while.

I think we were both sort of sick knowing that pretty soon we'd have a dead girl on the ledge. We fixed the frozen rope to a safe anchor and began to heave. We pulled until we were both exhausted and our hands were bloody from the thin, icy rope. We hadn't budged it an inch.

'What the bloody hell's up with it?' panted Joe in fury.

'It's stuck dead fast, must be jammed solid,' I replied between my teeth.

'That's all we needed,' said Joe and sank back against the rock.

'Somebody'll have to abseil down,' I said.

'It's not on,' Joe said. 'Not with just us two.'

If there had been any question of saving a life, we'd have had a go but it was obvious that after a 200-foot fall and six hours in freezing weather, the girl was dead.

'We'll wait for the lads,' I said.

'Right, in any case it'll be light in a couple of hours,' Joe said.

We settled down, teeth chattering, to wait for the boys who were climbing up the west face. When they got to within a rope length of us we chucked a rope down to them and got them over the worst bit. Ray Greenall arrived first with a bivouac sheet.

'Well?'

'The rope's jammed or something, we can't shift it,' I explained.

'She's dead, must be,' said Ray and we nodded in agreement.

The lads had brought a stove and they quickly had a brew going while we squeezed under the bivouac sheet and waited for the first glimmer of light.

After an uncomfortable hour, we thought it light enough to

make a start and Joe abseiled down with me holding him on a safety rope. Ray and the other three took up positions on the ledge ready to pull the jammed rope.

'It'll take a while,' Joe's voice floated up to us. 'Every place where the rope's on rock it's frozen over, that's what was holding it.'

Eventually, Joe freed the whole of the rope and we hauled the body up. The girl had a head injury and was dead.

The R.A.F. Mountain Rescue Team had arrived at Tower Gap with a sledge which would make the pull up to the summit quite easy. When we reached the Gap we decided to leave it to the experts. Much to the amusement of the lads, the R.A.F. officer who was in charge began to give me instructions on how to cross the famous ten-foot notch of the Tower Gap.

'Now laddy, if you move your left foot a little higher you'll find quite a good foothold. Don't worry, you'll be quite safe, you'll not fall off.'

'Careful, Don,' called Joe. 'Watch your right foot.'

'Do you want a hand, Don?' inquired Ray solicitously.

Gwen Moffat, the woman climber who wrote a book on the R.A.F. Mountain Rescue Team, later told Don that at the post-mortem on Betty Emery the doctor said that she would have lived had she been reached in reasonable time. If this implied that the rescue had been bungled, it was rather an unfair statement to make about an accident that occurred at a particularly inaccessible place at the worst time of day in almost Arctic conditions.

8 | The Red Slab

One Sunday afternoon, in April 1954, Don and Nat Allen stood at the foot of Cloggy and watched Joe as he packed his gear.

'I'm off then,' said Joe. 'Hey, Don, why don't you get yourself a nice, easy second ascent?'

'Like what?' asked Don.

'The Bloody Slab,' Joe replied. 'It'll be a doddle, won't it, Nat?'

Nat nodded. 'Looks okay to me,' he said.

'I thought you said it wouldn't go?' Don said, looking at Joe.

'Listen lad, me and Nat have had a look at it. We stood on the West Terrace and chucked stones on it and not one of 'em bounced. Just slid slowly off,' lectured Joe, describing the gentle descent of the stones with one hand.

'Slithered down,' said Nat in full agreement with Joe.

'All right, we'll have a go then,' Don said, and with a wave Joe set off towards the Halfway House, bound for an early train home.

I'd never had a look at the Red Slab myself, I much prefer crack climbs to slabs but Joe and Nat were both certain that it'd be a nice, pleasant climb.

'Bags of spikes for runners,' Nat said as we went up the Western Terrace.

We stood and looked at the huge, rust-coloured slab, dripping with water and slime.

'Piece of cake?' I said sarcastically.

'It can't be as bad as it looks,' said Nat with great certainty.

'Where's all your good spike runners?' I asked as I stepped on to the slab, not even sure where to start.

Nat waved an arm vaguely.

'There's one up there – and another about fifteen feet higher up,' he said, less certainly.

'You've got bloody good eyes, mate,' I replied, gazing up, looking for somewhere to make for.

About eighty feet up, there was an overhang and I thought I could see a karabiner hanging on a peg.

'Hey Nat, can you see a krab up there?' I asked.

Nat followed the line of my pointing finger.

'Yeah – that's a krab all right,' he replied. 'There you are, what did I tell you?'

'Great. How do I get there?'

'Streetly did,' said Nat, challenging me.

'Bloody Cambridge type,' I grumbled and started off up the wet rock.

After several moves I fixed a very poor runner on one of Nat's 'good spikes'.

'It's a sock job, Nat,' I called down to him and balancing very dodgily, I managed to get my ragged socks over my rubbers.

'Feel better now?' inquired Nat, grinning up at me.

'Get lost,' I replied.

I moved reluctantly up the slimy rock and at last reached a slippery ledge about ten feet from the piton and dangling krab. I looked at the move to the piton; if Streetly hadn't thought it necessary to put a peg in to protect this move, what the hell was the move after the peg like?

I looked hard and long for a line of holds which must be there, my respect for Streetly increasing every minute. My scrutiny revealed nothing except a small rib which could be used to semi-layback and so get the feet on to the slab where the peg was fixed.

'The fun will start when I try to pull from the layback to a position on the slab,' I thought aloud. As far as I could see, my position would be such that I would be completely dependent on the friction of my socks on the slab.

I glanced down at Nat who had obviously had second thoughts about this being a nice, pleasant climb. I returned to the problem in hand. Now, I told myself, Streetly had made this move and he hadn't been heading for a piton.

I grasped the layback hold and gingerly poked my left foot on to the faintest of dinges in the slab. The foot seemed to stick all right so I moved my right foot over to join it. Slowly, I pulled into a standing position, transferring my weight from my hands to my feet. Without any warning, my feet shot off. Luckily, I hadn't released my hold on the layback rib and with a great effort and a smile from the Almighty I managed to regain my layback position. Two minutes later I roped back down the slab and exchanged a few words with a subdued Nat. The Bloody Slab had won this time.

At least a year later, I did the climb with Joe who, in between times, had made the second ascent. When I reached the crux, the moves were still very hard but this time the rock was dry and the friction was there all right.

It's my favourite slab climb, this one, and I've done it several times over the years.

9 | The Blaitière

Joe, Ron and Ray were definitely going to spend the whole summer in Chamonix come what may, but although the problem of Don's military service no longer existed, there was one more major hurdle which he had to surmount – his father's attitude. To Don's father, the idea of working lads spending three months on holiday seemed completely unrealistic. Much to Don's surprise and greatly to his father's satisfaction, Don succeeded in getting permission to take three months off from work with the guarantee that his job would still be there when he got back. The final problem was purely financial and Don solved it quite simply by selling his motor-bike.

The first couple of weeks in the Alps were a shambles. For one thing the weather was atrocious, for another the Biolay had scrapped the communal straw bed and put up camp beds and, of course, the price. Ron was determined to do the East Face of the Grand Capucin, the 'Cap'. For days on end we wandered pathetically about among snow and mist getting more and more miserable. We actually managed to do the second ascent of a climb on the north-east end of the Albert but most of the time we were just sitting about freezing.

Geoff Sutton arrived, decided to join us in another attempt on the Cap, swallowed two raw eggs for energy, stepped outside the Requin Hut, spewed them up, and retired from the climb before he'd even started.

Eventually, the weather improved and just for a change we thought we'd have a go at the Cap. We went off, for about the fourth time, to the Requin Hut. As soon as we arrived the weather turned bad again and we spent two more boring days doing nothing. Ron suggested that we get to the foot of the East Face and build ourselves an igloo to save expense and also so that we'd be right there when and if the weather lifted.

Just as we were getting up after the first night in the igloo, we heard voices. Outside, the day looked like being a good one, but we were stunned to find that the voices belonged to four climbers who were quite obviously just about to start on the East Face. That was all we needed. The East Face was a three-day climb then and that meant that we'd have to spend the whole time behind this other lot and also meant that we might possibly have to bivouac in étriers. Anyway, we had breakfast and decided to give it a try.

The East Face is a magnificent sight – fifteen hundred feet of clean, solid granite with hardly a foot on it less than vertical. Almost the whole climb is artificial, which is a pity in a way because it means that progress is slow.

I led off up a slab which Ron compared to Narrow Slab on Cloggy, and then Joe began a vertical corner. We could see the two ropes of the party in front of us, they were getting on reasonably well, though slow by our standards. We later discovered that they were French.

The sun was hot, and the glare from the rock was hard on the eyes. The ring of pitons being knocked in indicated that the artificial stuff was starting in earnest. I was spending a long time sitting on the warm rock, bits of melting ice singing past me. I'd retrieve all the ironmongery that Joe put in, pass it up to Ron who'd pass it on up to Joe. It was a slow business.

After several hours we reached the first Bonatti Bivouac.

'These buggers are taking all the pegs out, not just their own,' Joe said, jerking his thumb at the party above.

'They're a bloody menace,' said Ron with heartfelt disgust.

We waited a further hour and a half, watching the French party swinging about on étriers.

'This is no bloody good,' Joe complained. 'I'm not climbing at this speed behind them for another couple of days.'

'Let's get down,' said Ron.

If it wasn't the weather, it was something else. The Cap wasn't for us that year. We rappelled down like spiders and spent the night in our igloo. The following morning the weather was really good again and we could see that the French party had speeded up a bit. It looked like they'd reach the summit that day, in which case we'd made a boob in coming down. We plodded back to the Requin Hut through the maze of the icefall. When we reached the Hut, the guardian had the bloody cheek to ask us if the climb had been too hard for us.

The climber is a strange being; on an uncomfortable climb he wants nothing more than to be enjoying the luxuries of valley life, yet once in the fleshpots he can't wait to be back on vertical rock driving himself to the end of his tether in abysmal conditions. After returning from their abortive attempt on the Grand Capucin, Joe and Don idled a week away, lounging in the sun, and telling each other how lucky they were to be alive and in the Alps. Then the itch began and demanded to be scratched.

'What do you fancy doing, Don?' asked Joe.
'How about the Cap for a bit of variety?'
'Get stuffed.'
'The Blaitière?'
'Now you're talking. Aye, that'd be all right.'
Nobody else was interested except me and Joe which suited us nicely. We were both on good form and we were a good combination in every way.

'We'll take some gear this time, too,' said Joe. 'Loads of pegs and we'll have to make at least one bivvy.'
'No sack rope,' I added, 'we'll use the 300-foot doubled.'
'Okay,' agreed Joe.
It was a fair idea this; the leader would have to pull one length up after him then chuck it down to the second who would tie on the sack. We would swop leads whenever we felt like it or whenever one of us was running out of steam.

We set off from Chamonix in the evening when the sun had

lost most of its heat and after a long flog we bivouacked on a ledge at the foot of the first crack.

I remember that night well; I'd overdone the sunbathing a bit and my blistered back kept me nice and warm in the cold air. Joe slept like a log as usual and I had the breakfast ready before he was awake.

It was a lovely day but cold because the sun hadn't got onto the Face when we started out. Joe led up the seventy-five-foot crack which was later to be called the 'Fissure Brown'. We hadn't much trouble with it because we'd learnt a lot from our efforts of the previous year. I remembered losing a fair amount of skin from the inside of my right leg and I was determined to use a bit more technique and a lot less brute strength this time. Pretty soon we reached the ledge where we had given up the year before. Now we had to decide on the route.

'There's nothing on the right, that's for sure, though it could link up with the old route,' I said, gazing at the huge, grey scar, away on our left, and recalling a recce I had done on the first attempt.

'Well, we'll have a go anyway,' Joe said and was soon jamming his way up a chimney.

'There's a great stance up here,' he called down. 'Come on up.'

On the stance, we were quite close to where the massive rockfall had crashed its way down. Joe disappeared round a corner and I prepared for a long wait. The sound of hammering echoed round the rock.

'It's getting a bit tough now,' Joe called and I searched around for a more comfortable position against the wall.

Much to my surprise, the rope was running out quite quickly and before very long I heard a confident shout from above.

'Hey, it's a doddle, come on.'

I found him sitting cheerfully on a good ledge, smoking like he'd never had a fag for weeks.

'How about that eh?' he grinned as I reached the ledge.

'Great,' I nodded.

Above us, a good crack ran up to an overhang, narrowing as

it went. The bottom part of the crack would go free but near the top some pegs would have to be used. Joe went up and banged a few in, stepped into an étrier and then took a stance on an exposed ledge. The brown rock with the original route on it was not too far off now. It looked like we had a new, major route in the bag.

We had no description of the old Allain–Fix route and we didn't expect it to be easy, for the Fissure Fix was reputed to be the hardest free climbing pitch in the Aiguilles and that was somewhere up above us. Moving well, we crossed some slabs baking in the sunlight and then climbed another long, jamming crack which fairly made the sweat squirt out. It was sapping both energy and will.

'Have you seen that?' Joe asked as we rested. He was pointing up at an extraordinary flake crack in the centre of a great wall above us.

'Aye, it must be the Fissure Fix.'

'It's like the flake on the Central Buttress of Scafell,' Joe remarked.

'Yeah. Except it looks a bloody sight harder,' I added.

We moved up the ridge overlooking the Couloir Reynier and stood beneath the wall. We traversed to the foot of the crack. The rock above was streaked with ice and there didn't seem to be any sign of previous parties. Joe began the crack and then after a few moves slithered back down.

'What's up?' I asked, disgusted at his weak effort.

'Can't do it, I'm too tired,' said Joe despondently. 'You have a go.'

I tied on to the middle of the rope and made a determined assault on the crack. Six feet above where Joe had stopped, I ran out of steam and like Joe I slithered back down.

'Hellfire!' I muttered.

'Fix is dead right,' said Joe.

'This can't be it,' I reasoned. 'We can do any free pitch in this bloody country so this can't be the Fissure Fix.'

'Where is it then?' asked Joe miserably.

'Hold on. Let's rappel down to the ridge and I'll have a look

round the other corner,' I said, trying not to get affected by
Joe's despondent mood.

Back down below, a fierce-looking crack ran round an overhang and disappeared round a corner. I laybacked out along
the crack.

'May as well make sure there's nothing out here,' I called
down to Joe and stuck my head round the corner. There under
my nose was a piton. Above me, a groove ran straight up for a
hundred feet with a good jamming crack all the way.

'Found it, Joe,' I called in triumph.

It was an excellent pitch, quite hard but child's play to the
crack we'd tried before. Another easy pitch led to a good
stance, and avoiding a wet, icy chimney we traversed right. Joe
disappeared into a small groove.

'There's a cloud on us, Joe,' I called after noticing that it had
suddenly gone chilly.

There was no reply from above, only the sound of much
scuffling followed by a slithering noise.

'What's up?' I inquired.

'I just fell off,' Joe replied in an incredulous tone.

'Stop fooling about and put a peg in, the bloody clouds are
blowing up,' I shouted, most unreasonably.

No reply except the clonk of the hammer as I simmered
down. This time Joe got up and I followed, finding the groove
very deceptive, awkward and constricting.

'An awkward bugger that,' I said to him on arrival.

'I'm glad you thought so,' he replied with a grin.

We were close to the completion of the first ascent now and
we'd regained our spirits.

'Just up the ridge and we're on the summit,' I said.

'Yeah, a good do that,' replied Joe.

But the summit was, as usual, farther away than we
thought. We fooled about after reaching it and it got darker
until finally we decided to bivouac on the ridge. We couldn't
find anywhere even reasonably comfortable and then as soon
as we got the cooker lit it burst into flames, singeing my eyebrows and hair. We retired to a safe distance until the fire died

down. As soon as I removed the safety valve it worked perfectly.

The clouds had cleared and the night was magnificent, still and starlit. I clipped myself on to the ledge and dozed off. I awoke to find Joe already awake, cursing and shivering in the cold. A point of light on the horizon cheered us up and we watched eagerly for the appearance of the sun. The light grew stronger and we were laughing and talking like normal human beings when suddenly the moon popped up.

'Hey – that's – what the – no, bloody hell, no,' stuttered Joe in dismay.

We spent the rest of the night in utter misery until the real dawn arrived and then we shot off down to Chamonix in what must have been a record time for the descent, reaching the Biolay at half-past seven before anybody else was even out of bed.

This magnificent first ascent, at the highest standard of rock climbing then achieved in the Chamonix area, launched Don and Joe as international figures in the climbing world. From then on the names of Whillans and Brown were accorded the same respect by the Continental climbers as those of Bonatti, Magnone, Rébuffat and Buhl. But the season was far from finished for Joe and Don; an even greater triumph was shortly to follow.

The weather had turned rough again and due to the new charges at the Biolay we were running a bit short of cash, so we made our lives even more miserable by moving under canvas about a quarter of a mile outside Chamonix.

I was sprawled out in the tent listening to the steady drip of the rain when Joe appeared in the doorway. He seemed to be quite excited in spite of being soaking wet.

'Hey, four Frenchmen have just done the second ascent of the West Face of the Dru,' he said, shaking water over me.

'Are they down yet?' I asked, wondering how they were managing in the lousy weather.

'No, somebody saw them on the top from the telescope up at Montenvers this afternoon,' Joe replied.

'Huh, they're going to have a struggle then,' I said. 'How long did it take 'em?'

This was the vital question because the first ascent by four crack climbers, Magnone, Berardini, Dagory and Laine had taken six days, spread over two separate expeditions.

Joe looked at me and grinned in anticipation of my reaction.

'Three days,' he said, knowing that we would both think the same thing. Six days was far too long on one climb but three days, now that was reasonable.

'Who are they?' I asked, hoping that I might know them then I could compare their capabilities with ours.

'You'll never guess,' Joe replied, still with a wide grin.

'Go on.'

'The same lot that held us up on the Cap. Now what about that, eh?' said Joe.

'Get away,' I scoffed, 'they were too bloody slow to catch cold!'

Joe shrugged. 'It's gen from Montenvers, so it must be right. Are we going to have a go?'

'Aye – as soon as we get a bit of sun,' I said, my gloomy mood completely gone.

Neither of us were under any illusion as to how difficult the climb would be. It would need more strength, stamina and determination than anything either of us had ever done before. The standard of the climbing, both free and artificial, was harder than anything on the dreaded Walker Spur; only the facts that the Dru was more accessible and at a lower altitude made it a safer proposition than the Walker. Nevertheless, we were convinced that if the four French climbers we'd seen on the Cap could do it in three days, we could do it in at least the same time. We began to plan for the climb.

That same night while we were playing table football in a café in Chamonix we heard that one of the French climbers had been killed during the descent. We felt sad about the news because we knew that for the rest of the party the tragedy would cancel out any sense of achievement they would get from having done the second ascent of a tremendous climb. We didn't get any details of the accident but the news impressed on us how seriously we must take the climb.

The following day we blew most of our money on equipment at Snell's shop.

'What do you wish to climb?' Snell asked us, sensing that it must be something big for us to flash our brass about.

'We're going to have a go at the West Face of the Dru,' I explained.

'H'm,' Snell lifted his eyebrows. 'You have any problems?'

'One or two,' said Joe. 'For instance, we don't know anything about the route.'

'That is a problem, yes,' replied Snell. 'Wait one moment.'

While we examined assorted wedges, krabs, hammers and whatnot, Snell disappeared from the shop and came back flourishing a paper-backed book.

'Have a look at this,' he said, handing the book to me.

'What is it?' asked Joe.

'Guido Magnone's book on the West Face,' I said.

We flipped through the pages and whistled at the photos showing soaring dièdres and vast, smooth slabs. There was only one trouble, it was in French.

'Don't worry,' said Snell with a grin, 'I'll translate the description for you.'

We thanked him for his kindness; we really appreciated it because such friendship for working-class climbers abroad isn't all that common.

Loaded down with gear and with French bread sticking out from the sacks, we had another splash and travelled up to Montenvers by the train, rubbing shoulders with the tourists. I often wondered what they thought of us. They would stare curiously at our tatty clothing and bulging sacks but whenever you caught their eye, they looked quickly away. We didn't exist in the same world. They looked out of the windows and made wondering noises at the sight of the graceful, aloof spire of the Dru. In a few hours' time we would be lost among the cracks and overhangs invisible to the tourists. They would probably think that we were mad. How could you possibly enjoy and appreciate nature when you were fighting for your life thousands of feet from comfort? Useless to try and explain that that is exactly the time and place when nature is at its most meaningful.

When we reached Montenvers, the sun was blazing out of a clear sky. The weather looked perfect at last. We jostled our way down the path to the ice-caves in the Mer de Glace and then left the crowds to begin the hard slog up the glacier moraine to the foot of the Dru.

After a hot, sweaty struggle we reached the great rock with the overhanging roof which is always used as a bivouac for climbs on the Dru and the Nant Blanc Face of the Aiguille Verte. We had decided to press on up the dangerous couloir to the lower terraces where we would spend the night. If the weather stayed fine we would be in a perfect position to start the serious climbing in the morning, and if the weather broke it would not be too difficult to retreat.

The snow cone leading to the foot of the couloir was pitted with stones – ammunition from the Dru – and we kept our ears open for the slightest rattle from above. Kicking our way up the snow, we reached the bergschrund.

We uncoiled the rope and armed ourselves with a few pegs and krabs. Because the Dru was essentially a rock climb we hadn't bothered with ice-axes and crampons, though Joe had bought himself a new hammer-axe which would see us through if we encountered much ice in the couloir.

'Let's have a shufti at that description then,' said Joe, and we both examined the piece of paper covered with Snell's handwriting.

'One pitch of Grade V and a peg to begin with,' I said.

'Where's the peg?' asked Joe, looking round.

We searched the rock.

'There isn't one here,' I said. 'The snow cone must be higher this year.'

'Typical,' sniffed Joe.

Joe stepped on to the rock and climbed up to a small cornice some twenty feet higher and then pulled over into the bed of the couloir. I followed him and we gazed up the couloir.

The route was obviously on the left bank because the thick ice which plastered the rest of the couloir was deeply grooved by falling stones. About 500 feet above us, the couloir narrowed, forcing both stones and climbers into the same path.

'I don't fancy that so much,' remarked Joe, when, even as we were looking up, a shower of stones came hurtling through the narrowed section and whined past us down the ice.

'Cross your fingers,' I said as he moved off.

We climbed quickly and very soon we were on the final pitch up to the safety of the terraces. Suddenly there was a dull rumble and we both froze, looking up the rock chute. Nothing.

'Joe, look,' I pointed back across towards Montenvers.

While we had been labouring up the enclosed couloir, great black clouds had descended. A cold breeze immediately started blowing up the couloir and the visibility began to worsen.

'That's all we needed,' I said in disgust.

'Well?' inquired Joe. 'Are we going up or down?'

I thought about it. 'Let's get up to the terraces first, eh?'

'Okay,' said Joe.

We crossed to the right wall of the couloir and Joe began cutting steps in the ice following a diagonal line to the terrace above. I listened to the ice chips tinkling away, shivering as the breeze started to swirl a clammy mist all around us. Joe climbed steadily, the rope moving jerkily as he moved on to each new step. Watching the rope, I suddenly noticed that it was rapidly running out; We must've misjudged the distance to the terraces.

'Joe!' I shouted. 'There's only five feet left.'

The rope movement stopped. I could imagine the expression on Joe's face.

'I've only about twenty-five feet to go,' he called back.

I waited, thinking furiously, though I knew that there was only one thing for it: I would have to move. As soon as I moved off the belay we would both be in extreme danger; right in the line of a stonefall with no protection at all. If a stone hit the rope that alone would be enough to pull both of us off to certain death. If I didn't move quickly, the couloir would soon be a combined stone and waterfall because even as I began to take off my belay, it started to rain. Cursing our stupidity, I started to climb the faint line of steps in the ice. Joe took the rope in carefully as I crammed as much vibram as I could into the ice steps.

'Is that enough?' I called up after what seemed an age.

'Not yet,' Joe answered in a quiet voice.

I didn't dare lift my eyes from the thin line of holds, I hardly dared to breathe as I moved up another few feet.

'That's it,' Joe called.

I lay against the ice, the rain streaming down as I carefully hacked two larger footholds in the ice with my peg hammer. I clung to the ice, pressing my wet woollen gloves into the holds hoping that they would freeze to the ice, head bowed against the ice slivers which rattled down on me from Joe's efforts 150 feet above.

Joe was safe now, out of the line of fire, moving swiftly towards the security of the rock terrace. I risked looking up to see where he had got to. I relaxed as I saw that he was almost on the rock. He reached out an arm then withdrew it and cut another step in the ice. Another reach and this time he pulled up onto the rock.

'Thank God for that,' I said aloud.

'Right Don, I've got a good peg here,' he shouted and with a terrific feeling of relief I started to climb, bringing feeling back into my wooden fingers.

By the time I reached Joe, the black clouds were pressing down all round us and the rain was obviously well set in. I struggled into my Pakamac, looking enviously at the expensive cagoule that Joe had managed to borrow. Determined to keep our legs and feet dry, we remained standing, staring out into the swirling cloud. Joe succeeded at the third attempt in lighting a soggy fag.

'Are we going down then?' he asked miserably.

'I don't fancy rappelling down that couloir in this,' I said.

'Well, it's no use going on, is it?' Joe said reasonably.

'We're going to get soaked whatever we do, aren't we? I think we should stop here till morning,' I replied.

I couldn't see why we should risk our lives on a dodgy descent when we were at least in a safe position. Joe smoked on in silence.

The storm was right over us now, a flash of lightning seemed to shatter the Dru and the thunder was almost simultaneous, deafening and frightening.

'Let's stop here and see what it's like tomorrow,' I said, having made my decision.

Joe shrugged. 'All right. Might as well get comfy then,' he said in his best flat voice.

A large lump of ice took up most of our ledge. We attacked the lump and the surrounding rock with great vigour.

'Christ,' Joe suddenly exclaimed.

I looked up from my hacking and scraping and saw Joe looking intently at his latest pride and joy – the new hammer-axe.

Then I noticed that the tool was not all it should have been: the hammer part had broken clean off.

'French workmanship,' he snorted.

We examined the now useless implement and discovered a flaw in the metal at its weakest part. It wasn't much of a consolation to know that Snell would replace it. If we did contrive to do the climb, which seemed unlikely, we would waste a lot of time if we'd to do much de-pegging with only one hammer between us.

After this latest disaster, there didn't seem much to say so we stood for hour after hour in the drenching rain, each of us lost in our own thoughts. As night closed in, the storm began to die down and then as it got really dark, a miracle happened, the rain stopped. We spread the rope out and sat down. With numb fingers, we got the cooker working and mashed the tea. After a meal of hard-boiled eggs, bacon and bread, things began to look a lot better.

Joe leant back and burped contentedly as he lit a fag.

'That's more like it,' he said.

We put on all our clothing and tucked our feet into the rucksacks. For me, it was a long night; I sat watching the clouds slowly breaking up, revealing the stars in a clear sky. Joe's regular breathing made me marvel at his ability to sleep anytime and anywhere.

I dozed on and off and woke with the first light of dawn. The day was cold with not a breath of wind, there was every chance of it being a good one. We stamped about the ledge, getting the circulation going as the cooker roared cheerfully and the sun touched the top of the Brevent.

We gazed upwards at the 2,000 feet of streaky red-brown granite above us.

'Well?' Joe inquired.

I nodded. 'Up,' I said.

Joe grinned. 'Right.'

As I climbed the friendly rock, I felt that surge of exhilaration and strength which means good climbing form. This was the life: no dodging out of the way of stray rocks and ice, no chancy moves on bad rock; just us with all our skill against formidable but reliable opposition. We thrived on technical difficulties, moving confidently and quickly, enjoying every foot of the climb.

' "The most difficult free climbing pitch of the climb," ' Joe read out from Snell's now soggy piece of paper as we reached the foot of the Fissure Vignes.

To me, it seemed like a good gritstone climb and I arrived at the top of the seventy-foot pitch without any difficulty; in fact the hauling up of the rucksacks took more out of me than the pitch did.

'If that's the most difficult pitch of free, then it's a cakewalk,' remarked Joe as he arrived on the ledge.

'Ordinary Very Severe,' I commented.

'Yeah, no more than that,' Joe agreed.

We were now taking alternate leads. Joe led up a tricky traverse under an overhang, which brought us onto a slab beneath a vertical wall up the centre of which ran a formidable crack. This was the famous forty-metre crack. A line of wooden wedges, soggy and dripping with icy water, decorated the crack, while away to the left a series of pitons indicated a false line tried by the first ascentionists.

'Your turn,' said Joe with a cheerful grin.

Twenty feet up, I found a much better stance than the one Joe was belayed on; it was quite obviously the stance used to climb the crack.

'Hey, you're on the wrong stance,' I called down to him.

'What d'you mean ?' Joe said in an injured voice.

'Come up here,' I replied, 'and see.'

Joe climbed up to me and surveyed the stance.

'Isn't it ?' I asked.

Joe scowled. 'You skiving bugger,' he said and prepared to lead on up the crack.

The pitch was all artificial and was therefore a slow, wet, cold job for the leader. I watched happily as Joe prepared to use the étriers. The slings on the wedges were swollen with water and exposure had weakened them. Also, the wedges looked very rotten and there was water running down the crack. Joe's hands quickly got cold and soon he was standing on his flimsy ladders blowing heartily into cupped fists. Slowly his swaying figure disappeared out of sight with a great jangling of iron-mongery. I heard him bang a wedge in and one by one the rucksacks were hauled up, only occasionally bumping against the steep rock.

Stiffly I stood up and straightened my clothes. I frowned up at the crack, not fancying it one bit. Then I had an idea.

'Joe? Keep the rope tight, will you?' I called and started to layback up the crack, using the protruding ends of the wedges, unclipping the krabs and slipping them on to the rope above.

I moved very quickly, but even so I had to stop twenty feet below the ledge to warm my hands. I noticed that the differ-ence in exposure compared to the previous pitches was a bit like stepping out of a skyscraper apartment on to the window-sill outside the building. I hauled myself thankfully up onto the ledge where Joe was standing among a rubble of empty tins and milk tubes.

'Did you enjoy that?' Joe asked sarcastically.

'Yeah, great,' I replied.

'Good, because your pitch is really bloody wet,' said Joe with a touch of venom.

Above us was a pitch which we recognized from a photo-graph in Magnone's book as the half-moon-shaped crack. A vee-gully above dripped a stream of melting snow into the crack. I had to put a peg in to get up this mild-looking pitch, but eventually I emerged out of the vee-gully into the shadow of a great, black overhang. This, we knew, was the last pitch before the most sensational feature of the whole climb – the ninety-metre dièdre. Joe took a stance below the overhang and I pre-pared to attack the verglassed roof.

I threaded slings and clipped to pitons until I was satisfied that we were perfectly safe from a fall. With feet pressed on one wall and shoulders on the other, I selected a wedge and, sweating with the effort, knocked it upside down into a wide crack. I clipped on an étrier and gently lowered myself into it and relaxed. A crack above seemed right for a peg, so with great effort I knocked one home, clipped on the other étrier and rested in what was now a cradle. I gripped the krab on the piton and strained upwards to peer over the block. A piton stared at me from a crack formed by the block and the gully wall. I stepped up another rung, still clutching the krab, trapping my fingers against the rock.

I reached up for the peg which would relieve all the strain in an instant but the more I stretched to reach it, the more my feet swung below the overhang. Exhausted, I dropped back into my cradle and considered the problem. Possibly the bloke who'd put the peg in had been taller than me and it could've been that he'd been at his limit of stretch. Well, I wasn't likely to grow any more so I had to think of another method of making up those few vital inches.

I launched out round the bulge again, this time pushing with my foot against the wall. I actually brushed the peg with my fingers but I couldn't manage to hook one through the ring. I slumped back again. After a rest, I unclipped a krab and tried again, using the krab as an extension of my fingers. I got it! Kicking my feet free of the swaying étriers, I pulled over the block and the most awkward pitch so far lay behind us.

When Joe joined me, we both noticed for the first time that the weather had worsened, dark clouds were closing in on the Face.

'Let's have a brew anyway,' I said, getting the cooker out.

'D'you know what time it is?' Joe asked.

'One o'clock?' I guessed.

'Five o'clock,' answered Joe. 'We've been at it nearly twelve hours.'

This meant that we had one and a half hours of daylight left. If we moved really fast, we could climb the ninety-metre dièdre and reach the bivouac ledge on the far side of a tricky rope move which entailed a pendulum swing.

'There looks to be enough pegs in there to start an equipment shop,' Joe remarked, indicating the vertical corner soaring above us.

'The more the merrier. Save us time,' I replied, drinking the hot, sweet tea.

'We're going to need them too,' said Joe. 'Look at the weather.'

We were definitely in for another storm, the cloud-covering was complete, we were sealed off from above and below. We had to reach the bivouac site before the worst of the storm hit us.

Refreshed, Joe climbed quickly and was soon sitting, suspended by étriers, below a bulge 150 feet above. I moved after him, hoping that the next rope length would be as thoroughly pegged as the first one.

In spite of the hurry, I took time to appreciate the position – it was certainly sensational. The left wall of the corner overhung steadily for 300 feet and the right wall had several great bulges in it and was capped by an enormous overhang. Two thousand feet below, I saw a small aeroplane through a tear in the cloud; it looked like a toy and hardly seemed to be moving.

As Joe attacked the second rope length, hailstones began bouncing down the rock and the cold grew intense. The hammering from above indicated that some pegs were missing and the ring of the hammer sounded out of place in this world of silent rock and dark mist.

We were reasonably sheltered by the overhang above but our position was far from pleasant. I wondered if we'd be forced to spend the night sitting in étriers.

'Don? I can see a rope hanging across a slab. What are we going to do?' Joe shouted down.

'We might as well try and get to the ledge,' I called back.

I sent up the sacks and climbed up, recovering the pitons that Joe had put in. When I reached him, he was sitting on a steep slab on the edge of the sheltered rock. One step away from him, the rock was streaming with water and hailstones were piling up on all the wrinkles. We had reached the point where, on the first ascent, Magnone and his party had abandoned the climb and transferred themselves to the North Face. A bleached hemp rope swaying in the wind above us indicated how they had left the West Face. To our right, another fixed rope led diagonally down farther right. This was the route to the bivouac ledge. The peg holding the rope didn't seem too brilliant, so I took a stance on two good pegs lower down and watched carefully as Joe descended.

'It's okay, it's fastened to two big wedges,' Joe called up, his voice muffled by the slabs.

I rapelled down and joined him. As bivouac ledges go, I've seen better; it was big enough – about nine feet long and three feet wide – but unfortunately, an immovable rock protruding in the centre ruined all chance of comfort.

'Going to be another lovely night,' Joe said as we unpacked the bivouac equipment in the pouring hail.

Joe sat at one end of the ledge and I perched at the other. We sat on as much of our equipment as possible to try and keep it dry. As darkness fell, the hail stopped and was replaced by soft, silent snowflakes. Soon we were both covered in deep, wet snow. I peered across at Joe, who appeared to be sleeping, head down on his chest. Beside him, his boots were full to the brim with snow. A trickle of water found its way through my Pakamac and gradually my duvet became flat and soggy.

'Lucky bugger,' I muttered to myself, thinking of Joe's expensive cagoule.

I sat listening to the drip, drip of trickling water all round us and tried to push all thoughts of the morning out of my mind.

The snow continued throughout the night, as we shivered and dozed the hours away. After an eternity, it began to get light.

'Joe?'

The mound of snow at the other end of the ledge moved and groaned.

'It's getting light.'

'Is it?'

'I'm half frozen and soaked to the skin,' I muttered through chattering teeth.

'What d'you think I am then?' asked Joe in a hurt voice.

'What? With your new cagoule?'

'It leaks like a bloody sieve,' moaned Joe, shaking snow out of his boots.

I looked at his pinched face and laughed.

'Just because you're wet doesn't mean I have to be,' he said glumly.

'Ah, it helps though,' I replied and felt a bit better knowing that I wasn't alone in my misery.

We got the cooker going and the brew was the best I'd ever tasted. The snow had practically stopped by the time we'd had breakfast and we got occasional glimpses of the valley below.

Joe fished the disintegrating paper out of his pocket.

'The next pitch is a good V, then there's one more pitch of VI left,' he said.

'Aye?'

'If you lead the V, I'll lead the VI.'

'Good old Joe.'

'It's fair, isn't it?'

'Okay.'

The worst thing was starting, of course, and we both knew this; even the harder pitches aren't so bad once you've got going. Still, somebody had to start and Joe obviously didn't want to.

The rock was cold and slippery and moving on it with already wet clothes was bloody unpleasant. Shivering and unwilling, I forced myself to climb. Gradually, life came back and I began to move with a little more enthusiasm. In spite of the coating of soft snow on the rock, we progressed quickly. Joe bombed up the VI pitch, which was surprisingly easy, and we soon had hopes of a quick finish.

The cloud cover hadn't lifted, however, and the higher we climbed, the colder, mistier and wetter it got. I started to climb a snow-filled crack in the angle of a slab. I sensed that I was extremely exposed though I could see nothing except grey mist below my feet. Technique went out of the window, I used clothing, elbows, knees and shoulders – anything that would grip on the icy rock. Thrashing snow down out of the crack, I found the inside wall covered with thick ice. The moves up the crack were hair-raising and it was with relief that I found a good peg near the end of my run-out. I took a stance and looked about me. Visibility was now down to a few feet, I had no idea what was above me and very little idea of what was below.

'Joe?' I called, my voice echoing strangely. 'Come on up.'

No answer, but the movement of the rope told me that he was climbing. After what seemed ages, a shadowy figure emerged out of the mist.

'This is a miserable place,' said Joe. 'Where do we go from here?'

'Let's see the description,' I said, and together we consulted our only source of information.

'What about this slab on the left?' I asked. Anything to get out of the crack.

Joe shook his head. 'Nothing. We'd better keep on up the crack.'

Snow showered down on me as Joe forged on, scraping and kicking his way up the apparently endless crack. I could just see us losing our way here, right when we'd finished all that hard part of the climb.

'Can you see any pegs?' I yelled up into the mist.

'Not yet,' came the answer and my heart dropped into my boots.

'There's a line of pegs crossing the right wall here,' Joe said in a doubtful voice.

'Well, that'll be it, get a move on,' I called.

The mist thinned for a few seconds and I saw Joe halfway across a wall, about seventy feet above me; a few feet more and it looked like he'd be on reasonable ground. Eagerly, I took off my belay and not wanting to stay a moment longer than necessary in the hostile crack, I climbed rapidly up to Joe. A couple more pitches and we were at the last pitch of V. I stared up at the rock in amazement; a long aluminium ladder was hanging down out of the mist.

'Look what I've found,' I said as Joe came up to me.

We both gazed at the ladder, trying to grasp the significance of this find. Magnone's party on the first ascent had used this pot-holing ladder to climb the Fissure Vignes some two thousand feet below. How had it got up here?

'Well, this explains how the French got up in three days, doesn't it?' I said to Joe. 'The leader must've lugged it all the way up while the others just shinned up it.'

He leaned out and gave the ladder a good pull.

'Seems all right,' he said, and with a rattle of rungs, he swung out.

When I had climbed up after him, we judged the ladder to be about seventy feet long. Amazing. An easy scramble over a few rocks and we looked out on to the North Face. We had done it.

But our troubles were far from over. Before we could start to descend, we had 800 feet of the North Face to climb, then we had to traverse across to the summit of the Grand Dru. Although the slope of the North Face looked almost flat in comparison with the West Face, it was plastered with snow and ice and we knew it would provide difficult climbing.

Ignorant of the correct route, we took a line leading to a sunlit shoulder – anything to get out of the cold, damp shadow. By this time the misty clouds had broken up and the weather prospects looked more cheerful, but before long we were in trouble. Joe couldn't manage a steep slab.

'I'm knackered, Don,' he said wearily.

I looked at him, his face was grey with tiredness and strain.

'Okay, give us the heavy sack,' I said.

We had been taking it in turns to carry the heavier of the two sacks but it was obvious that Joe wasn't going to be able to manage it any longer.

I climbed the slab and arrived at a line of traversing holds which had looked good from below but in reality were completely iced over. I couldn't descend the slab so I clawed my way desperately across the holds towards a ledge away on the right. Every move with the heavy sack sapped my strength and it was only with a tremendous effort and the last dregs of energy that I dragged myself on to the ledge. I stood there, trembling and gasping for breath, cursing my stupidity in keeping the sack on.

We reached the sunlit shoulder and lay, soaking up the warmth.

'Joe, we've got to shift unless we want another night out,' I said to the prone, relaxed figure beside me.

'Aye, all right,' he mumbled, half asleep, drunk with the sun.

Our clothing was still wet, we hadn't a dry stitch between us and the thought of another freezing night in the open was very uninviting. We had to move.

'Come on,' I said and scrambled to my feet, wanting nothing more than to lie down and sleep.

Joe slowly stood up and lifted tired eyes to look at the summit.

'Christ, it's miles away,' he said.

Pitch after pitch of strenuous climbing followed. I resoaked my clothing with sweat, climbing up never-ending cracks and struggling with the sacks. We reached the break between the Petit Dru and the Grand Dru and I soon squirmed up the final chimney to the summit. It was an immense relief to know that from here on the steps would be downwards.

Joe came to life again and found the point of the first abseil. Rope length after rope length, we zoomed down the Face, racing against the sinking sun. Just as we reached the bergschrund, the short twilight ended and darkness closed in. We stood on the edge of the bergschrund and tried to judge the distance across but it was too dark to make an accurate guess. Still, it wasn't going to get any narrower so I pulled plenty of slack in the rope and jumped for the faint, far edge.

I seemed to fall for ages and then I plunged waist deep into soft snow.

'I'm down,' I called, 'it's about eight feet across and maybe twenty feet down.'

'Are you sure?' shouted Joe who hated doing jumps even when he could see where he was jumping to.

'Ah, it's nothing,' I reassured him. 'Come on, it's a soft landing.'

After a bit more dithering, he finally jumped and plunged into the snow. We slid off down the glacier as fast as we could in the darkness. We found the danger spots by the effective method of falling into them. Blundering about, first on soft snow then on packed ice, we fought our way towards the Charpoua Hut and hot food, hot drinks and a comfortable bed. At last we reached a point horizontal with the rock bluff on which the Hut was situated. Between us and the Hut, two rope-lengths away, were a series of huge seracs.

'Well, that's it,' I said definitely.

'What?' asked Joe.

'We're not crossing that lot in the dark, it'd be committing suicide,' I replied.

Joe sighed. 'Yeah, you're right,' he admitted. 'If we had a torch –'

A great crashing noise high up on the Aiguille Verte caused us to stand absolutely still, ears pricked for the slightest sound of falling rock. We were standing in the débris chute – anything falling from the Verte would come hurtling down the chute.

'Nothing,' said Joe after a moment.

We began to reconsider the problem of crossing the tottering mass of ice. Suddenly, a thought struck me.

'Joe! Get down!' I yelled, and flung myself against the snow, smacking my piton hammer into the slope.

Within seconds, rocks of all sizes, chunks of ice and hard snow thundered all around us. The bombardment passed and we stood up, shaken and lucky to be alive.

'We couldn't hear anything because the bloody stuff was coming down soft snow,' I said. 'Let's get out of here.'

We moved out of the line of fire and hacked ourselves a broad seat in the snow, resigned to spending a third night in the open. We huddled together in the cold with chattering teeth, our wet clothes already beginning to stiffen up. I looked across at the black bulk of the Grandes Jorasses.

'I'd like to have a go at the Walker, wouldn't you?' I said longingly.

'Would I buggery,' replied Joe, and he sounded like he meant it.

'Let's have a brew,' I suggested.

'Can't,' said Joe, 'we've no matches. I've just used the last one to light my fag.'

'Bloody marvellous,' I said in disgust.

At the first sign of light, we got to our feet and stamped about, forcing the blood back into circulation.

Minutes after dawn, we were in the Charpoua Hut, but our desire for sleep had gone, all we wanted now was to get back to Chamonix as quickly as possible.

Soon we were beginning the long drag up from the glacier to the Montenvers Hotel. You run gaily down this path when starting a climb; coming back from one, it's all glassy eyes and gritted teeth.

Nothing had changed since we had left; the same tourists with the same ice-creams and badge-covered walking-sticks milled round, staring at us. Across the glacier, the Dru pierced the blue sky, supremely indifferent to the fact that two more tiny specks of humanity had beaten its challenge.

At the camp site we ate until we could eat no more and then crawled into our sleeping bags. In the middle of the night I awoke feeling very cold and wet. I struggled to make some sense out of the situation. Where was I? What climb was I on? Slowly, it dawned on me that I was in my sleeping bag in the tent on the camp site. Why was I cold and wet then? I sat up and was immediately engulfed in a great rush of water. Joe awoke with a yell as the flood which I was holding back swamped him.

Drunk with sleep, we staggered out of the tent into lashing rain. All around us were bobbing torches as lads dug channels or searched about for their belongings. The whole clearing was awash.

'Bloody hell, it's the second flood,' I muttered, searching dully around for a dry spot.

Thinking that another night of misery wouldn't kill me, I went across to the big tent and flopped down among a heap of other bodies. I slept through till nearly midday in spite of the sodden surroundings.

The third ascent of the West Face of the Dru was a great achievement. Don and Joe had cut the climbing time down to twenty-five hours – ten hours less than the time taken on the second ascent, which had included the dubious use of the pot-holing ladder.

The afternoon after the flood, they were visited by one of France's most famous climbers, Louis Lachenal, who, with Lionel Terray, had accomplished the second ascent of the North Face of the Eiger and had stood on the summit of Anna-purna. The dapper Frenchman chatted to them in the quagmire of the camp site and made notes as Joe and Don compared their ascents of the Dru and Blaitière.

Tom Bourdillon, the President of the Alpine Climbing Group, had arrived in Chamonix. Tom was a giant of a man in every way, hugely built and with a personality to match. He was a great companion, typical of the spirit in which the A.C.G. had been formed; no edge on him, nothing but straightforward honesty in everything. He'd been a member of the successful Everest expedition and, in fact, had been on the first summit attempt with Charles Evans. Walking into Chamonix that night, he casually mentioned that there was talk of a British expedition to Kanchenjunga.

'Would you be interested?' he asked us.

We both laughed, the Himalayas were not for us surely. The best climbers of past generations had struggled to get in the select circle of Himalayan climbers, we'd only just scraped the surface of the Alps.

'I hear it's all hard work,' I said while Joe walked on in silence.

I hadn't even dreamed of getting to the Himalayas; a long

summer in the Alps was about all I could hope for. I imagined what my father would have to say if I announced that I was off to Tibet for a few months.

Not much later, Joe got an invitation to join the Kanchen-junga expedition. I seemed to have missed out.

Don celebrated the completion of a successful season in the Alps by going into debt over the purchase of another motorbike. A huge, chrome-covered Gold Flash, the bike had a short life. Don and Joe, with a few weeks of their three months' holiday still left, decided to go up to Scotland and Don, loaded with gear, went round to collect Joe. Driving through Salford, Don pulled out to overtake a slow-moving car but failed to notice that a new traffic island had been erected during his absence. For a few seconds the air was full of flying bollards, 'Keep Left' signs and bits of the Gold Flash. Don flew across three lanes of traffic and landed on the opposite pavement. The accident cost him seventy pounds for the traffic island, the Gold Flash, the trip to Scotland and a badly sprained ankle. He counted himself lucky at that.

Back at work, Don encountered a phenomenon which was soon to become familiar: the resentment felt by people with steady jobs and a settled way of life against the man who prefers to lead his own, unorthodox existence. It was amazing how many of his workmates took it upon themselves to lecture Don on his responsibilities to his employer, his family and society in general. Don began to fret for his freedom and so, after an uncomfortable winter, chained to a routine which he now despised, he took his cards, left home and went down to Wales where Chris Briggs, landlord of the Pen-y-Gwryd Hotel, gave him work as an odd-job man. At least he was free from the daily grind and any financial disadvantages were outweighed by the proximity of the mountains.

But Snowdonia was changing. Each weekend, hundreds of

climbers and would-be climbers flooded into the Llanberis Pass and the Ogwen Valley. Since the ascent of Everest, the sport of mountaineering had surged forward in popularity. Climbing clubs flourished in every big city and at all the universities and colleges. The old miners' track from the Halfway House to the screes at the foot of Cloggy became as well-worn as the Snow-don path, but most of the ambitious ones who took the track simply stared in disbelief at Vember and the Black Cleft and then returned to the Glyders and Tryfan.

Like Colin Kirkus and Menlove Edwards, like Peter Harding and Tony Moulam before them, Don and Joe were ahead of their generation. Every so often in the climbing world, some-body – or more often it is a partnership – comes along and lifts the standard of the possible a little nearer to the impossible. With the exception of John Streetly, probably the only other rock climber of the early 'fifties who could have climbed hap-pily with the Rock and Ice was Arthur Dolphin, the gentle Yorkshireman. Tragically for the climbing world, Dolphin was killed in the Alps in 1953, leaving behind him a string of bril-liant climbs in the Lake District. In 1955, Don and Joe, un-approachable in Britain and proven Alpinists, had the eyes of the climbing world on them.

Towards the end of May we got the tremendous news that Kanchenjunga had been climbed and Joe had been on the sum-mit. We were all chuffed as hell and there were celebrations at the Pen-y-Gwryd as almost all the party were regulars there. It was a great achievement because the expedition hadn't been expected to make a summit bid, they were only doing a re-connaissance for another expedition due to go the following year. They had bagged the third highest mountain in the world.

Geoff Sutton called in at the Gwryd one night in June and said that he was off to Skye instructing on a Mountaineering Association course. I couldn't resist the 'call of the isles' and I collected my wage packet and went with him.

He drove his little van like fury and arrived at Kyle of

Lochalsh late on a Saturday night. We had just missed the last ferry.

'Well, that's done it until Monday,' said Geoff in exasperation.

'What d'you mean?' I asked. 'There's tomorrow, isn't there?'

'I doubt it. Ask if you want though,' Geoff replied.

I wasn't really with this, so I walked up to the nearest cottage and knocked on the door. A real sour-faced woman opened the door and glared at me.

'Excuse me, is there a boat tomorrow, d'you know?' I asked.

There was a short silence and the woman went bright purple.

'We keep Sunday here,' she snapped and slammed the door in my face.

She was dead right too, there wasn't a sign of life anywhere all the following day. On the Monday, we got on the first ferry and then drove round to Glen Brittle, camping on the beach close to where I'd camped on my first visit to Skye.

Geoff had to organize his group of ladies for guiding so I was left to find any stray who might fancy the idea of climbing. On the way to Glen Brittle, we'd picked up a lad and a girl who were hitching. The girl was home on holiday from her job in Tanganyika. She was a real tough-looking bird and as her boyfriend wasn't a climber, I took her out with me. She staggered the hard men by doing a series of difficult climbs in her bathing costume.

Eventually Geoff had a day off from his shepherding duties and with another guide, Jim Barber, we went round to Portree to have a look at the Old Man of Storr. This 200-foot pinnacle is a famous landmark and is an incredible piece of rock. It had never been climbed and looking at it for the first time, I wasn't all that surprised, as it overhangs considerably all round its base.

Round and round the pinnacle we marched, weighing up all possible routes but there wasn't any obvious line of weakness on the whole thing. As far as I could see there were two possibilities. Firstly, the back of the pinnacle, which faced a line of huge cliffs; the overhang for the first thirty-five feet or so was the main difficulty here. Secondly, the side which faced the sea; easy in angle for the first few dozen feet but then really steepening up. I decided to plump for the first possibility and tackle the hard bit first.

I placed a long sling round a bollard of rock for a start. It didn't seem too hot but there was nothing else available. I struggled into a sitting position on the sling. The rock in front of me was like coal, rotten and loose, you could prise chunks off without any bother at all. Twenty feet above me, it looked okay.

I tried to stand in the sling but my feet kept swinging under the bollard. I found a handhold and tried again; the handhold was small and my fingers began to weaken. I sank back into the sling. I had seen a hole above that might take a piton. I stood up again and put the peg in the hole and belted it with the hammer. The peg bounced straight back out of the hole and I caught it, pushed it back in then dropped down into the sling. So, the peg couldn't be hammered in but maybe I could use it as a handhold. I reached up and grabbed it and a few seconds later I was hanging comfortably from it.

So far, I hadn't been taking the climb very seriously; now I began to weigh up the chances of progressing farther. There appeared to be handholds of various kinds about five feet above but I couldn't see any footholds. I'd have to stand on the peg, that's all there was to it. I pulled up, being pushed outwards by a bulge in the rock, fully realizing that I'd have difficulty in reversing the move. To the left, the rock was sound and at an easier angle; carefully I leaned out leftwards and looked for holds. The only things I could see were two small ribs which offered a pinch-grip hold above the bulge. I put my left foot out on a wrinkle, stretched and grasped the pinch hold.

I was almost committed now, bulge pressing against my chest, fingers straining on the pinch grip, left foot doing very little and my right foot on the insecure piton. A small foothold on the lip of the bulge was the crucial hold. I would have to pull myself over the bulge without the assistance of footholds and then somehow get my foot on the crucial hold. I would then be in an almost doubled-up position, the pinch-grip holds being only inches away from the foothold. I heaved, summoning every little bit of strength I had, straining to get my foot up high enough. My fingers were tiring and with one final desperate effort I shoved my foot violently upwards and slapped it on the hold. I slowly straightened, shaking after the effort.

'Well done,' called Geoff from below. 'What's it look like from there?'

'Bloody hell, give me time,' I complained. 'I'm having a rest.'

Actually, the rock above looked much easier. After a few minutes, I mantelshelved on to a ledge, did a little gardening and progressed easily up to a grassy cave some seventy feet up. I couldn't find a decent belay so I climbed higher and found a good stance on the arete. The pitch had taken a diagonal right–left line across the back of the Old Man.

'Okay, I'm belayed. Climb when you're ready,' I called.

Jim Barber tied on and tried to climb up to the peg, but with little success. Eventually he prusiked up the rope to the point where the climbing got easier. Geoff followed suit and then we climbed on to the summit, about 120 feet of excellent rock. Standing on an untrodden summit was a new experience for me, even if it was only a pinnacle. In fact, the Old Man was a very good climb and, as far as I know, it has had only one other ascent and that was by Pat Walsh in the late nineteen-sixties.

Returning from Scotland, Don stopped off in the Lakes and spent Whitsuntide in Wasdale. There he met Johnny Sullivan, a climber from Derby who was a like-soul; hard, an excellent climber and with the blood of the wanderer in his veins. More than slightly eccentric, the red-bearded Sullivan lived on his own time-scale, rarely knowing what day of the week it was and never aware of the hour of the day. Sullivan proved himself to Don by partnering him on the first ascent of Trinity on the East Buttress of Scafell.

12 | The White Slab

Don returned to Wales where the weather was glorious throughout the month of June and the Rock and Ice gathered in force every weekend, repeating most of the new routes on Cloggy and planning the summer trip to the Alps. Early in July, Don, seconded by Vic Betts, put out a magnificent new climb on the West Buttress of Cloggy which they named Slanting Slab. Joe, after several months of load-carrying in the Himalayas, was finding the small-scale climbing very hard but like Don, was determined to have a good season in the Alps.

Even though Audrey was coming out with us, I refused to have anything to do with trains and so I set out a day or two before the rest of the lads and hitched it to Chamonix. Joe had set his heart on a warm-up climb on the North Face of the Charmoz and as nobody had any better ideas, this was the first thing we tried. It was a disaster.

There were four of us in the party – Joe, Nat, Eric Price and myself. Eric Price was a great lad. He'd been climbing with us on and off for a few years, ever since Don Roscoe had been on the scene in fact. He was from Manchester and he was the quietest bloke I've ever met. You could be with him all weekend and never hear him say a single word. Nobody could ever get into an argument with Eric, it was a sheer impossibility. He was a good climber though, nice and steady.

We set off from Montenvers in the evening, the idea being that we'd bivouac at the foot of the Face. None of us were too happy about the weather, which was unsettled, but Joe's enthusiasm for the climb made us carry on. We settled down under an overhang, the four of us in a row, squeezing together for warmth. I woke in darkness to the sound of dripping water and a feeling that I was being slowly squashed. I wriggled about, feeling the cold when damp patches of my clothing touched me.

'Shove up, youth,' the soggy figure on my left grumbled in my ear.

'How long's it been raining?' I asked.

'God knows,' replied Nat, 'I'm soaked through. It's them at t'other side of you, they're all right. Shove 'em up.'

Nat and I were under the narrow part of the overhang, while Joe and Eric were under a reasonable roof. I tried shoving Joe but it was no use, he was sound asleep and immovable. Nat and I shivered until first light.

'Well, that's it then,' said Nat as we packed up our breakfast gear.

'What?' inquired Joe.

'We're going down,' said Nat looking round uncertainly. 'Aren't we?'

'Why?' asked Joe.

'Don, tell him,' Nat said, appealing to me.

The rain had eased off but it had gone colder and already a few snowflakes were drifting haphazardly about. It was obvious that it could only get worse.

'It's daft, Joe,' I argued. 'We'll be snowed up to th'eyeballs before long.'

'Tripe,' said Joe, 'it'll take up – it's only an early morning shower.'

We continued to argue while Eric remained sitting on the wet rock, silently staring out into the mist.

'Come on, Eric,' Joe said, 'let's get going.'

Eric got to his feet and roped up with Joe. We watched them, baffled, as Joe kicked his way up the snow to the foot of the rock.

Nat stared after him with the look of a man who, having denied the existence of ghosts for years, suddenly sees one in his own bedroom. He tapped his forehead with a thick fore-finger.

'Bloody crackers,' he said sadly, 'th' Himalayas have gone to his head.'

We followed the intrepid pair, sometimes in snow, occasion-ally in sunlight. Pitch after pitch of reasonable climbing brought us nearer to the great feature of the North Face – an enormous ice slope.

The hours slipped by and eventually we stood at the foot of the ice. There was no further argument; wordlessly we started up the long slope. Rope length followed rope length as we kicked up the snow rib running down the steep ice. I was only hoping that we wouldn't have to descend by the same route. The weather worsened and by the time we had all reached a small rock platform, it was snowing heavily and a thick gloom hid the Face above and below us.

Joe led off and was soon out of sight in the mist, only the stream of snow which fell past us as he swept it from the rock indicated that he was still climbing. By this time, the snow was like a blanket in front of us and Nat was cursing everything from his ancestors to the cost of his rail fare to the Alps. A slithering sound from above, more chunks of snow and suddenly Joe was back with us, having slid down from a runner.

'It's no good that way,' he said, regaining his breath.

We were on the edge of the ice slope. If the rock was out of the question, it had to be the ice. I set out up the slope, cutting steps in the tough ice. Soon I was alone in a white, silent world, moving slowly through the powder snow which hissed in a continuous stream over the ice. I cut a handhold in the ice and put an ice peg in, dropping another as I fumbled with chilled fingers. The mist swirled away from the Face and looking back I saw the three spectral figures huddled on the ledge.

'Are you enjoying this?'

I almost fell off as I recognized the sound of Eric's voice.

'No,' I called back.

'Then let's go back down,' he replied.

I thought for a minute. If Eric bothered to talk then things were really desperate. I returned to the small ledge. Joe was preparing to descend, helped by a shivering Nat. Eric, impassive as ever, had resumed his silence.

The descent was dangerous as we climbed down the ice slope on steps that were half-filled with slippery snow. With tremendous relief we reached the rock and fixed an abseil. For ages, we slid down wet, snowy ropes, abandoning slings and pitons in order to get below the snow-line as quickly as possible. One last, long abseil took us out of the mist and sleet and into the rain and visibility. Now that we could see where we were going, our pace increased as we raced to beat the fast-falling darkness. Somehow we missed the gully that would have taken us clear of the mountain and became hopelessly lost. Wearily we struggled to retrace our steps, sliding about on slush-covered grass, hanging on to tufts of springy heather. After hours of misery, we reached the Montenvers Hotel and sat on a wooden form, eating the last remnants of our food and brewing up. Joe was almost asleep as Eric and I fumbled with the stove. Nat lumbered up out of the darkness.

'Want a drink, Nat?' I croaked.

'Can't stop, I'll never bloody well start again,' he replied in a hollow voice and disappeared into the blackness of the trees.

The nightmare descent continued until at last, at three o'clock in the morning, I ripped off my wet clothes and climbed into the heaven of a dry sleeping bag.

The failure of the warm-up climb did not deter Joe from putting forward as the next objective the latest 'last great problem of the Alps' – the South West Pillar of the Dru. A visit to Snell's produced no information about the climb, only confirmation that it was the great problem of the moment. Snell promised to give Joe and Don free rucksacks if they succeeded in climbing it. Joe bought himself a new pair of Louis Lachenal boots to show that this was going to be a serious attempt.

One great problem about the Pillar struck us immediately – the dangerous couloir which provided an entrance to the West

Face would have to be climbed to its top. Trudging across the Mer de Glace, heavily laden but in glorious weather, we could see part of the Pillar and we became very optimistic. We reckoned that if we could get up the couloir in one piece, the climb was in the bag.

This time, the couloir did not hold quite as many terrors for us as it had the previous visit. We had learned our lesson and both of us had ice-axes and crampons. We climbed quickly up the familiar, lower part of the couloir and then history began to repeat itself: the blue sky disappeared and snow began to fall quite heavily. We looked at the upper section of the couloir and realized that there was no decision to make, we had to retreat.

As we made preparations for the descent, we were surprised to hear voices from above. We stared upwards through the swirling snow and eventually picked out two figures rappelling down the Fissure Vignes. They were taking a long time arranging their abseils and were knocking a lot of stones down. With even more surprise, we saw that one of the pair was a woman. It was obvious that they would never get down the couloir before dark; they would have to bivouac on the ledge on which we were standing. We abandoned our six loaves of French bread and started to rappel down the couloir, shouting to the pair above to be careful what they kicked down.

New pieces of abseil cord hung from the pitons, left by Tom Bourdillon and Hamish Nicol after their attempt on the West Face a few days before. It was reassuring to see the new cord and we raced on downwards as the storm increased. I felt extremely sorry for the couple above us, I wouldn't've swopped places with the bloke even if the girl had been Sophia Loren.

The path to the Montenvers was a slick of mud and would have been easier in crampons. From Montenvers on the descent to Chamonix, we abandoned the path, which was more like a river, and took to the railway track – reminiscent of returning to Bryn Cork from Cloggy. Joe trailed behind, moaning that his new boots were crippling him. Sympathy from me was no good to him so I left him to proceed at a hobbling pace while I practically ran back to camp.

The following day we were in Snell's when several sun-burned men with a train of good-looking girls came in. Snell introduced them to us as Berardini, Paragot, Denis and Lesueur. They had all been on the French expedition which had climbed the South Face of Aconcagua in the Andes. I noticed their short boots and empty-looking suede shoes – evidence of the horror of frostbite. They were in Chamonix to give an illustrated talk and show some colour films. Much to our delight, they gave us some free tickets in honour of the fact that they had been unable to do our route on the West Face of the Blaitière. We enjoyed their grimaces as they talked of the Fissure Brown.

The holiday was over for Joe, Nat and Eric. Another day of rain convinced them that they might as well be soaked by the warmer rain of Snowdonia and they left Chamonix, glad to be away. Don and Audrey stayed on for a few days in the forlorn hope that the weather would improve.

On their last night, they called in at the Café Nationale and Don had a pleasant surprise.

Ted Wranghan's Jaguar was parked outside the Nationale when we arrived. I knew he'd been in the Dolomites and I looked forward to talking to him about his climbing there. Inside, he was sitting with a bloke I didn't recognize.

'Hello, Audrey, Don,' said Ted. 'I'd like you to meet John Streetly.'

So this was the lad. I shook hands and exchanged grins. I liked him instantly for his direct manner and obvious love of action. He was even smaller than me, with fair, wavy hair and an open, bronzed face. I looked forward to climbing with him.

Don hadn't long to wait. A month later while camping in solitude by the Cromlech Bridge in Snowdonia, he was sur-prised by the sudden appearance down the pass of a huge, two-seater car. The car stopped opposite Don's tent and a small figure leapt out and bounced over the wall.

I was sitting in the stream, trying to keep cool on a glorious summer's day, just contemplating finding a job, when John Streetly exploded on me.

'Right then, Don, come on. I've a few years' climbing time to make up. I've been doing nothing more strenuous than fishing in Trinidad,' said John, leaping backwards and forwards across the stream.

'Aye, right,' I replied, shaking the water off myself and scrambling about after my clothes.

'Arthur?' called John. 'Come and meet Don Whillans.'

Another man climbed out of the monster car and John introduced me to his brother, a quiet, pleasant character.

We climbed up to the foot of Clogwyn y Grochan and I suggested we try a climb called Nogombo that Joe and I had put out some time before.

'Anything you say fella,' said John, rubbing his hands with glee.

I stepped off and prepared to scramble up the easy first pitch.

'Doesn't it go up here?' asked John, pointing to the first pitch of a climb called Ochre Groove, which had first been climbed with many pitons but now was down to one that was considered to be essential.

'No,' I said, noticing that the essential peg was missing.

'Well, we may as well go up it, it's a nice pitch to reach the terrace. I soloed it yesterday,' John said.

I didn't mention the vital, missing piton but shrugged and stepped across into the groove. I managed to climb it free but only with great strain on my fingers. John followed, chattering cheerfully to his brother who was standing at the foot of the crag, watching a little apprehensively. On the top pitch of the climb, which is very exposed, I watched in amazement as he gaily pulled off the best holds and chucked them down, complaining that they were loose.

The next two weeks were the most hectic I can remember. We went from crag to crag, racing up and down winding tracks at suicide speeds in the huge Moon two-seater. The standard of our climbing was phenomenally high; second and third ascents of the most difficult climbs we could find were commonplace – Cemetery Gates, Erosion Groove, Surplomb, Suicide Wall and Suicide Groove.

'Got to get these things done now,' John explained. 'I'm thirty now, be too old next time I'm over here.'

With the possible exception of Joe, John Streetly was the best rock climber I had ever climbed with. His technique was incredible; he turned his lack of inches into a positive advantage and even though he could climb as delicately as a fly, moving fluently over seemingly holdless rock, he could also overcome problems requiring sheer physical strength with ease. Geoff Sutton wrote that, in his opinion, 'future advances in rock climbing will be made by men of less than medium height but of strong and lithe physique.'* His theory was that climbers of this build were likely to have the correct strength-weight ratio and the exceptionally strong fingers needed to advance the standards of free climbing. This was written in 1956 when most of us who were putting out or leading Extremely Severes in the normal run of thing were proof of Sutton's theory – Joe, John, Ron Moseley and myself.

Since 1956, others have come along to add weight to the theory – Pete Crew, Bas Ingle, Ian Clough and the great American, Chuck Pratt – but there have also been outstanding exceptions – Martin Boysen, Chris Bonington, Layton Kor – all of whom are well above average height. It seems to me that natural ability, an affinity with the rock and a desire to try for the impossible are qualities which will make a great climber, irrespective of physical characteristics, though, at the highest level of climbing, stamina and strength will always be essential.

At the end of summer, it became necessary for Don to find work if only to save up enough money to purchase another motor-bike. Johnny Sullivan suggested that the pair of them go up to Scotland and get work as labourers on one of the hydro-electric schemes. Huge excavations were taking place in Glen Garry, near to Glencoe, and Don and Johnny soon found themselves being given the once-over by one of the engineers.

*Snowdon Biography, by G. Winthrop Young, G. Sutton and W. Noyce.

'*We need two men for tunnel labouring,*' he said, looking doubtfully at Don.

'*Well, you've got two here,*' said Johnny.

'*I said "men",*' replied the engineer laconically. '*What about this little 'un here?*'

Johnny glanced at Don who was beginning to bristle at the engineer's derisory attitude.

'*When do we start?*' asked Don in a quiet, even voice.

The engineer thought for a moment and then grinned.

'*All right, you can start now,*' he said.

'*You just said the right thing there,*' remarked Johnny, breathing easily again.

The Glen Garry camp was primitive, but just about habitable. The men were hard and used to living and working in extreme conditions. Their needs were few and simple: a dry bed, a place to booze and gamble. Fights were a regular occurrence, often caused by the girls who worked in the canteen.

The work was tough and demanding and after a couple of months, Johnny had had enough and he left, considerably richer, for Derby. Don, determined as ever, stayed on until he had earned enough to buy a bike. Back in Manchester, Don found it difficult to get work as a plumber and so he and Pete Whitwell, a redundant bricklayer from Colne, went north in search of work.

We had a bad Christmas, wandering all over Scotland in sleet and snow, looking for work – any kind of work. We were both flat broke and bloody near the starvation line. Eventually we ended up at Haweswater in the Lakes, and got work on the Manchester Water Board project. A ganger, who must have been an all-in wrestler and who could have doubled for a gorilla, gave us a start as 'spannermen'.

It was good money but no fun: working at the face, deep in the hillside, with the drillers; twelve-hour shifts changing each week from days to nights. To say that the work was tough would be an understatement; a typical day went like this:

We'd leave our lodgings in darkness, slog to the point where the lorry picked us up, and stand shivering, half asleep, usually

1. Derek Walker and Don Whillans using a running belay on
Valkyrie, the Roaches, Derbyshire.

2. Don on The Mincer, the Roaches.

3. On Rivlen, a gritstone edge near Sheffield.

4. Don on the first ascent of the Frêney Pillar, near Chamonix.

5. Don on the North Face of the Piz Badile, Switzerland.

6. Layton Kor climbing the Cave Route, Leysin.

7. *Right:* The Aiguille Poincenot, Patagonia.

8. *Right inset:* Don on the ice ramp of the Aiguille Poincenot.

9. The North Face of the Eiger in winter. The continuous
white line marks the Direct Route to the summit, the

broken white the conventional route. The cross marks the
spot where Don and Chris Bonnington rescued Brian Nally.

10. Gauri Sankar, a 23,440-foot peak in Nepal.

11. Bob Downes's body being brought down from Masherbrum.

12. Don on the 'Little Eiger' of Gauri Sankar.

in driving rain or snow. The lorry would appear and we'd climb in, stumbling among dark figures and glowing cigarette ends. Every now and again, the lorry would stop and another passenger would climb in, rattling his bait box. Just as we'd get comfortable, we'd arrive at 'Belsen', as Pete called it. The lorry would stop inside a barbed-wire-fenced enclosure; great arc lights illuminating huge red-lettered 'Danger' signs.

A shambling, shuffling queue up to the small, lighted office window.

'Two hundred and six,' through numb lips.

A metal tag with the number on it from an anonymous hand and then up to the ramshackle hut to change into waterproofs, jostling with the night shift as they changed out of soaking, steaming, muddy, unrecognizable garments.

Then up the tunnel on the little loco to the face. The tangle of drills, compressed air lines, the foot of muddy water, the submerged rails of the huge digger which removed the debris and dumped it into the loco trucks.

Work would start and the scream of the drills filled your head and made speech impossible. Perhaps we'd be in a 'wet spot' – a fissure in the rock down which streamed gallons of freezing water – and in less than a minute we'd be soaked through. Then the face would be ready, plugged with gelignite to 'blow'. Everybody and every piece of equipment would be pulled back down the tunnel. We'd retire for a quick brew and a cheese butty in the draughty shed with the coke stove glowing warmly. Then back to the face and the whole thing over again.

A constant source of pain were hands, torn by the rock and then infected by the gelignite. The wage for the hours worked was £15 and the average weekly bonus was £12 – but to get that bonus, all work had to be done at the double, which increased the risk of accidents and completely shattered you physically.

Weekends were heaven. For one thing, we never saw any daylight during the week; for another, we could sleep and try to drive the sound of the drills out of our heads. Occasionally we'd have enough strength to try a climb or two. One excursion to Raven Crag near Thirlmere resulted in a very promising start to a good new route which we had to abandon due to ice, lethargy and blood poisoning – a present from the tunnel.

Pete eventually packed the job in and took a one-way ticket to Canada. I stuck it out until February and then went back home.

The thought of that unfinished new route on Raven Crag drew me back to the Lakes and I took with me a new recruit in the Rock and Ice – Joe Smith. Joe, known as Mortimer or Morty, to avoid confusion with Joe Brown, was a grand lad to have around. He climbed at the usual Rock and Ice standard and was always cheerful and talkative.

The route, which had been attempted first by Arthur Dolphin and later by Harold Drasdo, took a fine line up the cliff and included one or two exciting, exposed traverses. When Morty and I did it, the whole of the crag was plastered with snow although it was not frozen over. It was a magnificent climb which gave me great pleasure. We called it Delphinus. I think it made the long, tough weeks in the tunnel worth-while.

Joe, meanwhile, had received an invitation to join another expedition. This time, the object was the Mustagh Tower in the Karakoram mountains of Kashmir; a mountain renowned for its inaccessibility and frightening aspect. The expedition was a small one for such an intimidating peak and the leader, John Hartog, was an unknown quantity to both Joe and Don, though the other two members, Ian MacNaught Davis and Tom Patey, were familiar figures. Joe had to find £100 if he wanted to make the trip. He began saving up immediately.

Before Joe left for the Karakoram, he and Don solved one of the major problems on the Welsh climbing scene: they accomplished the Girdle Traverse of Dinas Cromlech. Previously, in March, the partnership had put out Sceptre on Cloggy and later, in July, Don led what was to be his last new route on the great, black cliff – Taurus.

In April, there'd been a bit of a shindig. One Thursday night in the Y.M.C.A., Joe asked me what I was planning to do that weekend. He and Ron Moseley and one or two of the others were going up to the Lakes for a change while Don Roscoe and myself were going to Wales.

'Well, I dunno,' I said. 'We might have a go at the White Slab.'

The White Slab was the big problem on Cloggy. For years, Ron and Joe had faffed about, talking about whether it'd go or not, doing a little bit on it every now and again but neither of them had made a really determined effort at it. They'd done a direct start to it but that was really as far as they'd got. I'd never even bothered with it at all, so I thought I'd give it a go and Don Roscoe was willing.

'You what?' asked Ron, who'd been listening.

'I'll have a do at the White Slab. Might as well,' I repeated.

'And the best of British,' Joe said.

We didn't get down to Llanberis till late Saturday night and we pitched the tent and went straight to sleep. While we were making breakfast on the Sunday morning, a head appeared over the tent. It was Ron Moseley and he was grinning fit to burst.

'Thought you were in the Lakes?' I said, surprised to see him.

'No, changed my mind,' said Ron, still with the big grin.

'Is Joe here?' I asked.

'No, he's gone up to the Lakes. Me and Morty came down here,' Ron replied.

I sensed that there was something queer going on but I couldn't figure out what it was.

'Know what we did yesterday?' Ron asked.

Then I got it. I knew very well what he'd done the day before.

'You and Morty?'

'Yeah. We finally cracked it. We did the White Slab,' he said.

I did the second ascent of the White Slab next day and enjoyed it as much as Ron did, I'll bet.

With Joe away, Don was at rather a loose end for the summer season. Most of the Rock and Ice were staying at home, unwilling to spend another annual holiday watching the snow and rain in the Alps. In Chamonix the previous year, Snell had shown Don some slides of the Dolomites and John Streetly had talked enthusiastically of the 'great, grey towers, straight as a guardsman's back'. Don began to think seriously about a visit, an added incentive being the assurance that the sun always shone in the 'Dollies'.

Earlier in the year, Don had climbed with two Lakeland-based climbers, Pete Greenwood and Paul Ross, both of whom were climbers of high calibre. He remembered that Pete had hired himself out as a guide to a dabbler in the sport who wished to climb in the Dolomites. Contacting Pete, Don found that the guiding engagement ended early in the season and would thus leave Pete free to do some serious climbing. The trip was on.

By this time, I'd got myself organized and bought a motor-cycle combination. Audrey was delighted with this as it meant that she could at last travel in reasonable comfort. Unfortunately, the bloody machine was the most unreliable contraption I ever possessed and on the way to the Dollies it was one breakdown after another.

Kneeling in sticky tar on some indescribable road in France, I finally chucked my tools down in surrender. It was blindingly hot and I was covered in oil and sweat.

'Bloody stupid machine,' I cursed. 'I've tried everything I know and the bloody thing's worse than ever.'

Audrey, knowing my mood, had remained silent during my futile labours; now she reached over and tried to pull the clutch in.

'You won't budge that,' I snarled. 'If I can't pull it in with two hands, I'm bloody sure you can't pull it in with one.'

I grabbed the screwdriver and poked hopelessly in the gearbox. I unscrewed a small stud a couple of turns.

'It works now,' said Audrey casually.

I looked up, prepared to tell her exactly what I thought of interfering women. She was moving the clutch in and out with nonchalant ease. Five minutes later we were on our way, singing at the top of our voices, praising the Lord for mechanical miracles.

We took the Brenner Pass from Austria over into Italy, the bike and the weather both behaving perfectly. I congratulated myself on deserting Chamonix, my excitement increasing as the kilometres rolled by. Just after leaving Dobbiaco, I saw something which made my eyes snap wide open. Slapping the brakes on, I pulled over to the side of the road and stared in wonder.

Framed by a steep-sided valley, two fantastic towers of yellow rock lunged to the sky. Inelegant and with a somewhat unfinished appearance, the Cima Ovest and the Cima Grande were a complete contrast to the orange and brown, snow-plastered spires of the Chamonix Aiguilles. But their effect on the beholder was just the same: awe and humility at such beauty. I could hardly wait to get to grips with the rock on those enormous faces.

We were to meet Pete at Misurina, a lovely village on the shores of a small, wooded lake. Due to our troubles with the bike, we were about four days late for the rendezvous and I had my doubts as to whether Pete would still be around. However, we hadn't been in the village more than a few minutes when I caught sight of a lean, slightly stooping figure dressed in a rag-bag of clothing wandering along the shore of the lake. In no time at all, we were pitching our tent by the side of his in the green, cool woods and swapping our stories of the bike's misbehaviour with his tales of the climbs he'd been on.

Few British climbers had ventured into the Dolomites before 1956, even fewer had done any of the hard, Grade Six routes. The main reason for this was that the British approach to mountaineering emphasized free climbing and was thus ill-suited to the steep, often overhanging and loose Dolomite rock. To climb the harder routes in the Dolomites, a climber had to be an expert in the use of artificial aids. In the nineteen-fifties only the young, almost professional climbers of the British Alpine Climbing Group were equipped with the techniques and knowledge necessary for Dolomite climbing. On the other hand, the French and Italian climbers had long been specialists in aid climbing and climbers such as Cassin and Comici had put out the famous Grade Six routes which bear their names as long ago as the nineteen-thirties.

Don and Pete had only scanty information about the climbs which they were going to attempt. Bob Downes had supplied Don with descriptions of some routes, craftily ensuring that he would have an extremely hard time of it, while Pete had gleaned information only about some of the easier climbs. Don's first objective was the Comici route up the North Face of the Cima Grande. This route had been climbed twice by British parties – members of the A.C.G. naturally – and was the hardest climb that had been done by the British in the Dolomites. Unfortunately, Don and Pete had no description of the route but a substitute was purchased in the form of a shiny postcard on which a broad, white line indicated the general direction of the climb.

I thought we'd use the Comici as a warm-up for the considerably harder Cassin route on the Cima Ovest for which we had a description.

It was nearly a finish-up. After getting supplies together I took the heavily loaded combination up the rocky track, while Pete took the bus up to the Hut where we camped. We had a cheap meal of spaghetti at the Lavaredo Hut and then the

following morning we stood at the bottom of the North Face
and looked for the start.

'Let's have a look at the postcard,' I said to Pete.

'You've got it,' he replied.

We looked at each other in silence.

'It wasn't much use anyway,' I said. 'We'll have to follow
our noses.'

I recognized a corner with some pegs in it from photos I'd
seen and I started up. The angle of the rock rapidly became
fierce and the climbing strenuous. As the exposure increased, so
did my enjoyment. There were bags of pegs in place and I
followed several false lines which petered out in the middle of
nowhere. The full sweep of the North Face looked extremely
impressive and the thought of the exposure in the middle of
that made our own position seem very unremarkable.

The quality of the rock surprised me slightly, it was about
the same as good limestone in England. The holds were good
and though I made it more difficult for myself by my reluc-
tance to use étriers, we moved quickly up the steep rock, only
now and again having to put in a peg. Soon the main difficulties
were over and we reached the great terrace which marks the
end of the technical problems.

Huge, dark clouds had crept in over the mountains and, as
we signed our names in the little book which sits in a tin box
on a tiny ledge, thunder rolled around us and the first heavy
spots of rain began to stain the rock. Cursing my luck with the
weather, I led on up to the summit, all pleasure at having done
a good climb rapidly disappearing as I battled on through torrents of water which streamed down my sleeves and soaked me
to the skin.

Luckily, or we might have wandered about for ages, Pete had
climbed the Cima Grande by one of the easier routes and was
familiar with the way down from the summit. We descended
the short chimneys and the maze of ledges into the couloir
through thick mist and it was a relief when we eventually
squelched into the Lavaredo Hut and got stuck into some tasty
'spag'.

Analysing our successful climb, we found that the time we had taken – nine hours – was more or less guide-book time, which was pretty good going considering our lack of information on the route. Anyway we decided to have a look at the next objective – the Cassin route on the Cima Ovest.

This was one of Bob Downes's chosen climbs and so we examined his description carefully.

'A magnificent climb, very exposed and on a big scale, where the rock and pitons are not always good. The hardest pitches are frequently traverses and a strong party is advised,' I read out to Pete. Looking up we could see an abandoned rope swinging about high on the face.

'Great,' said Pete, 'let's forget it.'

'It's been de-pegged too,' I said, having heard this sad news in the Laveredo Hut.

'Civetta, here we come,' Pete said with absolute decision and I decided not to argue.

Pete's girl-friend arrived at Bolzano, so we collected her and moved camp to Alleghi, a picturesque little place in the Civetta area. Shirley had come direct from England and she brought the great news that Joe's trip to the Mustagh Tower had been a success.

The climb we'd chosen to do was the North West Face of the Torre val Grande with the famous 110-metre overhanging dièdre which looked like it might provide a bit of a challenge. It was a short route but technically very difficult and I knew that the rock was not particularly sound. As it turned out, although the climb was far from easy and the rock lived up to its reputation, being in places like cube sugar stuck together with dried milk, we managed it in six and a quarter hours, an excellent time which provided us with the necessary encouragement to try one of the hardest and longest routes in the Dolomites – the North West Face of the Cima Su Alto.

Pete's enthusiasm had begun to wane a little with the arrival of Shirley but I managed to persuade him that after our success on the Torre val Grande it would be crazy to pack it in now when we were both extremely fit and with the mountain at our feet, so to speak.

The first ascent of our route had been made in 1951 by Gabriel and Livanos, two crack French climbers. It had subsequently been climbed on eight further occasions, the fastest time for an ascent being fourteen hours which, from what I'd heard and read of the route, seemed pretty good going.

We had no idea of the exact location of the route and we spent the best part of a day wandering along the meandering paths at the foot of the miles-long Civetta wall. Eventually we saw the unmistakable line of the Su Alto framed between two great humps of limestone. In our excitement we abandoned the path and attempted to plough straight through masses of undergrowth and brambles to the foot of the face. After hours of painful floundering which did nothing to ease tempers already tautened by the hot sun and tangled vegetation, we reached a decent bivouac site near enough to the start of the route. Suddenly, all was peaceful. We lay in the fading sunlight, leisurely cooked a much-needed supper, and then fell asleep, lulled by the sweet sound of distant cowbells.

At first light, we began to scramble up loose scree and crumbling ridges to the proper start of the climb. The going was uncomfortable; our rucksacks, laden with bivouac gear, were cumbersome and heavy but there seemed no alternative to lugging them along because neither of us reckoned that we would make it up and down without at least one bivouac.

At last, after an age of clattering up the corroding rock we reached the beginning of the first pitch. Two pitons indicated the correct line which seemed to consist mainly of a series of cracks and narrow chimneys. I pulled up over a small overhang with a piton in it and stood in a pleasant grotto. Tin cans hung by their lids from cracks in the wall and empty bottles stood in ranks along the ledge. This was the first Gabriel—Livanos bivouac and it was obviously a dry sort of place.

Pete arrived in the grotto, flushed and panting.

'An hour and a half, that little lot,' he said, regaining his breath and looking at his watch.

'Not bad going,' I replied, 'but we haven't really started yet. Have a look at the description while I sort the gear out.'

As I festooned myself with étriers, krabs and pitons and

organized the two climbing ropes and the sack-hauling rope, the first rays of the sun began to light the tops of the surrounding mountains. The Marmolata, highest of the Dolomite peaks, reached up through the blue haze of the morning. In the valleys, the heavy dew would be starting to vaporize and the early risers would be stirring in their comfortable beds.

'One pitch of Five before the start of the yellow dièdre – then it begins to get amusing – climb the yellow dièdre for six rope lengths. It says it's 500 feet, sustained Five and Six, steps of A1 and A2 and there's forty pegs in.'

Pete paused and looked at me.

'We hope,' I said with a grin.

Leaving Pete to his thoughts, I mantelshelfed on to a horizontal fault with a great jangling of metal and followed a natural line to the foot of the dièdre. As the corner steepened, so the climbing became harder. Generally, it was possible to make a few quick moves over a difficult spot in order to reach a piton already in, thus avoiding the effort of putting in some of our own. The only trouble was this method was very tiring and as my boots were rather on the tight side, my feet soon began to ache with the continuous squashing of my toes.

The sun was now on the massive wall and the air was already shimmering in the morning heat. The ever-present tinkle of the cowbells mingled occasionally with the unmusical tap and clunk of Pete retrieving another piton. Looking above, I felt half-relieved as I saw a wide crack splitting the overhang in the corner to my left. A long wooden wedge had been left in the overhang for which I was thankful because we had no wedges ourselves. I stepped out into space with the whole 500 feet of dièdre below me, casting an eagle eye on the wedge for the slightest sign of movement.

Once over the overhang, I'd expected the climbing to be less strenuous but I was surprised to find the rock still leaning gently outwards. Several cracks to my right seemed to be the line of least resistance but there was no sign of any of the fifteen pitons that the description had mentioned. According to the blurb, there was a sentry box some ninety feet above me.

Convinced that I was still on the right line, I started out up the cracks.

It took me a long time to gain the sentry box, due to the fact that I used only four pitons and that the sun was beginning to drain away my energy. At last I reached the bottom of the sentry box stance, and with my finger hooked through a peg below, I reached for the wire loop of a bleached wooden wedge driven into a wide part of the crack. Purely by instinct, I kept my left hand on the piton as I pulled up on the wedge. The next thing I knew, I was dangling from a severely strained forefinger, clutching a rotten wedge in my right hand. Dropping the useless log into space, I clawed my way back on to the rock, panting and perspiring like a four-minute miler. I clipped a krab into the piton, put a good, solid hand jam in the crack formerly occupied by the treacherous twig, and heaved myself and my accompanying junk into the haven of the sentry box.

I had just about recovered by the time Pete arrived at the stance. The sun and the strenuous nature of the climbing had obviously taken its toll of both of us; Pete's face was drawn and his clothing was soaked with sweat.

'You all right, lad?' I inquired.

'I'm knackered, man,' he panted. 'Watching your monkey act didn't do me any good either.'

I consulted the description and found that we were near to the Gabriel—Livanos second bivouac. I informed Pete and the prospect of a rest cheered him up visibly.

It was sheer bliss to sit dangling our feet off the sizzling rock, letting the sweat dry, relaxing our strained muscles. We were both hungry but it was impossible to eat without something to drink as well and that was out of the question: we might as well have been in the middle of a desert.

With a great effort, I stopped myself drifting off into sleep and squinted up at the shimmering rock above. One more pitch of hard artificial climbing and we would be on easier rock where we could free climb and thus move much faster.

I stepped out onto the top of a pile of blocks and reached

for the first hold. The wall above was steep and split by a crack higher up. One lonely piton decorated the pitch very near to the top. This wasn't going to be easy; we hadn't enough wide channel pitons for the job. I fought my way up the crack and planted a thick channel peg from which I hung, gasping and sweating, about ten feet below the solitary piton. To reach the peg looked horribly strenuous with no prospect of further artificial aid.

I looked down at Pete who was gazing serenely out over the magnificent scenery.

'Slack off,' I croaked through parched lips.

As he released the tension from the double rope, I launched up the crack hoping that I had enough strength left to complete the moves I had worked out. I snapped a krab through the life-saving piton with my last ounce of energy. After a short rest, I took up a comfortable stance in a chimney and prepared to bring up Pete.

The harsh, unfriendly sun had by now lost a little of its power and the chimney offered some welcome shade. Pete, almost spent after the nightmare of the last pitch, huddled gratefully into the cool stance.

Two pitches higher, it was necessary to traverse out onto the vertical left wall. Gingerly, I stepped out onto a small, crumbly ledge, casting anxious glances at the rope dropping freely down to Pete in the chimney. A group of splintered spikes above seemed to indicate the direction of the route, but they looked extremely unstable.

Thanking the Lord for my meagre nine stones, I put my full weight on the crumbly ledge and began moving slowly up on pressure holds until I was able to grasp the sound base of the spikes. Moving with as much care and delicacy as I could muster, I pressed directly down on the unstable mass and stretched for a good hold on solid rock. Seconds later I was safely belayed in a shallow gully and calling to Pete to come up.

I dropped into a quiet doze and was awakened roughly by a sudden tightening of the rope and a loud shout from Pete. Below me, he was cursing and struggling to get back onto the rock. The crumbly ledge was bouncing and rattling down the face. I watched anxiously as Pete approached the insecure spikes. Out of balance and temper, Pete grabbed the bad rock and with another shout and a crash, he was off in orbit again. Bleeding from a bump on the head and in an almost frantic rage, he flew at the rock and in no time at all was standing by me, wiping his face and uttering fearful oaths.

We had a brief rest in the gully, but with daylight fading quickly, we could waste little time. I ignored a line of pitons going up a most unlikely-looking wall and made a traverse to a zone of terraces covered in scree. A pitch of bad rock brought me into the final chimney and just as the last of the daylight flickered and died, I brought Pete up onto the summit of the Cima Su Alto. We had bagged a first British ascent of an extremely fine climb.

At the crack of dawn, we crawled out from under one plastic sheet and raced down a long scree slope leading to a tiny glacier at the head of a valley on the opposite side of the mountain. We followed the path round the great Civetta range and eventually arrived back at our original camp site. There we brewed gallons of tea and lounged in the now friendly sunshine before starting on the long descent to Alleghe. We bathed in every pool on the way down, and when we met Audrey and Shirley we looked and felt as though we'd just returned from an afternoon stroll.

Pete Greenwood was a fine climber who was always slightly competitive in his approach. He has many fine routes in Britain to his credit. Pete's home ground was the Lake District and the tales of some of his falls from those friendly crags are now part of climbing folklore. Pete, brought up in the traditional aid-free spirit of British climbing, firmly refused to countenance the presence of pitons on British rock even in their accepted role as protection. On occasions, he would jump for a hold. Brave it may have been, hair-raising it certainly was. Luckily it was never actually disastrous and Pete survived to become a successful businessman.

Don and Audrey saw Pete and Shirley off on their long hitch-

hike back home and then decided to move across the border to Chamonix for a last fling. Somehow the bike survived the Forclaz Pass and an outburst of torrential rain and they approached the familiar scenery with hopes of a good finish to the season.

Chamonix was almost deserted. The few British climbers who were still hoping for a break in the weather moped miserably around the sodden camp site. Don was surprised to see hardly any of the familiar faces; even allowing for the fact that the weather was so inclement, there should still have been more of the battle-hardened faithful around.

'Tom Bourdillon and Dick Viney have been killed in Switzerland.'

This news explained the absence of many of the Alpine Climbing Group. Bourdillon's death left a chasm in the ranks of British climbers, for men of his calibre were few and far between.

In the Nationale that night, Don got into conversation with Bob Downes who seemed determined to salvage something from the season.

He was a very quiet, reserved sort of man. I got to know him very well over the next few months and he was one of my kind. He had a strange scar running down one cheek, giving his face a kind of sardonic look which, I suppose, tended to discourage people from making friendly overtures to him.

I didn't know much about him then, except that he had a reputation as an excellent rock climber and that he'd done a few top-grade ice climbs. He was a very intelligent bloke and was studying at Cambridge University.

We talked about doing a climb and eventually I suggested that we have a go at my old bugbear, the East Face of the Capucin. I suppose I should have known better because this attempt went the way of my previous ones, only more dramatically.

It started off well though; up the familiar ground to the first Bonatti bivouac in good weather with everything going sweetly, then across a most impressive traverse on pitons to the famous forty-metre wall.

Engrossed in the climbing, it took me a while to realize what the noise I had been hearing for the last few minutes was. I looked up into a black, swirling sky and felt the sting of hailstones on my face. By the time Bob had climbed up to me, the storm had broken over us and we were being blasted by thousands of icy pellets.

Cursing my luck, but hoping that the furore would soon pass, we crawled into the large plastic bag that Bob and I had brought with us for just such an eventuality. Huddled together, sitting on coils of rope, deafened by the rattling hailstones, we watched the clouds gather round us, black and evil.

A great flash of lightning blinded us completely and the following thunderclap crashed with deafening ferocity against the rock. This was only an appetizer for what was to come. Lightning dazzled about us incessantly and the thunder beat at us in enormous waves of sound.

'The ironmongery!' Bob yelled. 'We've got to get it out of the way or we've had it.'

We struggled to separate ourselves from our krabs, pitons and hammers, thrusting the jangling shambles to the far end of our small ledge.

'This can't last for long,' I shouted during a slight lull in the pandemonium. I was over-optimistic.

We settled down inside the plastic bag and in spite of the tumult around us, we both dozed off. I awoke with a start and a horrible sensation of choking. Fighting for my own breath, the sound of Bob making the most frightening gurgling noises made me realize that we were suffocating. I tore at our plastic covering and gusts of cold air bellied into the bag and relieved the danger. While we had slept, the hailstones had become six inches deep on the ledge, effectively sealing us into the bag.

Meanwhile, the storm continued and as darkness came it became obvious that we would have to spend the night on the ledge. In all, we spent eighteen hours cowering there and even when we began to descend, the bombardment of hail showed no sign of abating. The descent was a torment of frozen fingers, icy rope and the stinging pain of the driving hailstones. I was never more relieved to see Chamonix.

After this racking experience, we both decided that we'd had enough; Bob left for Geneva and I collected Audrey and headed back home, hoping for a few weeks of good weather there.

The partnership between Don and Bob Downes was soon to be continued and this time with success. Before leaving Don in Chamonix, Bob had tentatively suggested that they spend a week or two climbing on Ben Nevis. The prospect of climbing the looming Carn Dearg buttress in hazy summer sunshine was heartening after the vicissitudes of the Capucins. The partnership made its mark in the annals of Scottish climbing in no time at all: the magnificent Centurion, with its never-ending series of overhangs, was Don's and Bob's first climb together on the Ben. Later in the week, they added the Shield, another new route of considerable quality.

With winter coming on and with no steady work to go to, Don began to take stock of his situation. One of the facets of his character which has, over the years, played an important part in his development as a climber and a man is his capacity for objective self-observation.

It seemed to Don that 1957 was the make-or-break year. Having reached the top of British climbing and also made an international reputation by his feats in the Alps, Don felt that this success must either be consolidated and if possible furthered, or it would soon be just a memory and a few words in the guide books. He had every intention of making climbing his only career, but the vision of the Himalayas and the Andes that had possessed him so vividly five years before as he looked in wonder at the Grandes Jorasses seemed no nearer to coming true.

Joe had been to the Himalayas twice with resounding success, John Streetly had been to the Andes and now Ron Moseley had been invited by the Rucksack Club to join an expedition to the Karakoram. When was it going to be his turn?

Don felt no bitterness or resentment for those lucky ones who seemed to have the money and know-how necessary to organize or take part in expeditions; but he suffered the outsider's frustration as he listened to talk of high-altitude equipment, coolies, transport and, worst of all, the thousands of pounds it took to get there at all. Don could see no solution except to go on climbing as well and as often as he could and wait until an opportunity presented itself.

I was sitting at home one night when my mother came in and said somebody wanted to see me. I couldn't think who it could possibly be because I'd got settled back in the weekday work, weekend climb routine and I was a bit out of touch with everybody except the boys. Then Bob Downes walked in. I was staggered to see him. We grinned at each other, standing there like cheese at fourpence.

'Come in, sit down,' I said.

'How's it going?' he asked, making himself comfortable in front of the fire.

I shrugged and for a while we talked about climbing and had a good laugh reminiscing about the Capucin. Then he dropped the bombshell.

'How would you like a trip to the Himalayas?'

I looked at him in amazement. Bob was no idle talker. He didn't waste words and he knew that I didn't.

'Who wouldn't?' I replied, wondering what was coming next.

'Well, the Rucksack Club are looking for another member for their Masherbrum expedition,' he said. 'I suggested you.'

All sorts of thoughts went through my mind. This was the expedition that Ron Moseley was going on. He'd never said anything. Perhaps he'd dropped out. How much money was it going to take? It was bloody good of Bob to put my name forward. What if they wouldn't accept me?

'What did they say?' I asked.

Bob grinned. 'They told me to ask you if you'd like to join them,' he said.

So that was it. All I had to do was to say yes and I'd be on my way to the Himalayas.

'You'd have to contribute £150,' said Bob. 'Can you manage it?'

'I'll manage it all right,' I said.

I was still too stunned by it all to work out how I would raise the money, but I knew I could do it somehow.

Eagerly, I questioned Bob about the details. I laughed to

myself as I recalled how, when Ron Moseley had talked about the expedition, I had kind of sealed myself off and not taken part in the conversation. This reminded me about Ron.

'What about Ron Moseley? What's happened to him? Is he not going or what?'

'No,' replied Bob, 'he's dropped out. I was asked to take his place. Then I suggested you.'

When Bob had gone, I thought about the great prospect ahead of me. First of all, the mountain itself: Masherbrum was an unclimbed peak of 25,600 feet; it formed part of the great chain of Himalayas known as the Karakoram. I knew nothing else about it at that time but that was enough. Then the expedition party: the leader was Joe Walmsley, a Lancashire climber I had never met but whose reputation as a good, steady climber was familiar to me. The rest of the party, apart from Bob, were unknown to me.

I felt extremely grateful to Bob for giving me this chance to realize my dream. I wondered if I would have had this opportunity had I come straight back home from the Dolomites instead of going to Chamonix. Then I thought about the actual climbing; expedition climbing was completely new to me, I'd almost be going back to school again. So what, I thought, the sooner the better. Of course, that £150 was a bit of a problem. It looked like the old bike would have to go again.

The expedition held its first meeting at White Hall Outdoor Pursuits Centre, near Buxton in Derbyshire. Don and Joe, who was going to the meeting to give his advice on equipment, spent a hard day on the local outcrops before making their way to the Centre.

'You'll get lumbered, you know,' said Joe.

'What d'you mean?'

'Paper work. They'll probably make you the equipment officer,' said Joe.

The meeting opened with introductions all round and Don had a chance to weigh up the strength of the party. In addition to Walmsley, Smith, Bob and Don himself, the other members

*were Ted Dance, an extraordinarily fit man who excelled in
the strenuous sport of fell-racing, and Dick Sykes, an under-
graduate at Balliol who was a good but relatively inexperienced
climber.*

*Don was impressed by the amount of work which appeared
to have been done already by Walmsley and the others. Sheets
of typewritten foolscap, maps, lists and inventories soon littered the rooms.*

I was completely lost among this welter of paper. To make
things worse, half the time I hadn't the faintest idea what the
hell they were talking about. Joe was in his element though :
he scanned through the complete list of the expedition's equipment and then, shaking his head, made a memorable criticism
of its contents.

'You'll need about half as many toilet rolls as that,' he said
with the air of a man who had judged to the very last perfora-
tion the toilet requirements of each member of the party for
six months.

Columns of figures were totted up, items were doubled,
others were slashed and the whole thing looked a shambles.
Over the years I've got used to the chaos which always sur-
rounds British expeditions and now I treat it as part of the fun
but then, well, it scared me stiff. I had to keep telling myself
that they really knew what they were doing. At the end of it
all, I emerged from the smoke-filled room clutching a list of
stuff which it was my job to get hold of on the best possible
terms.

For months I struggled with the unfamiliar task of writing
letters and bargaining. Every hour of my spare time seemed to
be occupied in niggling about all kinds of trivial detail. Then
just as I was getting the hang of it and progressing nicely, I
got fired from the firm I'd been working for. This was one hell
of a blow because I was saving every penny I could towards
my £150 contribution to the expedition's expenses. I'd no room
to grumble however because times were tough in the plumbing
world and a lot of men who'd been with the firm a long time
had also to go down the road.

Frantically, I searched around for another job locally so I could carry on living at home but there was nothing available anywhere in the district. I couldn't afford to lose even a week's wages so I handed my paper work back to Joe Walmsley with apologies and set off up north where I'd heard from Pete Greenwood that a big construction job was under way. He was working on the site as a labourer and he said that the firm was looking for plumbers.

On arrival in Carlisle I was faced with the same old sordid problem : if you've no job you can't afford to take digs, and if you've no digs, you've nowhere to sleep. Pete Greenwood turned up trumps however and found me a tiny bedsitter in the place where he himself was lodging. I was glad I hadn't lost him in the Dollies.

The construction site was the same as usual – filthy wooden huts, deep mud, biting winds and at that time of year, howling blizzards and sub-freezing temperatures.

The plumbing work wasn't due to start for another few weeks so I had to take a labouring job in the meantime. For two weeks, in atrocious conditions, I stuck it out, working under the thickest bloke it's ever been my misfortune to meet. Then I went to the boss.

'Look,' I said, fuming with anger, 'I can't stick this any more. I've had a bellyful of that stupid bastard out there. Either find me some preparatory plumbing to do or I'm off.'

Having said my piece, I waited for the boss to fly off the handle, mentally preparing my departure as I stood there in the warm hut.

'Okay,' he replied at last, 'wait in the small cabin till I find you something.'

Surprised but very pleased, I took myself off to the comfortable cabin with its huge, glowing stove. Three weeks later, the boss appeared in the doorway.

'Got a job for you, come outside,' he said.

With a sigh for my lost days of paid leisure, I donned my outer clothing and followed him out into the wild weather. We crossed to where a line of men stood among broken ice and rutted mud outside his office.

'Pick four out of that lot,' he said, waving a hand at the men.

I walked up and down the line, feeling like a cross between a power-mad army sergeant and an executioner. I chose the four toughest-looking and reported back to the boss. He nodded approval and set them to work moving three-inch pipes with me as foreman.

The days of struggling in trenches so deep in mud and water that it was impossible to keep the boots on your feet were relieved by the odd letter from Bob saying that the expedition plans were working out well. As far as I was concerned, the departure date couldn't come soon enough.

*   *   *

The final few days before the departure of any expedition are always hectic; the round of interviews, last-minute organizational checks and farewell parties make the time fly by and it comes as a relief when eventually Liverpool is left astern and ahead lie five weeks of uninterrupted, worry-free leisure.

Another expedition was also sailing for Karachi; led by Everest-man Alf Gregory, its objective was Disteghil Sar, another unclimbed peak in the Karakoram. Don was delighted to meet one of the expedition's members – John Cunningham. Don had wanted to meet the already legendary Scot who had done so many incredible things. At first glance, Cunningham, suavely dressed in blazer and grey slacks, seemed anything but the tough, resilient adventurer. It was hard to realize that he and that other Herculean Scot, Hamish McInnes, had set out in 1952 to scale Everest without any more equipment than was normally taken to the Alps.

'If we'd had another sack of potatoes we'd have had a go,' McInnes was reported to have said.

In Karachi we were assured that our baggage was right there on the train with us, and we began the cross-country journey to Rawalpindi. I'm not a great enthusiast for train journeys and this one was one in a million. Fighting our way through swarms of flies and beggars, we entered a compartment which was stacked high with blocks of ice, placed there to keep us cool on the two-day trip. Within hours, we were ankle deep in water with just the odd bit of ice gently floating on the swell.

We spent two days and a night crossing a vast, scrubby waste of sand, the temperature soaring and dust clogging up our throats and noses. It was dark when we arrived at Rawalpindi but the station was like a mad-house with hundreds of yelling Pakistanis fighting for the chance to earn a couple of bob by carrying our baggage to the waiting room. We struggled through the mob and reached the haven of the first-class waiting room where we spent the rest of the night on wicker cots.

The following day we booked ourselves in at a good hotel and began organizing ourselves and our personal gear. Relations were soon established with a retired colonel of the British Army – Buster Goodwin – from whom we received much generous assistance, and our liaison officer, Captain Rizvi, of the Pakistan Army. One outcome of this was that we very quickly moved out of the expensive hotel and into the Officers' Mess of Rizvi's regiment. This was a profitable move in more ways than one, because at the Mess we met Major Jhan Zeb Khan who had acted as liaison officer to the last expedition which had attempted Masherbrum. This was a New Zealand party in 1955, which, although a strong one, had not got as high on the mountain as the first expedition to Masherbrum – a British party in 1938.

So far, everything had gone smoothly with just one exception: we had lost all the expedition equipment. How this catastrophe had come about was a complete mystery; it had left Karachi with us and, as far as we were aware, the train had not been hijacked on the journey to Rawalpindi. The only possible solution was that it had been removed by mistake from the train at Lahore. Telegrams flashed back and forth between Rawalpindi, Lahore and Karachi. Eventually, two weeks later, it turned up, more or less intact.

The next step in our journey was the air flight from Rawalpindi to Skardu. No commercial airline will attempt to run a service between these two outlandish spots because the route, which is reported to be the most dangerous in the world, follows the course of the Indus river for the most part, hopping in and out of the deep gorges and narrow twisting valleys. We had to cadge a lift from the Pakistani Air Force.

Bob and I were very excited at the prospect of flying past Nanga Parbat and getting a bird's-eye view of this savage mountain which had fallen to the lone, heroic Hermann Buhl.

We were equipped with parachutes and instructed in their use and then, with a great rattling, we were on our way. The plane was a freight carrier and looked and sounded none too safe to me but I comforted myself with the thought of the parachute. It was only when we had been airborne for an hour or so that it dawned on me that the parachute was not the slightest bit of use.

The plane hadn't the power to rise above the towering ridges and so had to hedge-hop a couple of hundred feet over the tree tops. Suddenly the plane began to lurch and bump dangerously. The pilot signalled that the weather was closing in and that it was too misty to go on. The prospect of flying along the narrow valleys through cloud and mist didn't appeal to us either, so we made no complaints as the plane banked round and headed back to Rawalpindi.

A few days later we boarded another plane and this time all went smoothly. Gazing hopefully through the small windows, my heart leapt as the White Giant – Nanga Parbat – suddenly came into view. Intently, I studied the huge mountain rising above the early morning haze. I visualized Hermann Buhl toiling up the glaring snow slopes and ridges on his lonely way to the top. My eyes dropped slowly down from the White Summit, taking in the vast, high snowfield, then the tumbled mass of the glaciers and moraine to the bare, brown flanks of the mountain. At the foot of the dusty slopes, the river wound its way like a thin piece of cord. There was no doubt about it, it was a long way to the top of these mountains.

Skardu, at 7,000 feet, lay in a wide, brown valley. It was much cooler than Rawalpindi had been and seemed a decent enough place from which to set out on our 112-mile hike to the proposed Base Camp. We stayed at the Government Rest House and began to unpack the equipment and divide it into individual loads. We signed the visitors' book and looking back through it, it felt strange to see Joe Brown's familiar scrawl as part of the Mustagh Tower party. Just before our entries in the book, the names of Hermann Buhl and other famous Austrian climbers indicated that they had passed through on their way to Broad Peak at the head of the Baltora Glacier.

Selection of high-altitude porters from the crowd of coolies who were going to transport our equipment to the Base Camp was a difficult, trying job. Dozens of men, all shapes and sizes, waving bits of paper which were their testimonials from previous expeditions, all fought for these plum jobs.

High-altitude porters are the cream; receiving good pay, steady employment, free clothing and equipment and plenty of perks when the expedition is over. One man, sporting a badge with a tiger's head on it and an inscription 'Balti Tiger', had been on the Italian K.2 expedition. He took it upon himself to select the men he thought best; when he had done so, we sacked him.

The long slog began at four o'clock on a fine, crisp morning. I usually walked alone, being a one-pace man, quite happy to jog along behind the straggling caravan. Days passed and we drew steadily nearer to our mountain. We crossed the Shyok River in an unsteady flat-bottomed boat and arrived at the village of Mackilui where our coolies – over 300 of them – were routed by one woman brandishing a huge knife. The coolies had been helping themselves to the fruit from the woman's orchard.

At Mackilui, we left some of our supplies in the headman's house in the hope that we could use them on another mountain if Masherbrum succumbed easily. From Mackilui, the mountain was plainly visible; it looked very impressive and I thought that the leaving of the supplies was presumptuous.

The sight of the mountain made the frustrations of the last few weeks seem insignificant. If any of us had any doubts as to whether the worry and struggle of getting the expedition this

far had been worth-while, they were completely dispelled as
we turned into the Hushi Valley and saw the enormous,
shapely bulk of Masherbrum filling the skyline. It was difficult
to believe that we were still forty miles from the peak.

*Approach marches, base camp building, the establishment of
a chain of camps stringing up the mountain, are routine pro-
cedures for every expedition. But they are not without danger
or excitement; avalanches, route-finding, strikes by the porters
and a thousand and one other incidents keep the expedition
members on their toes.*

*The assault on a mountain the size of Masherbrum requires
persistence, determination and stamina. There is no easy way
to climb a Himalayan peak; men who challenge these mountains are putting themselves to a supreme physical and mental
test. Each man must consider those in front of him and those
behind him. Unity of purpose is essential to success.*

*On 15 June 1957, the Masherbrum expedition established a
comfortable Base Camp at 13,000 feet. A few days later Don
and Geoff Smith started up the mountain with the object of
finding the route and selecting safe sites for the various camps.*

Our first summit bid from Camp Six failed mainly because I
lost all track of time and made a miscalculation of the sun's
position.

Geoff and I had struggled up from Camp Six for what seemed
an eternity. I decided that it was too late in the day to attempt
to climb the steep, soggy snow slope up to the col between the
twin summits. Returning to Geoff, who had a watch, I was
amazed to find that it was only eleven o'clock in the morning,
but even so we had been labouring upwards for six hours and
we were both very tired.

The snow was in a terrible state as the sun beat blindingly
down on it. I reckoned that it would be too much for us to
make the summit and back that day, so we dragged ourselves
to a tiny serac where we relaxed in the shade.

'We'll bivvy here,' I said. 'The weather looks settled; if it's
good tomorrow, we'll make it easy.

Geoff agreed. We reckoned that we were at about 24,500 feet, some thousand feet from the summit. The snow would freeze hard during the night and apart from the rock step very near to the summit, which we thought we could avoid anyway, it looked like it would be plain sailing.

We settled into our hacked-out ice seats in the grotto and while I was making a tremendous effort to light the Primus, Geoff discovered the beginnings of frost-bite in his hand. Combined with the inability of the stupid matches to light, this news was a bit shattering. We resolved to keep close watch on our extremities as we settled down to face the freezing hours of darkness.

I awoke with a screaming pain in my right foot. Hastily I ripped off the clumsy high-altitude boot and rubbed frantically at my foot until I nearly wept at the agony of returning life. Outside our plastic covering, I could hear the moan of the wind and my heart sank as I realized that we were enveloped in thick cloud.

At first light, we disappointedly kicked our way back to Camp Six. The spell of good weather had obviously broken and it looked like a great storm was about to break over the mountain. In fact we had no sooner climbed stiffly into our sleeping bags than the storm arrived and we could hear the hiss of the snow-slides racing down at either side of the tent.

Just as I was dozing off, I heard voices outside; only just audible intermittently in the wind. Quickly, we wrapped up and struggled out of the tent. Down the slope, two dim figures were wallowing in the seething mass of snow.

'What are you doing?' I yelled against the wind.

Camp Six was only a two-man tent and in any case we had little food left. As the figures drew nearer, I saw that it was Ted and Dick.

'Throw us a rope,' they called up.

'Get back to Camp Five, this is crazy,' I shouted in reply.

But it was no use. They refused to return to Camp Five and so we had no alternative but to throw them a rope and for the four of us to crush into the tiny tent.

Five days of absolute purgatory followed. Unable to stretch, soaked with condensation, without food, and fighting to hold back the tide of snow which streamed continuously over our flimsy covering, we crouched miserably together.

When the storm finally quietened down enough for us to emerge from the tent, Ted had become a liability, the altitude and the cramped conditions causing him to lose the powers of speech and co-ordination. Leaving Geoff and Dick to follow my trail, I set out into the thin film of cloud, moving across a steep snow ramp between two sets of ice cliffs.

Visibility was practically nil in the white clinging mist and I groped blindly forward, moving from instinct and memory. Suddenly I realized that the snow underfoot was turning to ice and that the incline was steeper. Certain that I had somehow got too high and that I was above the ice cliffs, I took one more step to see if the slope steepened any more. A crampon caught in the canvas overboots I was wearing and with a neat dive, I went head first over the 100-foot-high ice cliffs.

Convinced that I would go sliding over the ramp and down the really big ice cliffs farther down, I idly wondered how long I would stay conscious as I crashed on to the back of my neck and somersaulted off again. Then with a great thud, I landed in a huge drift of new snow at the top of the snow ramp. Wearily, I dragged myself to my feet and, without any feeling or emotion whatever, I shook my head to clear it, and set off again towards Camp Five.

It wasn't long before I noticed a sharp pain in my right ankle and I supposed that I must have sprained it in my glorious tumble. Quickly making up my mind, I determined to push on to Camp Four, which was much more comfortable than Camp Five. As I limped through the deep snow, the cloud cover cleared and the sun turned the mountain into a blaze of white light. I turned and looked back up the glittering face. High above me, three black dots were stationary above an ice cliff.

'Work that bugger out,' I said to myself and enjoyed a quiet chortle.

I arrived at Camp Four in considerable pain and settled down to examine the extent of my injury. I wasn't left to my own devices long, however, because much to my pleasure Joe Walmsley and Bob arrived eager for news.

'Did you get there?' asked Joe.

'No, sorry Joe. We got within 400 feet then that bloody storm put an end to it.'

'Tough,' said Joe. 'Rizvi saw you. He sent two cigars up. Felt sure you'd make it.'

'There'll be another time,' I said.

They filled me in with the news from the Base Camp. Bob, who had not been well when we arrived at the foot of Masherbrum, had spent several weeks recuperating at the village of Hushi farther down the valley and now looked very fit again.

I suggested that for the next summit bid, a small camp should be set up where Geoff and I had bivouacked. I felt certain that, granted a few hours good weather, the summit could be easily reached from there. Joe agreed and he, Bob and one of the high-altitude porters set off on the upward trek.

Geoff, Dick and Ted, a trifle amazed at the speed of my descent, arrived and then continued on down to Camp Three leaving me once again in solitude.

I decided to brew-up and searched around for some matches. I rummaged through every possible pocket and container; there wasn't a single match in the place. Of all the things to be short of, this was the worst possible. Most of the food was dehydrated and so without water there wasn't much one could do. I pondered the situation.

Five tortured days in Camp Six without a decent drink and nothing much to eat, a swollen ankle which would not allow any movement for at least three days, and now, no matches. I decided to sleep.

During the night, a fierce wind battered the tent and I awoke to find everything covered in fine snow which had blown in through a tear in the canvas. Miserably, I picked at some concentrated food blocks and contemplated raw porridge oats with horror.

I remembered the advice given in some medical reports on high-altitude climbing.

'Every climber should drink at least eight pints of liquid a day.'

I shook my head in disgust. 'Bloody lucky to get eight pints a week,' I thought. In any case, it takes two hours to melt enough snow to make two pints of tea. You'd be brewing up all day to get eight pints.

The blizzard roared on outside and another crisis arose inside. This time it was a question of nature taking its course. Normally, it's a quick dash outside and head into the wind, but for me that was out of the question. Doing my best to forget I had such things as bodily functions, I forced myself to sleep.

Another morning dawned and I could shelve the problem no longer. Luckily the storm seemed to have calmed down, so at least I wouldn't get blown down the mountain. Gingerly testing my ankle, I crawled outside the tent. The swelling had subsided but as I put my weight on the foot, the pain shot up my leg with the same old force. I resorted to hopping along on my hands and my one good foot, leaving the injured leg trailing behind me. I lowered my trousers and stared out across at some tremendous ice cliffs which, just to add the finishing touches to my torment, chose that exact moment to avalanche.

Lumps like blocks of flats keeled over in slow motion and crashed down on to the plateau. Anxiously I judged the distance of the holocaust from the camp.

'No, it'll never reach here,' I said to myself.

A wall of fine snow was rising high in the air and I made another quick calculation.

'Impossible,' I muttered.

The billowing clouds of snow continued to rise skyward and I could see that they were travelling quite quickly. I wondered if there was any solid stuff behind the snow. Deciding that it wouldn't be wise to hang about and find out, I clutched my trousers and shot off like a wounded hare as fast as I could across the crusty snow. I didn't make it. A great blast of air bowled me over and I was enveloped in the snow cloud. Luckily that was all it was, and even with my pants full of snow and my ankle giving me hell, I saw the funny side of it and laughed till my empty stomach ached.

The time had come for some more action. I tied up the tent door and began the painful trek down to Camp Three. This journey was far from easy, as the vast snow falls of the past two weeks had altered the landscape considerably. Luckily I hadn't gone far when I arrived below the cloud ceiling and saw Camp Three in the distance.

Much to my disgust, Dick and Geoff were just finishing the last of the food. To add to my dangerous frame of mind, three high-altitude porters arrived carrying a minimum of equipment. I blew up.

'What the bloody hell's been going on down here for the last six weeks? Look at that lot they've just brought up, I could've brought more in my bloody pockets.'

I buttonholed the panic-stricken porters as Geoff and Dick looked on in silence.

'I'm going down to Base Camp tomorrow and you're all coming with me and when we get there, I'm going to load you with 100 pounds apiece and you're going to get it up here.'

A day later, the three porters and myself arrived at the Base Camp. Things had changed during my six weeks' absence; the tents now sat on a glacier completely cleared of snow and the surrounding scenery was like paradise; colours that would normally appear drab had taken on a new lustre; the grey granite and the patches of lichen seem brightly-hued after the endless white glare of the snow slopes.

Rizvi greeted me warmly and was rather taken aback when I took him to task about the lack of supplies on the mountain.

'What the hell do you think Bob and Joe are going to eat while they're making the summit bid?' I asked.

I had a hasty meal and then began to make up the loads for the three porters. They stood around, their eyes growing larger and larger, almost keeping pace with the loads.

Rizvi remarked in a worried voice that the porters were not going to stand for the size of the loads. At this I really lost control.

'The trouble with these lazy bastards is they've had it too

cushy for too long. This is an expedition to climb a mountain, not a bloody rest camp. And you can tell them this; any one of 'em who isn't intending going up tomorrow can take his bloody hook now.'

At the crack of dawn, Ted, now fully recovered, the porters and myself set off for Camp Two. We stopped for a rest at Camp One but I forced the reluctant porters on and up to Camp Two. I spent a weary, sleepless night in Camp Two and was greeted by the sight of gently falling snow in the morning.

It had been my intention that Ted and I should leave our loads at Camp Two, letting the porters take theirs up to Camp Three and then return for ours at Camp Two. The new snow looked like putting an end to any movement at all. While I was trying to think things out, I noticed that the porters were preparing to move. I pointed outside to the falling snow.

'Look. No good,' I said.

'No. O.K. sahib,' said one, and the others looked at me and grinned cheerfully.

It was with mixed feelings that I watched them trudge off into the snow, shirt tails hanging below their anoraks. I felt responsible for them and yet I couldn't help but admire the fact that they had taken some of the responsibility on their own shoulders – and taken it cheerfully. I decided that they'd manage it to Camp Three and back all right.

Ted and I retreated to the luxury of the Base Camp and the prospect of a good rest. I stood on a flat stone on the edge of the tumbling stream and stripped off, looking forward to my first wash for six weeks. I had a shock as I looked down at my body : I was like a skeleton, dried up and almost muscleless. Effort at altitude certainly drains away strength and physique. Even so, it was great to be in reasonably civilized surroundings; the heat and smell of the wood fire and the piles of scrambled egg were comparable to central heating and caviare.

'Sahib,' Gulam, one of the porters routed me out of my warm sleeping bag, 'the sahibs are coming.'

I went outside and took his binoculars. Two figures were on the snow just below Camp Three. Another figure appeared beside them. One, two, three. Where were the other two? A sigh of relief as another black dot appeared against the white backdrop. Four. I waited, eyes straining against the binoculars. Minutes ticked by and the four dots moved slowly down towards Camp Two. Something had happened, one man would never have been left alone on the mountain.

'Don sahib?' queried Gulam.

Joe, Bob, Dick, Geoff and Hussein, one of Gulam's own kin, had gone on the mountain; only four were coming off. A tragedy must have happened.

'Only four, sahib,' said Gulam, holding up four fingers.

I nodded, unable to say any more. We'd just have to wait until the morning, they would never reach us by nightfall.

I spent a sleepless night wondering what could have gone wrong and at first light I dressed and walked up the glacier to where the four would descend. My heart sank as I saw the fatigue and sadness in their every movement. Joe, Geoff, Dick, Hussein.

I stumbled forward towards them.

'Where's Bob?' I managed at last.

Joe met my stare, his eyes dull and tired.

'Bob died in Camp Six,' he said quietly and moved slowly past me to the tents.

I stood shaken and numb. Life, climbing, money, worry, suddenly seemed trivial. To Masherbrum to die. Memories of Bob flooded back: the scar on his face, the bivouac on the Capucin, the triumph of Centurion on Ben Nevis, that moment in Salford when he had presented me with the opportunity of a lifetime. I looked up at the great, white bulk of the mountain, so peaceful, so beautiful. I remembered how we had scrambled up Table Mountain when the boat to Karachi had docked for twenty-four hours in Cape Town. How we'd laughed when, on the flat summit, Bob had come across a notice board:

'Do not throw stones on the climbers below.'

No one spoke for the rest of that day. The next morning we held a meeting to discuss our plans. It was agreed that Bob's body should be recovered and taken to the Army Hospital in Skardu and the cause of death ascertained.

Camp Six was high on the mountain and with all the other camps empty of provisions, the recovery of the body virtually meant another assault on the summit. I suggested that we might as well make it one and try to claim at least something from this mountain that had cost us so much.

A few days later, heavily loaded, and dragging the crude sledge on which Bob's body would be brought down, we began the hard grind back up the mountain to Camp Six. Six days later, Joe, Geoff and I, with two porters, reached the tragic camp.

As we approached it, up the steep and treacherous snow slope, the porter who was roped to me began to flounder and behave in a peculiar manner. Looking at his face, I could see that he was in a state of extreme fear, and I fervently hoped that he wouldn't crack. Watchful for any hysterical movements that would send us both to certain death, I hauled myself into the crevasse where Camp Six was situated. I took in the rope from way back in the crevasse, wedging myself in preparation for a sudden jerk. Steadily the rope came on and slowly the porter's head appeared over the icy rim. Without looking at me or the tent, he pulled into the crevasse, stumbled past me to the far end of it, and trembling with fear, began a weird chanting and wailing that set my teeth on edge.

Quite suddenly, however, he stopped, turned, and calmly untied himself from the rope. There was no trace of his former terror and his expression and movements were completely normal.

That evening I walked to the edge of the great ice cliff and gazed across at a scene of fantastic beauty and tranquillity. The moon flooded the vast panorama with cold, white light and the stars flashed and twinkled in the deep black night. The grandeur of the surrounding peaks was awe-inspiring; Chogalisa, the Masherbrums and K.2 stood massive, immovable and eternal, dripping with ice and snow, lording it over the world. Turning to look at the tiny, green tent glowing with candle-light, I felt an inner peace which was profound and intense. Up here, at 24,000 feet, it was hard to believe that down below in the dark valleys, men scratched a living from the soil; there seemed to be nobody else in the whole world but the mountain gods and us – the fools who tried to challenge their supremacy. I walked back to the tent in search of warmth and companionship; sometimes the mountains are at their most frightening when they are at peace.

The peace had disappeared by the morning, however, and it was snowing hard as we battled to get the sledge down to Camp Five. We managed after a hard struggle, and Joe Walmsley and I wearily retraced our steps back to Camp Six to prepare to throw a last gauntlet at the mountain.

Laden with the smallest of the tents and with only sufficient fuel and food to last two meals, we approached the crevasse which guarded the entrance to the long, steep, snow slope at the top of which was the bivouac where Geoff and I had spent the night so long before.

At just after midnight, I peered out at the twinkling stars and scooped up some snow to make a brew.

'It's a great night,' I said, feigning enthusiasm. 'If it stays like this, we can't fail.'

Joe nodded, and carried on crumbling snow into the pot. I longed for the night to pass and the weather to stay fine.

Just before dawn we began to prepare for the struggle ahead. For ages, in the freezing, grey light, we fumbled with wooden fingers at the icy crampon straps until, at last, we stood on the hard snow, ready to give everything to reach the top of the mountain that had taken so much from us.

My feet quickly went solid on me. Before we could even start to move, I had to spend half an hour kicking my toes against the crusted snow to draw the warmth back into them. Throughout my activity, Joe remained standing, staring ahead, holding a few coils of rope in his hand.

'Joe,' I panted, exhausted by the exertion, 'what about your feet?'

'They're all right,' he replied.

I shook my head but could think of nothing to say that would have done any good.

I stepped from the tiny crevasse and on to the snow slope. The going was firm and we moved reasonably quickly. Suddenly I was optimistic.

'If the snow's like this in the gully, we'll be on the top in two and a half hours – and that's taking it easy,' I called to Joe who grunted non-committally.

We paused at the bergschrund at the foot of the critical 500-foot gully leading up to the col between the twin summits, and Joe belayed me with his ice-axe as I stepped on to the slope.

To my dismay, the snow was soft – the floury kind from which it's impossible to make snowballs – and I sank into it up to my knees. I looked back at Joe.

'It doesn't matter. We've got bags of time,' I said.

I floundered through the powdery, crunching mass towards a rock buttress bounding the left side of the gully. A good, sound belay was essential before I dared move out into the centre of the gully; a slide from there would take me thousands of feet to a death on the rocks below.

I banged in a piton and sighed with relief. I brought Joe up and we had a short session of rearrangement. I took out a few pitons and some krabs; the next section was the critical one and I meant to take no chances. If we could reach the col, nothing would stop us.

Six hundred feet above and to the right, the summit was bathed in sunlight. It looked near enough to touch. I made sure Joe was ready and alert, took a deep breath and plunged up to my armpits in the snow, traversing into the centre of the gully.

I tried to make some upward progress, stepping delicately as though I were walking on eggs. But it was no use, I slipped back time and time again. It became obvious that this game of snakes and ladders was no good; if we were going to get up the gully, it wouldn't be via the snow slope. I turned my attention to the rock buttress.

The rock was sound, pretty steep but with plenty of cracks and a sort of chimney in it.

'I'm going to do a bit of rock climbing, Joe,' I said.

Joe was not enthusiastic; the buttress would have been difficult at sea-level, at over 25,000 feet it was absurd.

'There's no alternative,' I said. 'The snow's hopeless, there's only the rock left.'

From the first touch, I knew it was going to be a supreme test of my skill and strength. The sun was now full on the gully and it was stifling inside our wind-proofed, padded clothing. I sweated my way up the rock, oblivious to everything except the few feet ahead. I banged in pitons and hung from them, gasping for breath for minutes on end, my heart thumping and sweat blinding me.

At last the angle eased slightly and I was able to take a stance. Joe, convinced that I'd boobed, tried to climb the snow slope. After half a dozen, strength-sapping slides, he gave up in disgust and began to climb the rock. Two or three times he fell off and only grim determination got him up to my stance.

The next pitch looked harder still and I decided to remove my crampons. It began with a twenty-foot tongue of ice running up to a big flake which would have to be laybacked and looked remarkably like the Right Unconquerable Crack at Stanage Edge. I cursed the bad snow in the gully – if it'd been sound, we'd be on our way down now.

Carefully, I cut steps in the tough ice until I was perched on the top of the tongue, my hands grasping the underside of the flake. This was it: a strenuous layback in high-altitude gear at 25,000 feet. I moved as swiftly as I could, fighting my way up.

'Bastard!' I gasped as I made the discovery that the top of the crack was jammed with ice.

But I had burned my boats, I had to get up, a fall would mean an injury and that would do for both of us. I made a desperate heave and somehow pulled up on to a small, ice-covered ledge on top of the flake. I lay panting, waiting for the strength to return to my body.

Putting in a piton, I began to review the situation. Looking above, I saw that it would be impossible to climb without crampons. My crampons were down below with Joe; that meant that I had to bring Joe up to my tiny stance. I weighed up the chances of Joe managing the climb : it wasn't on, and I couldn't possibly haul him up. An alternative was to tie the two ropes together and for me to go on up to the col on a single rope. If it was easy going from the col, I could climb to the summit alone; it would be only one or two rope lengths and Joe, meantime, could stay where he was. He wouldn't object, I was sure.

'Joe? What time is it?' I called, my mind racing as I thought of reaching the summit.

My heart sank when Joe told me what the time was. I looked round for the sun. He was right. With dismay and incredulity I realized that my 300-foot rock climb had taken seven and a half hours.

It was hopeless, we were beaten. I looked across at the summit, hardly a stone's throw away. If I climbed on, got there in quick time and then got back to Joe at the double, we'd still have to spend a night in the open which would mean certain frostbite and possible amputations. If I climbed on alone and fell, it would mean the end for both of us. I looked down at the silent figure, gazing at the world's most fabulous mountain scenery with unseeing eyes. If I called down to him, he would slowly get to his feet and face up to the agony of a struggle which would surely finish him. No, if we couldn't make it together and return safely, I had no decision to make. We would have to go down.

I thought about breaking the news to the others who would even now be struggling down the mountain with Bob's body. I looked at my feet in the clumsy high-altitude boots; not long before they'd been new and shiny and exciting to look at. So : the years of planning, the time and money spent by countless people, the death of a close friend; it had all been in vain. So much effort and tragedy to put me on a little rock ledge 300 feet from success. I looked across once more at the glittering summit; it would have to wait for somebody else.

I tried to get some saliva to my parched throat and swallow but I couldn't manage it.

'Joe?' I croaked.

The blue figure, vivid against the brown granite 100 feet below, stirred slightly. His face turned upwards.

'We'll have to pack it in,' I said slowly.

There was a long silence.

'Okay.'

That was it. All that remained was to get down safely.

The retreat from the mountain was accomplished safely. Back in Skardu, nothing had changed; it all might never have happened. The cause of Bob Downes's death was established as pneumonia, and he was laid to rest on a small hillock overlooking the Indus.

The five remaining expedition members set their faces towards home. For Don, this first experience of expedition climbing had been invaluable: he was now a mountaineer in the true sense of the word.

15 | The Bonatti Pillar

1957 was a bad year for mountaineers the world over: Gregory's expedition to Disteghil Sar had been repulsed by avalanche danger; an Oxford University expedition to Haramosh had met with appalling tragedy; Roger Chorley had contracted polio on Machapuchare; and the North Face of the Eiger glowered from the front pages of the world's press, the body of the Italian climber Longhi dangling horrifically from the face, and somewhere among the jumbled mass of rock and ice, the bodies of two Germans, Northdurft and Mayr. Most tragic of all, Hermann Buhl lost his life on Chogalisa when a snow cornice collapsed beneath his feet. Buhl, perhaps the greatest climber ever, had at last run out of the luck so essential for continuous high-pressure climbing.

For Don, the trip to Masherbrum provided an unexpected source of income – lecturing. Not a voluble man by nature, Don nevertheless found the job to his liking, after a few sleepless nights before the first lecture. From then on, a camera became a vital piece of his climbing equipment.

In May, Don and Audrey finally got married and departed for Scotland to spend a climbing honeymoon. John Cunningham teamed up with Don, and they spent a glorious week climbing in Glencoe. Marriage has been the end of many fine climbers; wives who willingly encourage their husbands to spend three months of the year in the Alps or on an expedition and every weekend in Wales or the Lakes are few and far between.

In Audrey, Don knew he had one of the rare ones. Throughout the years of their marriage, Audrey has sacrificed her own

interests in order that Don should continue to climb. Year after
year she has worked long hours the twelve months round to
keep a home together and to ensure that whatever money was
needed, it was there. As expedition followed expedition, she
must have wondered whether each parting would be the final
one. None of this shows in Audrey; she remains serene and
unchanging, friendly and content. In truth, no mountaineer
ever deserved such a wife.

A lecture at Oxford University Mountaineering Club in June
presented Don with another opportunity. Colin Mortlock, the
President of the Club and a fine climber himself, asked Don if
he was interested in a return visit to Masherbrum.

I was very surprised at this. I remembered back in Skardu
taking a last look at those great mountains and wondering if I'd
ever have the chance to come back. Now here was the chance
handed to me on a plate. I thought about it for a few minutes.
All that way back for a couple of hundred feet which I'd seen
anyway? On the other hand if I turned the chance down I
might not get another. I asked him what he was planning and
he told me of a proposed University expedition for 1960. Thinking that an awful lot could happen before 1960 – not least that
Masherbrum could be conquered by some other party – I said
I'd be willing. Then I pushed it out of my mind and began to
think about the summer season in front of me.

The problem of what to do during the summer was easily
solved: there were a dozen climbs in the Alps I wanted to do.
The main problem was who the hell was I going to do them
with? 1958 was a turning point in the Rock and Ice Club. Joe
got married, Ron was married, Nat was fed up with the bad
weather in the Alps, and most of the other lads had got steady
jobs and were saving up for one thing or another. The general
attitude was that it was a waste of valuable cash and time in
the Alps. Joe had suddenly developed a yen for climbing on sea
cliffs and as wherever Joe went, everyone else followed – 'the
curly-legged shepherd', Doug Verity called him – it looked like
the whole troupe was bound for Cornwall. I contacted young

Paul Ross who had asked me if I fancied going to the Alps and I arranged to meet him in Chamonix. However, when Joe saw that I was determined to go to the Alps, he decided that he and some of the others would come along after all.

The weather in Chamonix was perfect when I arrived and it looked set fair. I met up with Paul and we discussed possible climbs. In 1955, Joe and I had made an attempt at the South West Pillar of the Dru which had been foiled by bad weather. Since then, this 'last great problem' had been climbed in a most incredible manner by Walter Bonatti, who had done it solo. Renamed the Bonatti Pillar, the climb had since been repeated several times by strong continental parties who had all expressed amazement and admiration at Bonatti's achievement. Bonatti had taken six days to conquer the Pillar, during the last three of which he had been without food and water. I marvelled at the man's daring and courage yet at the same time I was baffled by a climber of Bonatti's stature wanting to risk his life in such a way. Bonatti must have had dozens of climbing friends who would have been only too eager to share the adventure with him and yet he had chosen to do the climb alone. Presumably, he had to prove something to himself or to try and set a standard which would plainly say, 'beat that if you can'. Whatever his motives, it was a fantastic accomplishment.

We went down to Snell's to see if we could get a description of the climb.

Donald Snell greeted us warmly and listened to my request.

'Can't help you I'm afraid,' he said, shaking his head. 'Bonatti never writes descriptions of his climbs and I can't find the French one anywhere.'

'Has somebody else asked you for it?' I inquired, wondering how he was so sure that the French description was missing.

Snell nodded and smiled.

'Two other climbers only yesterday,' he replied. 'McInnes and Bonington. You know them?'

Interesting, I thought. I knew both by name and reputation and had seen them on various occasions. Mention of Christian

Bonington among the Rock and Ice Circle usually produced a few smiles. We had been sitting near the Cromlech Boulder, sunning ourselves, when a climber came running down the scree from the crag.

'First aid, I must have some first aid,' the man called out as he neared us.

'Got a bloody plum in his mouth and he can't get it out,' remarked one of the boys, propping himself up on one elbow.

We watched with amusement as, still crying out for first aid, he plunged past the Boulder and started up the Pass. It turned out that it was Chris Bonington and that in rappelling down Cenotaph Corner, he had burnt his shoulder rather badly. (For some peculiar reason this is a common occurrence on a first rappel down Cenotaph). At the time, we thought the posh accent and the appeal for first aid indicated a certain softness. Later, Chris showed me the burn mark and it had been severe, worse than any of the lads had suffered.

Hamish McInnes, the gaunt Scot with the wild eyes and the straggly beard, seemed to have been around for donkey's years but was still relatively young. Johnny Cunningham had told me many stories about 'Big McInnes': apart from the famous Creagh Dhu Everest Expedition, Hamish had many other equally eccentric exploits to his name.

*   *   *

Bonington the public school climber and McInnes the Scottish mountain goat; a good combination. I remembered hearing their names linked together in connection with some first winter ascents in Glencoe. At the time it had seemed very unlikely. Anyhow, they were obviously interested in the Bonatti Pillar and when we'd made some further inquiries it seemed that the pair had got a description of sorts from somewhere and had disappeared into the mountains.

Paul and I, in spite of diligent searching, failed to find anyone who could help us; so that finally, as the weather looked settled, we set off loaded with provisions and gear, resolving to follow our noses. It was late evening by the time we reached the big bivouac rock at the foot of the Dru and we weren't all that surprised to find the bivouac already occupied by Bonington and McInnes. They had joined forces with two Austrians, Walter Philip and Riccardo Blach.

No information on the route was forthcoming – in fact the only thing we learnt was that the Austrians were the fastest things on two legs. We moved on a little farther up and found a reasonable bivouac place.

'D'you reckon the weather'll keep up?' Paul asked anxiously.

'Well, it's a bit nippy and with the sky so clear, it should be okay,' I replied.

We snuggled down under the glorious granite architecture of the Dru and quickly dropped off to sleep. I awoke early, chilled and stiff, and was disgusted to see that the great spire was shrouded with cloud.

'Here we go again,' I groaned and promptly fell back asleep.

It was after six o'clock by the time we had had breakfast and packed up. Paul was obviously disappointed at the bad weather. I gazed up at the blanket of grey cloud.

'Could do anything this bloody weather,' I said. 'It could fine up or it could develop into a storm. In any case, we should have been up the couloir by now.'

'The others aren't moving,' Paul remarked, nodding towards the boulder below us.

'They're probably waiting to see what we're going to do,' I said.

'I'd like to start up,' said Paul. 'We could always retreat if it did turn out bad.'

We discussed the question and then agreed to start the climb in the hope that the weather would improve. Soon we were kicking our way up the stone-pitted snow at the foot of the couloir.

I reckoned that five hours' climbing should see us at the top of the couloir providing all went well. This was the third time I'd been in this dangerous chute and it was not a place to which I'd grown attached. There'd been stories that Bonatti had avoided climbing the couloir by abseiling down from the ridge of the Flammes de Pierre to the foot of the Pillar. How true this was I didn't know, but there was a lot to be said for it.

Hardly had we begun to cross the bergschrund when four figures arrived on the moraine below – McInnes and Co. Two rope lengths up the couloir, with Paul way up on a rock rib in spite of my advice that it was easier farther left, I heard a commotion below and saw that Walter had fallen into the bergschrund, only saving himself from a serious fall by an instinctive, desperate, bridging manoeuvre.

I watched Paul dithering on the delicate rock. I knew that it was difficult from my own previous experiences. I could only wait for the inevitable appeal for help.

'I'm stuck. Can you take the belay off and climb above me?'

Great, I thought, two rope-lengths up and we were in trouble, a good start to a big climb. Walter, completely recovered from his trouble, suddenly appeared beside me and I stepped to one side to let him pass. The party below us were all climbing solo and moving quite fast. I followed in Walter's wake, taking care that the rope between Paul and myself didn't catch on any projecting rock and so pull him off his precarious stance. A scuffle and scrabble above me was quickly followed by the rapid descent of Walter. Unable to get out of the way, I made sure I had a handhold and braced myself to take the full weight of Walter's body. Before I had recovered, Walter had picked himself up, apologized, thanked me and started on his way again. I was left wondering whether I'd got involved with a troupe of acrobats.

By the time I had extricated Paul from his dicey position, we were at the rear of the caravan and there we remained until the leaders struck the first of the large ice patches. At this point McInnes took over the lead and I noticed that the Austrians had neither crampons nor ice-axes. Paul and myself, fully equipped, moved out on to the ice patches near the centre of the couloir and left the others to cut steps between the rock outcrops. Strangely, nothing was coming down the couloir but I wanted to get out of the unhealthy bottleneck as quickly as possible before our luck broke and a stonefall descended upon us.

About three hundred feet from the top of the couloir, I banged in a good peg, which would be useful if by any chance we had to make a rapid retreat, and brought up Paul. Two rope lengths on thin ice lead to a long pitch of mixed work on icy rock. While taking photographs of the figures strung out below me on the ice slab, I noticed with pleasure that the sun was creeping gently down the clean, brown granite of the Pillar. Looking at the sky, I saw that it was a glorious, cloudless blue; the day promised some really good climbing on warm rock.

By the time we reached the foot of the Pillar, we had become a party of six. We had a short discussion as to the order of march and decided that Walter and Riccardo should take the lead, putting in any pitons that were necessary, that Paul and myself would do the sack hauling and that Chris and Hamish should bring up the rear and do the de-pegging.

'Hey, look,' Walter was shouting and brandishing something in his hand.

'What's he waving?' Paul asked.

'Looks like a walking stick,' I said, incredulously.

Walter began climbing the first crack and we traversed across to where Riccardo was standing. There, leaning against the rock, was the walking stick. Who had left it there was anybody's guess; what with ladders on the West Face and walking sticks on the Pillar, it seemed that the Dru was the setting for a revolution in aid climbing.

After a rope-length or two of pleasant free climbing, we assembled on a large overhang. It was grand to be out of the dark couloir and sitting in the sunshine, smoking and admiring the view. When it was my turn to lead I discovered just how drowsy I was. It required a lot of effort to climb up to the overhang so, to get myself back in the climbing mood, I climbed the pendulum move and arrived at the foot of a long, wide crack. Eighty feet above me, Riccardo's feet dangled over the ledge at the top of the crack. The pitch looked strenuous but straightforward and not thinking too much about it, I started up. Twenty feet from the top I began to realize that this was no piece of cake; the crack was becoming an awkward width, too wide for the boot, and I was having to expend a deal of energy. By the time I'd reached the ledge, my respect for Bonatti had doubled and when Chris came up leading Hamish he confessed that he'd had serious thoughts about asking for a top rope. Hamish arrived on the ledge and looked at us with a jaundiced eye.

'Aye,' he said, 'have you looked on the right?'

Just to the right of the crack, a groove bristled with wedges. We had climbed the wrong crack.

We made good, steady progress and eventually reached a fine ledge beneath a steep chimney. Chris consulted the description of the route.

'This is the Grade Six chimney I think,' he pronounced and we gazed skywards. Walter and Riccardo had already climbed it and were out of sight.

'D'you think I could take the lead, Don?' Paul asked. He'd been seconding all the way and was just itching to have a go.

'Sure,' I said, glad of the extra rest. 'Off you go.'

Hamish, Chris and I sat on the ledge and gazed across at the West Face as Paul set out up the chimney. I pointed out the West Face route to Hamish and talked a bit to Chris. I had been watching Chris climb and I was quite impressed. This was only his second season in the Alps and the Pillar was his first major route. I suppose we made a peculiar trio: Hamish recounting his exploits in the Himalayas with Johnny Cunningham, Chris chatting about his Army career, and me telling them that I was a plumber by trade.

'Okay, come on up.'

Paul's shout from above broke up our enjoyable yattering and I stood up reluctantly. I looked at the chimney and at the ropes swaying against the rock. Slowly, I shook my head, more in sorrow than anger.

'What the bloody hell have you been doing?' I called up.

Paul's head appeared over the top. 'Why, what's up?'

'You've put the sack rope through all the krabs and it's stuck,' I yelled.

I had no alternative but to climb the chimney loaded with

two sacks. I didn't fancy the idea but at least I could have a pull on the rope if it got too strenuous.

Jamming up the chimney was a struggle but the real fight came when I had to leave it. I found myself hanging on by my fingers from krabs with nothing at all for my feet.

'Pull,' I shouted but the rope stayed slack.

I noticed that the peg I was hanging from was beginning to work loose.

'Pull the bloody rope,' I yelled in despair but still nothing happened.

I hauled on the loose peg and reached for the peg farther up. I just got my hand on it as the lower peg came out. Reaching the ledge, I sank down exhausted. That pitch had cost me more in strength and stamina than the rest of the climb put together. After that, I led all the way.

Above us, the climb had become very open and exposed. Walter was directly above us, engaged in heaving Riccardo bodily up a steep chimney. A wide crack with four wooden wedges in it soared upwards for about sixty feet, and led to a most entertaining pitch : an exposed swing across the bottom of a large flake from a piton high on the left; then a crack up the right of the flake followed by a short, steep chimney.

The six of us assembled at the top of the chimney on a ledge which although spacious was in a very airy position : below us two thousand feet of rock fell away to the snow slopes; above, a thousand feet of vertical wall soared to the sky. We consulted the description and had a look at the time. As it was late in the afternoon, we decided to bivouac on the ledge and be assured of a comfortable night. The two Austrians pushed on another pitch or two and settled themselves on another roomy ledge directly above us.

Soon we had the stoves out and, clad in our warm duvets, we set about making the ledge as comfortable as possible. After a meal, a drink and a smoke, we stretched out and watched the lights of Chamonix twinkling in the dusk.

'Bet there's some fun going on down there,' remarked Paul.

'You don't know when you're well off, man,' replied Hamish.

'Take a look about you : a beautiful mountain, a deep, starlit night, air like champagne. You've got a full belly, you're warm, you're tired and you've got a great day ahead of you to-morrow. What more do you want?'

Hamish was right, it certainly was a night to remember. Such nights make even the most strenuous day worth-while.

'Well, time to give the old station-master the signal,' said Hamish, producing a torch.

I stared at him in surprise.

'Station-master?' I echoed.

'I said I'd signal the station-master at Montenvers at nine o'clock to let him know we're okay,' said Hamish.

I dropped another piece of ice in the brew can as Hamish began flashing his torch in the direction of the cluster of lights round the Montenvers Hotel.

'There it is,' Hamish said in triumph as a light winked back from across the Mer de Glace.

Other lights flashed from the area of the bivouac rock way down beneath our feet.

'Must be a party going on the West Face,' said Chris.

As Hamish returned to his place, the most tremendous crash sounded from the couloir below. We all edged forward to the lip of the ledge and peered over.

Great showers of sparks leapt about as granite struck granite and the huge rockfall tumbled down the couloir.

'Good job that lot waited till now,' I said to no one in par-ticular.

As I moved back from the edge, an old feeling suddenly came over me. My mind went back to the Rannoch Wall, Eric Worthington and the dead student. I felt sick with fear and I couldn't understand why : we were perfectly safe on the ledge, nothing could happen. I drew myself to the back of the ledge and sat in silence. The conversation was resumed and Chris made another brew. Suddenly, without any warning at all, the peace was shattered by a series of high-pitched whines and the crash of falling rock. Everyone dived for the back wall and cowered under its slight shelter. Stones plunged past us, rico-

cheting from the rock and zooming off into the darkness. There
was a sickening thud followed by a low groan and then everything was quiet again.

Confusion covered us all as we scrambled around on the
ledge. Someone struck a light and I saw Hamish slumped over,
his head in his hands, blood flowing freely through his fingers.

'Lie down, Hamish,' said Chris, trying to examine the wound.

'Och, I'm not so bad,' mumbled Hamish but I'd heard the
thud and I knew it must be at least a fractured skull.

'Better tie him on,' I said. 'He might faint or something.'

Chris miraculously produced a thick Army field dressing and
tied it round Hamish's head. My heart sank as I saw the blood
soak through the dressing in a matter of seconds. We jammed
Hamish in a wide crack and secured him to the rock. At least
he was safe, but he was bound to have an uncomfortable night.
The rest of us, shocked and worried by the freak accident,
huddled at the back of the ledge and tried to sleep. I pondered
for ages on the problems we would face the following morning: if the weather broke and Hamish proved to be incapable
of helping himself we would be in real trouble. We had no
acceptable alternative but to continue with the climb, we were
about halfway up and the face with its ledges and belays was
certainly safer than the couloir below. With these thoughts
chasing each other in my mind I dozed through the interminable night.

In the grey light of the morning, we struggled to get life and
warmth into cold, aching limbs. The ledge was a shambles of
scattered equipment and it seemed to be ages before we had a
brew going. Hamish was at least conscious and seemingly
aware of the situation but he looked a terrible sight with his
hair and beard clotted with blood and his face pale and
strained. He thought that he'd had several fainting fits during
the night, which didn't seem too encouraging.

'D'you think you can make it to the top?' I asked him.

'I'll do my best,' he replied, and I knew that he'd give everything in the effort.

While we packed the gear, Chris and I decided that it would

be best if I climbed with Hamish while he and Paul brought up the rear. Above us, the two Austrians had already started up and we could hear Walter hammering away somewhere out of sight.

I led off up a rather awkward groove-cum-chimney and arrived at the top with numbed hands. Although the sun was just out, it would be an hour or two before it would reach us with its friendly warmth. Meanwhile everything would remain frozen.

'I'll prusik up the rope,' Hamish called out.

'Okay,' I replied. 'Come on then.'

I had taken a solid stance and I waited anxiously; we would soon know just how much of a liability Hamish was likely to be. For several minutes the rope tightened, stretched and went slack again and it was obvious that progress was not satisfactory.

'You all right, Hamish?' I called down.

There was a pause and I peered over my ledge and saw that Hamish was unknotting his prusik loop from the rope.

'I'll have to try and climb it, Don,' he replied, looking up with blood-crusted face.

'Aye, come on then,' I said.

'Keep a tight rope, will you?'

'Don't worry, lad.'

I watched as he slowly, and with all the signs of weakness, stepped on to the slab. However, he gave us all more heart by climbing the pitch reasonably quickly.

Two parallel cracks split the face above and by using both I reached a small ledge and stood there, enveloped in grey cloud. Some steep slab climbing landed me in an awkward niche and I hauled up the sacks and watched Hamish struggle up to me. There was no doubt that he was feeling the strain now and I could only hope that his strength and will-power would hold out until we reached easier ground. Luckily, the climbing began to ease almost immediately and we reached a zone of terraces beneath a huge red wall where we found Riccardo just about to follow Walter's lead. He was visibly shaken by

Hamish's appearance and seemed to have some doubts as to whether we could carry on. We assured him that we were managing all right and with one last look of concern at Hamish, he set off up a crack in the great wall.

Actually, in spite of our troubles, this pitch provided us with some magnificent free climbing, well-protected the whole way. At the top of the crack, a wide ledge allowed the three of us to lie and relax in the sun, which by this time was full on the face. As Walter's rope crept out above us, I had a chance to find out something about our Austrian companions.

Riccardo was only nineteen and he wasn't the only climber in his family: his elder brother had made the tenth ascent of the Eiger North Face some six years earlier. Walter was twenty-one and had a reputation for doing big wall climbs in fast times. He'd done the West Face of the Dru the previous year with a fellow Austrian.

'What a view, what a day,' commented Hamish, gazing at the wonderful panorama of the Grandes Jorasses and the Chamonix Aiguilles.

I remembered what had happened on the last occasion when Hamish had waxed poetical, and I cast a wary glance skywards in case he'd started another stonefall; but all was sunlit peace. Dozing on a pleasant ledge wasn't getting up the mountain, and once Riccardo had started up, I prepared for action.

The pitch above looked quite strenuous. The route took us off the Face and into the side wall of the great couloir which separates the Dru from the Flammes de Pierre ridge. It was artificial climbing all the way up and very exposed. Walter had placed the pitons very wide apart and I, with my lack of inches, had to struggle to make the distance. At the top of the pitch, there was another spacious ledge and from there the route seemed to follow a line of pitons up a rather smooth wall. Hamish and I settled down for another welcome rest as Walter started on the wall.

By the time Chris and Paul arrived, Walter was standing in étriers in an exposed position in the centre of the wall. Thinking that it was likely to be a long stay on the ledge, we made ourselves comfortable, leaving Riccardo to keep an eye on Walter.

Three hours later we were all watching Walter and beginning to get worried. We had sent up our total collection of ironmongery and still Walter had made little progress. He was trying to follow a thread-like crack which shot straight up the wall for at least a couple of hundred feet.

'There's summat wrong here,' I said at last. 'We must be off the route.'

Telling Hamish to belay me, I set off to look for the correct route. I tried several possibilities which led nowhere and then I traversed across a big slab and peered round a corner. There above me was a tremendous overhang with a line of pitons running up to it. The overhang and the route up to it was out of sight from our ledge, so it was no wonder Walter had missed it.

'Hey, I've found it,' I shouted. 'I'll bring you round, Hamish, and then we'll have a look at the description.'

A short chimney and crack led up to a good stance under the overhang.

'It's the biggest overhang in seven kingdoms,' said Hamish in awe as we stood beneath it. 'I've seen pictures of it; it's the variation made by the lads who did the second ascent.'

Walter meanwhile had returned from the wall, retrieving all the pegs on his way down. Chris and Paul had come across and were gazing up at me as I tried the overhang for size.

All the pegs were in place and all were sound, so although not technically too difficult, it was fantastically exposed. I was soon standing in étriers thirty feet from the rock wall, directly above the couloir running to the foot of the Face some three thousand feet below. I reached a small ledge on the very tip of the overhang which had obviously been used for a stance and surveyed the way ahead. A long groove continued upwards for some distance and I couldn't see what was beyond it.

'It's getting late, Don,' Chris called from below.

I hadn't realized that the time had gone so quickly and that it was already seven o'clock. Soon it would be dark; it was obvious that we'd have to spend the night on the comfortable ledges below rather than continue upwards into the unknown. Before I retreated from the overhang, I hauled up all the iron-mongery which Walter had retrieved and clipped the lot to a piton ready for use in the morning.

One of our greatest torments throughout the day had been the lack of water. Everyone was desperately thirsty and a good brew of tea would have made even the poor progress of the day bearable. Down in the couloir, patches of snow were tanta-lizingly close but the risk in reaching them was too great. We'd just have to stay thirsty.

Hamish, unwilling to lose any of the ground he'd so pain-fully gained, jammed himself into a chimney and prepared for another uncomfortable night. Paul, Walter and Riccardo spread themselves out on the big ledge, leaving Chris and I sharing a smaller one slightly lower down. The night was cold and a dark mist swirled about us as we talked and dozed. Chris coughed and choked as I filled our plastic bag with smoke.

At dawn we stamped about on our respective ledges, breath steaming in the chilly air. Breakfast was no problem as there wasn't anything to eat.

I suggested to Walter that he take the lead as I knew that Hamish was going to need time to surmount the overhang. Lucky Walter, for great icicles hung down from the roof of the overhang and he sat comfortably in his étriers, licking them with evident relish. We shouted to him to leave some for us and urged him to get a move on.

When Hamish arrived at the stance below the overhang he looked definitely seedy and promptly announced that he was going to faint. Quickly, I lashed him to a good peg; it wasn't a very comforting thought to know that my second might roll off the stance while I was up on the overhang. I lit a cigarette and settled down to wait for Hamish to finish his slumbers.

'You all right?' I inquired, stubbing my fag.

'Aye,' he replied without any great conviction.

'I'm off then,' I said and promptly began the assault on the overhang.

Riccardo had long since disappeared out of sight and earshot above the overhang. Without too much trouble, I arrived at the tiny stance on the tip of the overhang and found that it was covered with verglas. Changing places with Hamish on such a stance would be extremely dangerous, so I decided to climb on with the hope that I'd have enough rope to reach a more comfortable stance above. A groove provided really enjoyable climbing and I silently thanked Walter for reducing the distance between the pegs. I found a good ledge, and expecting some trouble with Hamish, I made myself comfortable and secure.

Looking up, I saw that the sky had cleared and we were obviously in for another hot day. I thought longingly about a pint of good bitter; my throat was still parched even after sucking a few icicles.

'Take in,' Hamish called from below and I pulled in the bit of slack that I'd allowed to accumulate. At least he was on the move.

'Don, take in tight, I'm going to faint.'

I grabbed a cigarette which I'd laid on the rock ready for just such an emergency. Puffing away contentedly, I hauled on the rope.

'Right, Hamish, faint away.'

Time passed and all was silence. A rather nasty thought crossed my mind. What if Hamish didn't come round this time? I was working on possible solutions to this frightening problem when the rope jerked and I heard a muffled voice from below.

'Coming on again.'

'Good lad,' I called, pleased and relieved.

It took Hamish a long time to reach the stance, twice more he fainted before he slumped down beside me. His face was pale and drawn with fatigue; the struggle had almost used up his last reserves.

'Thought I was finished there,' he mumbled through cracked lips.

'You're doing great, Hamish,' I said and meant it.

The voice of Chris, cursing Paul for something or other, floated up to us but we had our own problems: I couldn't work out the route that Walter had taken. I climbed a short, wide crack while Hamish moved into the belay position. I was in a zone of slabs topped by steep walls. Climbing a small wall, I looked up at the slab above and there, right in the centre, was a piton. I cursed the route description which said that this was a pitch of Grade Four. Because I'd thought that it was going to be fairly easy, I'd brought my heavy sack with me. The position wasn't too well protected either; the peg was a good ten feet away and the moves to it were very delicate. However, it had to be done and that was it. With a heave, I pulled on to the slab and moved quickly and decisively to the peg, clipped on, and now, convinced that the description was completely at sea, prepared myself for some hard climbing.

At the foot of a wide crack I noticed some ice. I smashed a few chunks off with my peg hammer and stowed them away in my sack. I felt much better as I climbed the crack and arrived at a nice ledge on the very edge of the buttress. When I'd brought Hamish up, I got the stove out and soon had the lumps of dirty ice melting into delicious, filthy water.

A shout from below disturbed our brewing-up and Hamish went to investigate. Chris was clinging desperately to the peg in the centre of the slab politely asking for a top rope. While Hamish obliged, I drank my share of the hideous brew and immediately felt a new man. By the time Chris arrived at the ledge, I was on my way again.

The climb was beginning to break up now; the sheer section of the Pillar lay below us, above, although many hard pitches still remained, good ledges were more frequent. Route-finding became more difficult, however, and we took several false lines in our eagerness to find a familiar landmark. Eventually, in the late afternoon, we reached the shoulder where the West Face route meets the Pillar. From this point on, I knew the route.

A long chimney with ice in the back almost finished Hamish and it was only by telling him convincingly that each pitch was definitely the last, that I could keep him going. We reached the summit just as darkness closed in, bringing with it a few snow flakes and heavy cloud.

Walter and Riccardo, who had had no food or drink worth mentioning for three days, shared our meagre supper – one packet of soup. We settled down for a third, freezing night.

During the night the weather began to break and we woke to find the whole mountain in cloud, which swirled by on the bitterly cold wind. The descent was going to be unpleasant and it would have to be done quickly. Only Walter had used this descent route before, Joe and I had made our descent by way of the Grand Dru.

'Can you find it, Walter?' I asked.

'I think so,' he replied, 'but it's hard to see anything now.'

Walter had a point: snow was falling thickly and heavily, the wind blowing it directly into our faces as we faced down the mountain. We began the long series of rappels in abominable conditions; communications became impossible and on the third rope length down, the very thing I'd feared happened. Walter was a dim shape below me and I struggled to hear his shouts.

'We are – wrong way – to the right.'

Chris slid down beside me and we uncoiled the spare ropes, fumbling with our icy fingers. I slid off, heading for an almost invisible ledge below. There didn't seem to be any frozen corpses around so I assumed that there would be a reasonable way off from the ledge. Chris came down and through a break in the cloud we caught a glimpse of the Flammes de Pierre below us. We were on the right route again. Above us, however, things weren't going too well; Riccardo had collapsed from fatigue and cold and Hamish was trying to assist him. Walter had fallen twice while trying to climb up from his position after going down the wrong route and Hamish had held him. It seemed that the brave Scot had his hands full. It was obvious that we'd have to get organized or something serious would happen.

'Send Walter and Riccardo down first,' I yelled up into the mists above.

The ropes were in position and I wanted to see what condition the Austrians were in. Riccardo came down first and slumped down on the snow-covered terrace, white-faced and silent. Walter arrived and began babbling hysterically. I gave him the rope and instructed him to fix the next rappel, hoping that having something to do would calm his shattered nerves.

The others came down and it looked like we were an organized party again and I turned to see Walter go off on the rappel. Within seconds, the sling he had fixed over a razor-sharp spike of rock had snapped and he had gone hurtling down the Face. I felt sure that that was the end of Walter but I was wrong; a voice floated up to us on the wind and a minute or two later, Walter himself appeared back on the ledge. Miraculously, he had fallen into a chimney and jammed there.

I blunted the edge of the spike with my hammer, fixed a new sling round it and sent Walter off again with instructions not to bounce.

'Ja, ja,' he nodded, eyes wide and staring.

After numerous rappels in conditions which improved with every rope length, we emerged from the cloud and snow and felt the rain on our faces.

Riccardo and Walter both appeared to have recovered and they went bombing off down the snow slope to the haven of the Charpoua Hut. The rest of us, forgetting our weariness at the thought of a meal at the Montenvers Hotel, pushed on across the Mer de Glace. Above us, thunder rolled and the sky darkened as a great storm brewed round the Dru. It was good to be out of it.

That night, we celebrated the end of our four-day famine with a huge meal and plenty of ale which I, the only one with any money, paid for.

The Bonatti Pillar had been an epic climb, not least for Hamish McInnes who had done the greater part of the climb with a fractured skull. The partnership of Don and Chris Bonington seemed, on the face of it, an unlikely one, yet during the next few years it was to be completely successful.

Chris Bonington, Ex-Army officer, professional photographer, explorer and journalist, is a man who has turned climbing into a successful business. Behind the plummy accent and impeccable manners, Chris is a warm, sincere man whose infectious enthusiasm makes him a lively companion. Anyone who challenges the world's highest mountains needs a will-power and determination beyond the average and in Chris these qualities are outstanding.

16 | The Petites Jorasses

Returning to Chamonix after their ordeal on the Bonatti Pillar, Chris and Don waited for Joe to arrive. Don had some doubts as to whether Joe would be fit to do a big climb, as his ankle, broken earlier in the year, had not fully recovered. Meanwhile, Simon Clark and Ronnie Wather, two members of the successful Cambridge University Expedition to Pumasillo in the Andes, were camping near by. Clark had also sustained an ankle injury and Wather was without a partner. Knowing that Joe would not be arriving alone, Chris decided to join Wather and the pair went off to the Leschaux Hut with the intention of doing the West Face of the Petites Jorasses, a rock climb of the highest standard. Don hung around Chamonix, hoping that the good weather would continue.

Joe eventually arrived with Morty and Dennis Gray. Morty was his usual cheerful, clumsy self and Dennis Gray seemed to have lost none of his volubility on the journey from Manchester. This was Dennis's first visit to the Alps and he was obviously excited and a little overawed by the prospect of doing a two- or three-day climb. I remembered my first trip and I knew what he must be feeling. I hadn't done much climbing with Dennis previously, but I knew him to be a persistent, unrelenting type whose determination outweighed the disadvantages of a slight physique. Funnily enough, the first time I had seen Dennis was on my first visit to Cloggy when I had noticed this tiny lad among a group of climbers in the Halfway House. Since then, he'd climbed all over Britain and had eventually worked round to becoming a member of the Rock and Ice, though he actually lived in Leeds.

'What've you done then?' Joe asked.

I told him about the Bonatti Pillar and what a great climb it was.

'Wish we'd done it when we first tried it,' he said regretfully. 'Ah well. What do you fancy next?'

I said that I rather fancied the West Face of the Petites Jorasses which Chris and Ronnie Wather were attempting. It was supposed to be a tremendous modern rock climb and would be a good introduction to the Alps for Dennis. Joe looked a bit doubtful but eventually agreed.

The only snag to the climb was that we would have to descend the other side of the mountain into Italy which would involve us in a wearisome and possibly expensive trip back to Chamonix. I decided that we'd have to find a way back down the West Face if it was at all possible.

We trekked up to the Leschaux Hut which had been partly wrecked by an avalanche. Still, there was a fair chunk of roof remaining and the magnificent panoramic view of the Chamonix Aiguilles, the Petites Jorasses and the Aiguilles de Leschaux made up for the occasional gust of wind.

Taking enough provisions for one bivouac, we set out by starlight and began the long haul to the foot of the climb. Dennis, who had been complaining for some time about not feeling well, decided that if he carried on, he might become a liability and so he returned to the hut. A party of three was a bit awkward but we all wanted to do the climb so off we went. Joe wasn't keen on doing any leading because of his ankle, so I agreed to lead the whole climb.

The first few hundred feet were pleasant and we moved fairly quickly in spite of Morty, who fell asleep on every stance and could only be wakened by a hefty pull on the rope. On our way to the foot of the climb, I'd eyed up the chances of a possible line of descent and thought I'd seen one; now from a vantage point high on the face, I could ascertain that the line was feasible. The only difficulty seemed to be what would be the final abseil; a free drop over a great cliff down to the glacier beneath. If our ropes were long enough, we'd be okay.

For the next few hours we moved up a series of vertical

chimneys which ultimately became cracks. The climbing and sack-hauling were strenuous and Joe, in particular, seemed to be feeling the strain. Eventually we gathered on a ledge beneath an overhang and took a look at the description of the route.

'We're at the crux pitch,' announced Joe. 'It's graded A3.'

This meant the highest standard of artificial climbing and obviously a good deal of effort. I donned the necessary paraphernalia and stepped up below the overhang. Above it, I could see a piton sticking from the rock. I waved a hand in an exploratory manner over the overhang and it dropped surprisingly into a great jug handle of a hold. Gratefully, I did a monkey-like swing and stood on this excellent hold looking for a place to put a peg. No possibility presented itself, however, and so I made a couple of moves up in search of a crack.

'Bloody queer this, Joe,' I said, 'I can't get a peg in anywhere. No wonder they said it's A3, there's just no place to put a peg.'

'Can you climb it free?' Joe asked.

I studied the rock ahead and weighed up the move.

'Yeah, I'm sure I can,' I said.

'Well, go on then,' said Joe.

And I proceeded to climb the pitch free.

'It's all psychology, this climbing lark,' I said to Joe at the end of the pitch.

Several pitches higher, we arrived on a shoulder and it became certain that we would have to bivouac. The route description mentioned a bivouac place but due to a mistake in our route-finding, it was almost dark before we were settled on a comfortable ledge. After a brew and something to eat, we watched the moon flood the mountain with pale light.

I thought I'd mention the Walker Spur on the Grandes Jorasses to Joe again.

'The Walker doesn't look very steep from here, does it?' I commented.

Joe twisted his neck and pulled his anorak hood out of the way. He studied the shadowy outline for a few moments.

'No,' he said and snuggled back into his hood.

It began to get chilly and the three of us huddled together inside our plastic bag. Soon, the combined warmth of our bodies plus the fug of cigarette smoke had us nodding off to sleep.

The grey light of dawn filtering through the plastic shroud stirred me to action. I stretched and the bag crackled, disturbing Joe and Morty.

'What time is it, Joe?' I asked through a yawn.

Joe, proud possessor of the party's only watch – a present from Kanchenjunga – struggled to look at his wrist. Morty groaned and I noticed that he didn't look too well.

'What's up wi' you?' I asked.

'I feel sick,' he replied and with a sudden movement, dragged up the side of the bag and lurched to the edge of the ledge. The dixie rolled over and disappeared over the edge. We listened as the can bounced musically down the face.

'That's the last,' Joe said as we heard a faint tinkle from below.

'And again,' I said as another clink reached our ears.

'That's definitely it,' said Joe after a few moments. He turned to Morty. 'See what you've done, you clumsy little bugger.'

But Morty wasn't listening; he was hanging over the edge, his face a delicate shade of green.

We packed up the gear and took stock of our whereabouts. In the search for a bivouac place the previous night we had wandered off the route and were now practically at the top of the crag. We decided to cross an icy couloir to a gendarme on the ridge to our left and find a line of descent. Half an hour later we began to rappel down the wide, easy-angled couloir. It was evident that we would be able to reach the Leschaux Hut, and without too much difficulty, sometime during the afternoon. There remained only the problem of the final abseil to the glacier.

At last we reached the top of the great wall rising vertically from the glacier. I banged in a good piton, tied two 300-foot ropes together, and dropped a double length over the edge. It hung clear of the rock all the way down and just reached the

ice below. I felt pleased that I had estimated the distance cor-
rectly and soon I was speeding down in a glorious free slide.

'Aye, impressive that,' commented Joe as we coiled the ropes
and set off for Dennis and the Leschaux Hut.

*Several days later, Joe and Morty decided to attempt the
Bonatti Pillar and Don persuaded Dennis to accompany him on
yet another try at the Capucin. Once again the hoodoo struck
when the Montenvers railway went out of order; now the
climb would have to be prefaced by the interminable grind
through the pine forests to Montenvers. From then on things
went perfectly: the weather was ideal, every piton was in
place. It was a great moment, a reward for persistence, when
the summit was reached and the whole of the Capucin lay
beneath Don's feet.*

*Returning to Chamonix, Don and Dennis found that Joe and
Morty had been repulsed in the couloir leading to the Bonatti
Pillar. As usual, the couloir was a death-trap and the pair had
wisely chosen to retreat rather than risk death or serious injury
from the incessant stonefall. At the Nationale, Nat Allen had a
shock in store for them: taking from his pocket a cutting from
the* Manchester Evening Chronicle, *he read out the following
article.*

CUPID BREAKS UP NOTED CLUB

Cupid has helped to kill what was once one of Britain's leading
climbing clubs. For Manchester's Rock and Ice Club, which produced the two 'climbing plumbers' – Joe Brown of Rusholme, and
Don Whillans of Salford – is to be disbanded.

The club was once all-bachelor. But Joe and Don have both
married. So has 'leading light' Nat Allen. Others have gone to the
altar – and left the club.

And now treasurer Ron Moseley (married) and Doug Belshaw
(engaged) are to share the club's assets among fewer than twelve
remaining members.

'Most of the past and present members still climb, but no longer
as a group,' one of them told me today. 'I blame women for the
break-up. Please don't mention my name ... my wife-to-be might
object.'

Why Moseley and Belshaw took the decision remains a puzzle. It is significant that the winding-up of the Rock and Ice took place when the majority of its members were in Chamonix and could therefore do little about it.

The demise of the Rock and Ice, however, was one in name only; the friends who were now ex-members continued to climb together. Then Nat Allen and Dennis Gray decided to circularize old members and their friends with a view to re-forming the club. The response was enough to justify the birth of a new Rock and Ice, and so at Hathersage in February 1959, after a break of only a few months, the Club was reformed.

The name of the first president was drawn from a hat and the lucky man was Don. Some new faces had joined the Club and the membership list presented a formidable array of climbers: Nat Allen, Joe Brown, Vic Betts, Eric Beard, Fred Gough, Ray and Pete Greenall, Dennis Gray, Ronnie Cummerford, Eric Price, Don Roscoe, Steve Read, Harry Smith, Morty Smith, Alan Taylor, Charlie Vigano, Don, Les Wright and Doug Verity.

Of the new members, Harry Smith from Birmingham was probably the most outstanding climber, along with Steve Read from Derbyshire. Doug Verity, son of the Yorkshire and England cricketer Hedley Verity, had climbed with Arthur Dolphin and Pete Greenwood and was a good companion on or off a climb. To Eric Beard climbing was secondary; his forte was long-distance running in which he had considerable success. The point was that he was well liked by the other members and this was the main criterion for membership. Sadly, 'Beardie' was killed in a car crash in 1969.

Since 1959, the Rock and Ice has seen little change. New stars have risen, but the friendly spirit of the Club has remained through the years. Nat Allen had worked selflessly as secretary, and Dennis Gray has demonstrated his skill as an organizer. The Rock and Ice Club will never again come so near to the point of collapse as it did in 1958.

17 | The Walker Spur

With the onset of winter the problem of work cropped up once again. Slum clearance and rebuilding had started in earnest in Manchester, enabling Don to take a job close to his home, but even so the work was heavy and unpleasant; its only advantage being that it kept Don at the peak of fitness. Don was heartily glad to see Easter come round. A visit to Glencoe resulted in a partnership for the Alps during the summer: Hamish McInnes, his skull well on the way to recovering its former knobbly solidity, was full of plans for the forthcoming season.

Several days before leaving for Chamonix, Don was in Wales doing a few warm-up climbs. Calling in at the Gwryd, he glimpsed a familiar figure huddled in a chair, staring morosely into a drink: John Streetly was back in circulation. The news that Don was about to leave for the Alps sent John into a torment of frustration. He badly wanted to make the trip yet he had no gear and had not touched rock for nearly three years. However, making hurried arrangements to met Don in Chamonix, Streetly shot off to collect the essential equipment.

I didn't really expect to see John for another five years, it seemed so unlikely that he'd be able to lay his hands on enough gear. It was a pity; but Hamish was already over there and I couldn't keep him waiting. We'd also fixed up to meet Walter and Riccardo and as I knew that they'd be raring to go, I just said 'So long, see you, John', and left for Chamonix.

I arrived at the 'Chalet Austria' – the woodcutter's hut near the Montenvers Hotel that Walter and Riccardo had taken over the year before – and found Hamish, alone, replete with salami sausage and potato jam.

'They're gone off to do a wee ice climb,' Hamish informed me as I unloaded my gear.

'What?' I asked, wondering if I could catch them up and get in a bit of training myself.

'The Nant Blanc face of the Aiguille Verte – not very difficult, a nice ice route,' mused Hamish.

'Why haven't you gone?' I asked.

'Ah, well, I'm already trained,' he replied with a grin.

I decided that I could reach the Rognon bivouac below the Dru before it went completely dark. This shows how keen I was; I was tired from the long drive across Europe and the three thousand foot slog up from Chamonix, but I thought, well, another three hours won't make all that much difference.

When I reached the bivouac site, it was pitch black and I was almost out on my feet. I kicked the sleeping pair awake, we exchanged loud greetings and Riccardo made a brew. Afterwards, I tried to get a couple of hours' sleep before our proposed one o'clock start but I simply couldn't nod off. By the time we had started the long haul up the crisp snow of the glacier I was on the point of giving up and returning to Hamish, but somehow I kept going.

After a few hundred feet of cramponed climbing, the strain on my calf muscles became almost unbearable. I called to Walter to ask him to take a rest but I received no reply. For twelve hundred feet, the agony remained at full pressure. It was obvious that the Austrians were extremely fit and that I should have had a day in bed.

Resting on a small rock spur, I had a chance to talk to my two companions. I noticed that Riccardo's face seemed somehow subtly changed and he explained that he'd had a bad fall on his local rocks. Walter was chatting happily about how a party of French climbers had done our 'wee ice climb' a week or so before and had had two bivouacs. I cursed Hamish under my breath.

Soon we were stabbing up the glassy surface again, ice piton shredding the woollen mitt on my left hand, ice-axe in my right hand. Walter pressed on mercilessly, thrashing ice chippings down on to my head. Up and up we went, up a rock ridge – pleasant after the ice – then more ice ridges until we confronted a big wall of ice. Walter battled up a narrow chimney which split the wall and I reckoned that the summit was almost in our grasp. A final wall of soft snow barred our way. Walter's weight was too much to enable him to pull out from the wall on to the slope above. I took both ice-axes from Walter and Riccardo, plunged one into the wall, stood on it, plunged the other two into the slope and pulled myself up. The summit greeted my gaze. I couldn't remember when I'd been so glad to see the top of a mountain.

Almost immediately, we set off downwards, scrambling over mixed rock and ice until we emerged into the Whymper Couloir. A quick descent brought us on to the Glacier de Talefre and in gathering darkness we reached the Couvercle Hut. There we found that none of us had any money so away we went down the long track to the Mer de Glace. By the time we should have been leaving the glacier, we had become separated by the continuous, tiring process of weaving in and out of the jumbled ice, leaping small crevasses, avoiding the big ones. We had been on the go for twenty-five hours; this on top of a sleepless night, the drive over and the Montenvers slog was too much. I wasted another hour in trying to find the path and then resolved to climb the shaly hillside for just another fifty feet before giving up and spending the night under the watery moon. My last, tired efforts brought me to a large boulder with a nice overhang on it. In two minutes flat, I was in my bivouac gear and sound asleep.

I was awakened by the hideous sound of pneumatic drills. There, fifteen feet from where I lay, workmen were drilling holes for the foundations of a new tourist cafe. The path ran alongside the newly dug holes.

Years before, on the first visit to the Alps, Don had gazed in wonder at the huge, black mass of the Grandes Jorasses. Don

Cowan had pointed out the soaring line of the Walker Spur and
Don had silently vowed that one day he'd climb that formid-
able route. Over the years familiarity with big mountains had
not lessened the healthy respect Don held for the Walker Spur.
The route had had no British ascent, partly because of difficulty
and partly because the North Face of the Grandes Jorasses was
so rarely in good condition. Now, with companions capable of
doing the climb, the route apparently having little snow on it
and with the weather fine, the opportunity had arrived.

We'd been discussing the possibility of having a crack at the
Walker and only one thing was stopping us. Much to my surprise and pleasure, John Streetly had arrived, full of bounce
and enthusiasm as usual, and had thus created a problem of
numbers. Walter and Riccardo were sticking together which
left Hamish, John and myself; we had to have a fourth member.

Looking around for a likely lad we pounced on Les Brown, a
Burnley climber who had a good reputation on rock. Les, a
lanky, easy-going character, hadn't done all that much in the
Alps but we felt that the combined experience of the four of us
would be enough. Les had a problem himself though : on his
last climb, while sack-hauling, the securing strap on his sack
had broken and all his equipment had been lost. We solved this
one by having a whip round, which produced enough essential
gear for the climb even if some of it was of doubtful worth.
We completed the outfitting by presenting Les with a magnifi-
cently decrepit trilby hat, a veteran of many campaigns, which
we discovered high in the rafters of the Chalet Austria.

We trekked across to the ruin of the old Leschaux Hut from
where we were going to start the climb and were surprised to
find two Czech climbers already established in the derelict
shack. Hamish somehow contrived to learn that the pair had
retreated from the Walker that day when one of them had
damaged a hand. They had friends still on the climb and they
intended resuming their own attempt the following day.

We lit a great fire from timber hacked from the shattered

hut and rudely disturbed the peace of the night with a selection of choice songs. The two Czechs struggled to get some sleep, no doubt thinking unpleasant thoughts about the idiotic English. It was a great night; we should have been resting in preparation for the long day ahead but the roaring fire and the pleasure of companionship plus the excitement of the prospect in front of us were too much.

High up on the black silhouette of the Grandes Jorasses, a spark of light flickered intermittently.

'Must be their friends,' Hamish said, indicating the two huddled figures lying outside the ring of firelight.

'Bet they're wondering what the hell's going on down here,' I said, chuckling to myself.

'Probably think their mates have set the hut on fire,' said Les laconically.

Eventually, as the fire died down and even John stopped talking, we each of us drifted off into sleep, a few short hours away from the climb of a lifetime.

Although we were up early, our two companions had silently disappeared. In all probability they wanted to catch their friends before they had made much progress. For over two hours we trudged up the Leschaux glacier, Hamish wielding his piolet nicknamed 'The Message' with great relish at every opportunity. Our spirits soared as daybreak came and with it the promise of a fine day. As we approached the foot of the Spur, I picked out the figures of the two Czechs just emerging from the first rock difficulty – the hundred-foot crack. We scrambled up several hundred feet of easy, iced rock and reached the beginning of the serious climbing. I took off my rucksack and prepared myself for the attack on the 4,000 feet of the famous Spur.

It had been decided that I would climb with Les and that we would take the lead. As I started up the hundred-foot crack, I felt the familiar exhilaration, spiced this time with the knowledge that I was at last attempting a climb I'd dreamed of doing. With the morning sun already beginning to warm the rock, we climbed quickly and with great pleasure. The difficulties were sustained but not desperately hard and as the hours passed only one thing worried us: John and Hamish were climbing very slowly below us, we were already hundreds of feet above them. We held a short discussion and concluded that as we hadn't received any appeals for help, the pair must be all right but not fully warmed up as yet.

Above us we saw four other climbers – presumably the two Czechs had reached their friends – engaged in some rope acrobatics. Consulting the description we decided that they must be at the Pendule about which the description said: 'It is thought that beyond this point, a retreat would be impossible.' It looked and sounded interesting.

We waited a while but there was still no sign of John and Hamish and although we didn't want to get too far ahead in case there was something seriously wrong, eagerness got the better of us and we continued to climb. A pleasant traverse from the top of an icy chimney brought me to a length of rope hanging vertically down the face to a ledge about forty feet below. This was the 'Pendule' and I quickly slid down the rope to the ledge and traversed right, to the point where we had observed the Czechs. An overhang composed of iced-over blocks had obviously provided the setting for their acrobatics and I arranged some protection to avoid repeating their performance. Above the overhang, I belayed on a long, comfortable terrace and as Les began the pitch I decided that I'd been in positions of far greater commitment than this. I concluded that in an emergency it would be possible to reverse the pitch without too much difficulty.

As we rested on the terrace, John appeared below and across from us. Relieved to see him, I shouted across and inquired if everything was all right.

'It's Hamish,' John called, 'he's not feeling too well, it's his head.'

This sounded serious, because I knew that during the year since the accident on the Bonatti Pillar, Hamish had suffered several blackouts.

'Can you go on?' I asked anxiously.

John called something down to Hamish and we heard the faint voice of the iron Scot.

'Och, it'll pass off. Tell 'em to push on.'

'We go on,' John shouted.

Although we were only climbing steadily, we were gaining rapidly on the Czechs and it wasn't long before we caught them up. They were progressing slowly up the slabs of the Grey Tower, the feature of the Walker which contains the greatest concentration of difficulty. I was soon waiting patiently behind the last man of the party. There was no reason to ask whether we could pass or not; if we went through we would be separated from John and Hamish.

The climbing technique of the party in front seemed to be that when the first man had climbed a pitch, he secured the rope and the other three hung prusik loops from one rope and climbed using those while the leader hauled mightily on the rope fastened to the second man. Standing comfortably on adequate holds, I watched with interest and amusement the antics of the last man, as, with torn hands and bruised knees, he swung crazily about. For a long time he fought and thrashed about, then, with a final desperate lunge, he pulled himself, bloody and exhausted, on to the desired ledge. Amazingly enough, he didn't seem at all demoralized by his incredible performance but immediately began calling up instructions to the leader in a very commanding voice. His whole behaviour indicated that this was normal procedure. It was, without doubt, the worst exhibition of climbing that I had ever seen. God only knows what he was doing on one of the most serious Alpine climbs.

The next obstacle was a steep wall which gave climbing of about Very Severe standard. I waited at the foot of the wall until my friend above disappeared over the top after another crashing, smashing ascent. Halfway up the wall, I was very surprised to discover a piece of nylon rope jammed into a crack to form a running belay. It was undoubtedly British nylon rope and the jammed knot was a peculiarly British method. I could only conclude that, as no British climber had ever made an ascent of the Walker Spur, some continental climber had picked up the trick. The pitch brought us to the crest of the Grey Tower just as the light was beginning to fade.

The party above had already chosen the best bivouac sites and we were left to spend an uncomfortable night on a small ledge. As John and Hamish had the stoves and the provisions, and as there was no sign of them below, we were forced to do without the pleasure of a brew. I fell asleep wondering if everything was all right with Hamish.

A breakfastless morning dawned and away in the distance masses of dark clouds were gathering. I reckoned that we were about three or four hours from the summit; we might just make it before the storm reached us.

The Czechs were already moving up the easy ridge as Les and I leisurely packed our gear. It was still very cold as we started moving but we were heartened to hear a shout from below and to see the tiny figure of John appear at the top of the Grey Tower. Hamish had completely recovered and they were now moving very quickly.

Ahead of us was the huge wall of the Red Tower, split at the bottom by a fairly easy-angled gully and at the top by a very steep chimney. Both of these features were choked with ice, great icicles stabbing downwards out of the chimney, and I hoped the route didn't take that particular line. We arrived at the heels of the Czechs and waited for them to complete a traverse which led to the point in the icy gully where the angle eased. As we stood and shivered in the thin air, John and Hamish arrived, both going like bombs.

'How are you, Hamish?' I asked.

'Great, how're you?' grinned Hamish.

'Bloody thirsty,' I replied.

In no time at all, we had a welcome brew going. Above, the Czechs had obviously run up against considerable difficulties and our own position wasn't looking all that healthy. Cold, grey cloud was stealing swiftly and silently up the Grandes Jorasses and creating a very menacing atmosphere. If the

Czechs didn't get a move on, the weather would certainly break before we reached the summit. Through thickening cloud, we could see the two tail-enders of the party above standing at their posts like sentries. They remained immobile for almost three hours during which time the weather became decidedly nasty and I gave John and Hamish a detailed description of the climbing skills of the four heroes above us. There was no doubt that they were physically very fit; I could imagine them spending endless days on a climb which had a schedule of one day, suffering stoically in abominable conditions, slowly grinding their way to the summit. Right now though, they were in the way.

The storm gathered round us and our patience began to be exhausted. Suddenly, the last man began to move and we all sighed with relief.

'Thank God for that,' said Les dryly. 'I thought they'd decided to bivouac.'

Soon I was hard on the heels of the last man, waiting for his every move, stepping into a hold as soon as he'd left it, effectively stopping any time-wasting dithering. He didn't like my tactics very much but at least we were moving at a reasonable speed. We reached the foot of a steep gully, clogged with ice and bad rock; about seventy feet up, the third man was in a most awkward exposed position. This was obviously the reason for the delay. Due to my pushing method I had almost landed myself up the creek; I had to stand on a very dicy, ice-coated knob of bad rock with nothing but space beneath my feet while the two Czechs in front exchanged positions. Luckily, they managed this manoeuvre quickly and as soon as one man had left, I was able to clip on to a good piton and bring Les up.

The pitch above was iced up enough to cut steps in and so we had nothing to do but follow the line of steps disappearing into the damp cloud above. We reached the ridge above the Red Tower and the Walker Spur was almost conquered, the summit being only 500 feet above us. Through a gap in the swirling mist we glimpsed the Czechs approaching the last, steep pitch to the top. We stopped and had a brew and something to eat while they battled out the last couple of hundred feet. As we ate, the first snowflakes began to float down; the storm was almost on us but we knew that we were virtually safe, we wouldn't be trapped on the Spur.

The Czechs had disappeared by the time I pulled out onto the summit after some very unpleasant final pitches. A strong, cold wind swept Pointe Walker and the view was restricted to the swirling cloud but I relished the moments on the summit. I had enjoyed the climb more than any I'd ever done. The great Walker Spur had not let me down. The route was far from being the most difficult I'd climbed, there had been no rock gymnastics over horrifying expanses of space, but there had been the feeling that this was a great mountaineering route where the length, the altitude and the consequences of bad weather combined to give the climb a serious atmosphere. Except for the re-occurrence of Hamish's injury and the party in front of us, we could undoubtedly have completed the climb in one day but this was of minor importance; I had accomplished a dream.

At Courmayeur, a surprise awaited Don and the boys. Standing in the main street, surrounded by smart, gaily dressed tourists, the four were suddenly greeted by two equally scruffy climbers.

'Robin Smith and Gunn Clarke,' said Hamish as his two compatriots approached. 'And I know what they've just done.'

'The Walker,' said Don.

'Aye,' said Hamish, nodding his head gravely. 'I was a mite suspicious when I saw a couple of Smartie packets and that jammed knot sling.'

Smith and Clarke had indeed completed the Walker Spur on the previous day but, more important, they had found a cheap lodging house with lots of good food. The two parties combined for a celebration.

For several weeks, Don fretted and fumed as the clouds rolled by only to be replaced by more clouds. A meeting with Steve Read, one of the newer Rock and Ice members, resulted in a trip to the Dolomites. Walter and Riccardo had already left for Civetta where Walter had been engaged to do some guiding, so Don decided to make Civetta the first port of call.

They arrived in the midst of a thunderstorm; toiling up the track to the Vazzoler Hut was like walking up a waterfall. At the hut, Don was surprised to learn that Robin Smith had arrived the day before and had disappeared with the intention of soloing the Tissi route on the Torre Venezia. Although this climb is by no means a route of extreme difficulty, it is a serious undertaking and the fact that Smith tackled it solo gives an indication of the young Scot's confidence and ability. At this time, Robin Smith was developing into a climber of the highest calibre; possibly he would have become the finest climber ever to come out of Scotland had he not met with a fatal accident in the Pamirs in 1962.

Walter was delighted to see Don and immediately began chattering about the route he wanted to do: the North Face of the Cima della Terranova, which was reputed to have pitches harder than anything on the Cima Su Alto. The first ascent had been done in 1954 by Gabriel, Livanos and Da Roit. It had had only one subsequent ascent by the crack Italians, Guidice and Georgio Radilli, who had completed the climb in two days, one day less than the first ascensionists. Don and Walter set out prepared for the worst, with enough food for three bivouacs and enough ironmongery to open their own equipment shop.

Much to their surprise the difficulties of the climb appeared to
have been exaggerated and with Don leading the whole way,
they finished the climb in one day, using only twenty-eight
pitons where the first ascensionists had used 129.

A desire to see new rock and contrasting scenery took Don
and Steve across to the Marmolata Group. Don had recently
read Herman Buhl's book Nanga Parbat Pilgrimage *and had*
been interested in Buhl's struggle up the South Pillar of the
Marmolata di Penia in wet, icy conditions. He and Steve de-
cided that they would like to try the route, assuming that the
conditions Buhl had experienced were somewhat unusual. It
was a decision which almost cost them their lives.

The weather was fair though certainly not settled but we
reckoned that as the climb had a time-schedule of ten hours,
we would have no difficulty in finishing it off in a day. We set
off for the South Pillar unable to see the South Face because of
heavy, low cloud but I thought that it'd clear once the sun got
out. Crossing the col to the foot of the South Face, we saw a
great cache of equipment – crash-hat, pegs, étriers – beneath a
boulder.

We looked around for signs of other climbers but everything
was quiet in the grey mist. A mystery to start with, I thought.

I found the small overhang which marks the beginning of
the climb and soon I was climbing on cold, wet rock. It was
very miserable and after doing several pitches we had a talk
and decided to do just one more pitch in the hope that it would
improve. As is often the case, the pitch brought us on to good,
dry rock and the climbing became really pleasant.

A ferocious jamming session up a long crack led directly to a
big ledge with many signs of habitation. Above, a crack literally bristled with wedges and pegs. I was very suspicious of the
number of abseil loops hanging from almost every peg. According to the description, we had already done the technically
difficult pitches, yet there must have been some very good
reason or reasons for all these retreats. My mind went back to
Buhl's account of the climb and I began to wonder about the

conditions that he'd met: were they going to prove to be the normal on this particular route?

Steve was climbing much better than I had anticipated but I always prefer to have a known quantity on a really tough climb. I began to have more thoughts about retreating. Consulting the description, I saw that the upper section of the route usually had ice in the cracks. We had neither crampons nor ice-axes. It was a pity that we hadn't been able to see the top for cloud. Still, it couldn't be all that bad. I decided to push on.

I stepped into an easy gully and a shower of ice whined past me, leaving me in no doubt that the upper section would be iced up. We were standing looking at the pitch which would give us entrance to the final couloir.

'Usually wet,' I read from the description.

Above us, water streamed from every crack in the icy armour of the rock. This looked like being the worst pitch of the climb. According to the description, it was the last pitch for ice. What I now know is that we should have turned and followed the abseil loops back down. Still, ignorance is bliss and we were enjoying the climb.

A powder snow avalanche hissed down the gully catching me in a perilous position as I clung to icy holds. I moved slowly up towards the great chockstone mentioned in Buhl's account, knowing that things were going to get much, much harder and that we were now in a very nasty situation. Six inches of ice covered the walls and the gully bed. There was not much difference between this climb and Scottish winter climbing. I wished hopelessly for my crampons and ice-axe.

It began to snow as I reached the shelter of the huge block. I looked down at Steve standing on iced footholds a full rope-length below. There wasn't a single runner between us. The roof of the block was bedecked with rotten slings. I remembered that Buhl had tunnelled through at the back of the chockstone and thrown a rope to the other side. In the conditions we were experiencing, this was impossible; there would be six feet of snow and ice on top of the block.

I brought Steve up beside me to the only dry spot in the

gully. He stood, blowing on frozen fingers and I thanked the Lord that I'd brought my gloves.

'We're going to have to go very carefully,' I said, deliberately understating the case so as not to panic Steve.

I knew that Buhl had taken two and a half hours to overcome the chockstone in more watery, less icy conditions. I rubbed the dull ice and saw a wedge beneath the surface and chopped away until I could clip an étrier to the soggy cord.

'Watch it,' I said to Steve, 'it looks rotten.'

I stood in the étrier and the cord stretched and groaned under the strain. Exactly at the moment that I had decided it was safe, the cord snapped and I swung back under the chockstone. I climbed back and banged a piton in at the side of the wedge and clipped on the étrier again. This time it held and I leant out and cut steps as far out as possible on the wall. With my feet pressing into the slippery holds, I moved out with my shoulders against the roof. I thrashed down the snow which filled the gap between the chockstone and the wall and cut two more steps to use for the final push which would take me over.

Above the chockstone was a steep chimney and a great overhang of ice which did not bear thinking about. I looked about for a belay, snow falling gently about me. I began to experience the feeling that had become familiar after many years of climbing: that as far as enjoyment was concerned, the South Pillar was finished. From now on it was a life or death struggle and if we didn't get up before dark, it was quite likely to be death.

I slashed steps up a ribbon of hard snow running up the ice slope in the gully bed and had just reached rock when Steve shouted that there was no more rope. I looked around and could see no sign of a peg; unwilling to waste time putting one in, I threaded a sling round some pebbles in a small crack and with my left foot in a hold on the ice, my right foot pressed against the inclined wall and my back on a sloping wall, I called for Steve to come up.

There was not an inch of rope left and he would have to

move a few feet before I could put the rope over my shoulder but I reckoned that with the steps already cut, he should have no trouble. I looked down at the twin ropes lying against the ice, disappearing beneath the chockstone 150 feet below. I had belayed in continental style, the rope tied around the shoulders instead of the waist, with the knot in the centre of the breast.

Without warning, a yell, accompanied by a great jangling, sounded below and the rope went as tight as a bowstring. Steve had come off and was swinging in the middle of the vertical ice wall. Slowly but surely, his weight was dragging me over and I fought with all my strength to stop myself from turning upside down.

'Can you climb the rope?' I called, trying to keep the panic out of my voice.

I knew that if I turned over, the pebbles in the crack would never hold our combined weight.

'I can't climb it, it's too icy,' Steve replied calmly, totally unaware of our desperate position.

'Try man, it's only about eight feet and you're up,' I shouted.

The weight on my chest was killing me, yet I daren't ease a fraction or I'd be over. I knew that I couldn't hold out much longer.

'For Christ's sake, climb the bloody rope and take the weight off my chest,' I exploded in desperation, panic taking over.

'I can't. I'll try and put a peg in,' Steve called.

That seemed to be the death blow. I had no rope to lower him, he couldn't climb the icy rope and the chance of his finding a crack beneath six inches of ice was one in a million.

Slowly I keeled over, staring at the dirty ice coming up to meet me. Soon I would be slithering down the steep slope to catapult over the chockstone, out into the swirling mist and down to certain death on the screes below. At least Steve would be spared the horror of watching death approach slowly. I pictured him calmly tapping about the ice and then suddenly, without a second to realize what was happening, plunging ahead of my flying body. Even now, he'd be wondering what was happening as he slipped, little by little, down the glassy wall.

Fighting to avoid a jerk on the belay, I eased gently downwards, listening to the pebbles grating in the crack. I was convinced that this was the end for Steve and me. I looked down at the great chockstone. I had taken barely twenty minutes to surmount the huge obstacle. I was now lying flat on the ice. Another sickening grating sound and I slipped forward a little more.

I knew what would follow the next grating noise.

'If there's anyone up there, help us now because in one second it'll be too late,' I muttered.

Immediately the murderous pressure eased and I heard Steve's voice through the drumming in my ears.

'Okay, I've got a peg in and I'm standing in étriers.'

Dazed and bewildered, I stood up. Steve had found a crack in the ice. Miracles happen. Quickly I banged in two pegs and clipped on.

'I'm back under the chockstone,' Steve called, his voice muffled by the snow.

I stepped up to a rock ledge and took a cigarette from the peak of my cap and lit it gratefully. I pulled in the slack and making an overhand loop, dropped it over a bollard of rock. The belays were almost at foot level and if Steve came off again – which was unlikely – he would hang directly from the bollard while I was safely belayed to the pegs. When enough slack came in the rope, I could take it in.

'I'm trying again,' Steve called.

A moment later the rope round the bollard went taut and Steve was off again.

'Let me down a bit,' he shouted.

'I can't,' I replied. 'I've taken up more rope now.'

After a while the request was repeated but this time a little less calmly. I suggested that he hammer some steps in the ice and use the rope. A short silence followed and then Steve asked again for more rope. This time there was a touch of hysteria in his voice. Slowly I rolled the taut rope to the lip of the bollard and pushed it off. The next second was a blur as the jerk of the rope pulled me from my ledge back onto the ice. My cap, with its precious cigarettes, rolled down the ice and disappeared over the chockstone.

As soon as Steve was safe under the chockstone, I fastened the end of the sack rope to the piton and descended to the top of the chockstone and took a stance with a belay 150 feet long. When Steve came off again, only eight feet of rope separated us and I was able to haul on the rope. Our combined efforts eventually got him onto the top of the chockstone. The pitch had taken us two and a half hours and we were now desperately short of time with an unknown number of ice-covered pitches above us.

I attacked the chimney at the top of which was a great mass of ice, with icicles hanging down like a crystal portcullis. I calculated that we had about an hour and a half of daylight left. I couldn't see us ever overcoming the ice overhang in that time.

Walter's words came back to me as I began bridging up the glassy walls: 'A great climb; we had no ice, just a little water. When you've done it, mention my name to the guardian of the hut and he'll let you stay for nothing.'

In places, the ice gave way to verglas which was far more dangerous. I battled on, determined that nothing should hold us up. I looked down between my feet as I bridged on the treacherous rock. Not a single runner between us, one slip and that would be the end. I took a stance on a chockstone which looked like a marble with its coating of ice and clipped onto a wobbly piton sticking from the back of the chimney. My fingers had worn through the woollen gloves and the ends were numb and wooden.

Sometimes a climber has to make a move in a desperate position when he knows that failure to complete the move will result in death for his companion and himself. Now I was having to make an endless number of these moves, unable to relax for a split second, for even when I was bringing up Steve, the belay positions were nerve-wrackingly bad.

After seventy feet of incredibly perilous climbing I gazed out from the head of the chimney through the great ice teeth which hung from the overhang. Here the danger was greater than it had been at the chockstone; there I'd had belays to safeguard a fall, now the rope hung clear through space to Steve standing on the glass marble seventy feet below.

It was impossible to climb over the yard-long teeth so I hacked them off with my hammer, leaving one to use as a grip. Steve cowered into the chimney as the great swords of ice smashed in pieces around him. Using the remaining icicle, I leant out and looked over the overhang. A steep slab lay on the right, with an overhang left wall forming a dièdre. There was no sign that the climb was easing, but surely the top couldn't be far off. I glanced at the description and saw that we had reached the last line.

The pull over the bulge looked dangerous without protection and I guessed that even in good conditions there would be pitons in place. I rubbed at the dull ice and peered hopefully into the grey mass. I shouted with relief when I saw what could only be a peg far below the surface and I smashed at the ice until I could clip on and relax my tense nerves.

Chipping a hold in the thick ice on the outside of the bulge, I moved out and stood on it with my left side pressed on the left wall of the chimney. Using the icicle as an underpull, I chipped a good jug over the top and made two footholds on the steep slab. I then abandoned the icicle, hauling myself up and stood above the bulge. Things were still bad, but the overhang wall was dry and the slab had thick ice on it in which good steps could be cut.

It was growing dark as I brought Steve up to join me above the bulge. The cold was intense and our soaking clothes were freezing up. We would have to reach easier ground in the next rope length or our numbers would be up. It would be impossible to climb in such difficult conditions in darkness and the only alternative was to sit or hang in our unbearable position and hope to be alive when daylight came twelve hours hence.

I set off again, sending ice showering down on Steve who, no doubt, was thinking his own thoughts on the situation. Suddenly, an opening appeared in the left overhanging wall and a snow gully appeared in the mist. I was just able to make out a long cornice above my head.

'We're nearly up,' I shouted to Steve, excitement and relief showing in my voice.

I turned up the gully and came across a roll of wire fencing jammed across the gully and frozen to the ice. Now I knew we were almost there. We kicked steps up the snow for one more rope length and then we stood on the summit as the last glimmer of light disappeared.

Hurriedly, we crossed to the summit hut. The hut was empty but we found some blankets and a further search produced some bars of chocolate. Beneath six woollen blankets I shivered the night away, hardly sleeping a wink because of the intense cold.

Next morning the sun streamed through the double-glazed windows and, donning our wet clothes, we walked stiffly out into the welcome warmth and started on the long descent.

Walking along the path at the foot of the Face we met the owners of the cache of equipment that we had stumbled across the day before. They were lowering the frozen body of a climber from the South West Face. He had decided to bivouac on the Face and wait for the weather to improve.

In February 1955, before Don's epic on the Marmolata, he had finalized arrangements to take him on a return trip to the Himalayas. Colin Mortlock's tentative suggestion about an expedition to Masherbrum had resolved itself into the Anglo-American Karakoram Expedition 1960, objective Trivor, leader Wilfred Noyce.

The decision to abandon Masherbrum had been taken by Noyce, who disliked the idea of retracing other men's steps. The expedition then considered Kanjut Sar, a peak of around 25,500 feet, but a party of Italians conquered the mountain in July 1959. They next turned to Disteghil Sar from which Alf Gregory's expedition had been repulsed in 1957 by avalanche danger. Raymond Lambert, the Swiss guide, had also attempted the peak by a different route and had met with no success. Noyce decided that the mountain, like Masherbrum, was too well known. Finally, via Eric Shipton's map of the Hispar-Biafo area, Noyce discovered Trivor, which he aptly named 'The Unknown Mountain'. It reaches a height of 25,370 feet and was absolutely untrodden.

Wilfred Noyce was something of a unique figure in modern mountaineering: he was probably the last of the scholar-poet-mountaineers. A fine all-round climber, he had the traditional approach to climbing which contrasted strongly with that of the members of the Rock and Ice. He amazed Don, when, on their first climb together on Dinas Cromlech, he insisted on climbing to the summit of the Glyders after completing a relatively short rock climb. To Noyce, mountaineering meant mountaineering, not brief, fierce assaults on rock buttresses.

Tough and possessing immense stamina, Noyce climbed not for the physical challenge but in search of self-knowledge and for the aesthetic pleasure that high mountains can bring.

Of the rest of the party, Colin Mortlock, a good rock climber, lacked experience on snow and ice but had the qualities necessary to make him a fine mountaineer. Sandy Cavanagh was the medical man of the party and had climbed in the Alps. Jack Sadler, an American, was a man of phenomenal strength but a gentle, quiet individual. Finally, an old friend: Geoff Smith from Burnley, who, at Don's suggestion, came along as food and provisions organizer.

Don decided to try out an idea that he had toyed with before the Masherbrum expedition: to return from the Karakorum overland on his motor-bike. His Triumph was crated and left with the rest of the expedition gear on board ship bound for Karachi. Don, in his role of equipment officer, sailed with it on 16 May 1960.*

I waited at Karachi for Colin Mortlock who was to help me transport the gear to Gilgit. From Gilgit we were to do a reconnaissance of the mountain, recruit porters and generally smooth the way ahead.

We left Gilgit by jeep for the village of Nagar, 8,000 feet above sea level, on the northern bank of the Hispar River. On the opposite bank lay Hunza, a mirdom and the deadly rival of Nagar.

We'd heard plenty about both places and their peoples. The Nagars apparently were not much better than useless as porters, while the Hunzas were far from being Sherpas. We stayed as guests of the Mir of Nagar on our way to Trivor and for diplomatic reasons we were forced to take on two Nagars as high-altitude porters.

Colin and I had a difficult time establishing Base Camp, forcing a route up a valley and then onto the glacier over difficult, strength-sapping terrain. Not far out of Nagar, a series of vast

*A detailed account of the expedition can be found in Wilfred Noyce's fine book, *To the Unknown Mountain* (Heinemann, 1962).

mud slopes frightened the Nagar porters so much that they refused to go on.

'No way, no way,' they chanted, sitting down and dumping their loads.

I lost my temper and kicked the main trouble-maker up the arse and then set off to find the way. We fixed ropes along the dried mud and, after much complaining, the Nagars slowly and reluctantly began the traverse. The journey was one long moan but eventually we got them so far that they were committed and had no alternative but to push on.

We established a Temporary Base Camp and then, a day's march away, Base Camp proper. It was sited perfectly, off the glacier on a stretch of lush grass with a stream running by. From Base, Colin and I explored the lower slopes of Trivor. It looked a fine mountain which would only succumb to a sustained effort. The obvious route lay up the long, north-west ridge, which would contain pitches of hard climbing but these would only occasionally be on very steep ice or rock. In good time, Colin and I pushed our way up to the col at about 22,000 feet. On our way, we selected sites for Camps One and Two and reckoned that Camp Three would go on the col itself. By this time I was ready to return to Nagar to meet Wilf and the rest of the expedition. I was well satisfied with our reconnaissance as we had done most of the route-finding necessary.

With everybody established at Base Camp, the real labour began. For a fortnight we ferried loads, first to Camp One and then to Camp Two. This was tedious work and I was glad when I could start pushing up to the col to establish Camp Three. We fixed about 500 feet of rope up soft snow and set Camp Three right on the col. From here on the route lay up and along the ridge which led to the summit a mile and a half away.

From Camp Three, Colin and I reconnoitred a spot for Camp Four and then Wilf and I established it. The difficult stretches now lay immediately in front of us. The ridge plunged about 500 feet down to a small, snowy col and then rose steeply about the same height in a rock tower with a snow cornice.

Wilf and I explored this major difficulty and I found the rock climbing enjoyable.

The day after our exploration, it snowed heavily and we spent the whole day in the tent. This snowfall hindered Geoff, Colin and the others who were bringing supplies up from Camp Three. As soon as the weather cleared we had to retrace our steps in order to haul some of the dumped supplies to Camp Four so that we could push on and establish Camp Five.

The following day we climbed down to the small col and again ascended the rock tower but this time we were carrying large loads. Having regained the height lost from Camp Four, we proceeded to lose it again down another steep slope. A long slog up through waist-deep snow and we slowly reclaimed the height. A rock buttress, which I had christened 'The Castle', seemed to be the ideal spot for Camp Five in spite of it being only a few hundred feet higher than Camp Four.

Suddenly, as I was plodding up the last few feet to a snowy hollow which would provide a perfect camp site, my legs gave way. I floundered about in the snow, struggling to remain upright. I'd never felt so weak in my life. All at once my head felt light and my legs like liquid lead. Somehow I managed to reach the snowy hollow and I sprawled on top of my load, limbs aching.

'What's the matter, Don?' Wilf came into the hollow, looking at me anxiously.

'I dunno,' I replied. 'My legs have gone.'

I couldn't understand it at all. I was perfectly fit and I'd never had any similar experience before. I recalled that the previous night I'd felt a couple of twinges in my legs but they had quickly passed and I'd thought nothing about it.

'Can you get back to Four?' Wilf asked. 'It can't be anything serious.'

I was thinking about Roger Chorley on Machapuchare. He'd contracted polio and he'd been with Wilf. I pushed the thought out of my mind – after all, I'd had inoculations against the disease.

'D'you think you can manage it?' Wilf asked.

'I'll have to, won't I?' I answered.

I did manage but it was a terrific struggle. I was more than relieved to sink down at the camp where Colin had a drink waiting for us. I hauled myself gratefully into my sleeping bag. We discussed the plans for the next day; Colin and Jack agreed to return to Camp Three there and then, get an early start next morning and bring on more supplies for Wilf and myself to take on to Camp Five. After they had left, Wilf took my temperature. It was 101 and felt every degree of it.

'What were Roger Chorley's symptoms?' I asked.

Wilf looked worried. I could see that the idea of polio had already occurred to him.

'Look, it can't be polio,' he said. 'We all had inoculations against it.'

'Well, it's bloody funny, that's all,' I replied.

The following morning, Jack and Colin arrived and announced that Sandy and Geoff were coming along later. My temperature had dropped slightly but I still felt extremely weak. It was obviously impossible for me to go with Wilf to the summit. Colin, who hadn't been all that well himself, agreed to stay with me, leaving Jack to accompany Wilf.

I was disappointed; I had seen this mountain through from the beginning, led the whole way and now, within reach of the summit, this had to happen. Still, unlike Masherbrum, it was odds on that somebody was going to get up and that was the main thing.

When Sandy Cavanagh arrived, he examined me and said that it looked like a mild case of polio. I had to stay on my back for two days; if no further symptoms had developed by then, I would be all right; if they had, well, that was it. I sweated it out, dozing, sleeping, thinking.

Meanwhile, Wilf and Jack were well on their way. They spent one night in Camp Five and then, even though Jack was feeling ill, they forced a way upwards and established Camp Six some two thousand feet below the summit. A day of snow must have taken a lot out of the pair but they stuck it out and on the following day, they reached the summit. Wilf's persistence and determination had been fully rewarded.

Back in Camp Four, in spite of a complex system of torch communications which Wilf and Colin had arranged, we knew nothing of the summit bid. Colin flashed his light at the appointed hours and waited in vain for replies. Wilf told us later that he too had faithfully adhered to the schedule yet had seen nothing from Colin. Something went wrong somewhere, probably our watches were not synchronized.

My two-day incubation period passed and at the end of it I felt fit and well. The bug obviously hadn't fancied me all that much. Arrangements for a support party for Wilf and Jack had been made but after we had watched them start to descend steadily, we decided that they weren't going to need any help. Without waiting for news from above, but knowing that there were enough fit men on the mountain to act in case of emergency, I left Colin at Camp Four and shot off down to Base Camp. I didn't wish to experience a re-occurrence of the strange symptoms.

On the return journey from Trivor, we spent an interesting time in Hunza where the hospitality of the Mir was superb. By the end of September, I was ready to start my motor-bike trip home from Rawalpindi. I had suffered no ill-effects whatever from my frightening illness, and hoped to be soon back among the big mountains.

Don's account of his epic journey by motor-cycle forms an appendix to Noyce's book To the Unknown Mountain, *and so it would seem pointless to include it here. The trip, accomplished with the aid of a map of the world in the back of a diary, was not without danger, incident and humour and it took the best part of six weeks.*

20 | The Frêney Pillar

Don's desire to return to the big mountains seemed destined to be fulfilled in double quick time. Joe Walmsley, whose taste for the Himalayas had not been dulled by his experience on Masherbrum, proposed to lead an expedition to Nuptse, third peak of Everest, height 25,750 feet, and Don was invited to join it. The organization of the trip started almost before Don had shaken off the dust from his 7,000-mile solo trek. Mountaineering was becoming a full-time occupation. Then, in January 1961, disaster struck.

The Nuptse expedition's gear was being packed in Stockport and one rainy night, Don, with Audrey on the pillion, was driving from Manchester to the packing place. On Stockport Road, a lorry turned right without signalling and Don and Audrey smashed into the side of the heavy vehicle. Audrey sprawled under the back wheels of the lorry, Don was somehow trapped in its belly. The result was a broken leg for Don and a shattered leg for Audrey. For him, the Nuptse trip was definitely off.

Four months later, Don crashed the bike again, this time almost losing an eye. He began to have serious thoughts about abandoning motor-cycles and turning to the safer, four-wheeled mode of transport.

Walmsley's expedition succeeded in climbing Nuptse and afterwards, Bonington, who had arranged to meet Don in Chamonix in July, arrived, like Joe had done years before, in a very weakened condition. Don himself was reasonably fit and had given his leg a thorough testing on gritstone before leaving for the Alps. Forsaking the bike, Don had hitched out, loaded with provisions but with a minimum of money. He was dismayed to discover that Chris was equally insolvent.

Chris decided on a training climb. The main objective of our season was to be the North Face of the Eiger and Chris reckoned that before he could attempt anything so serious, he had to get in reasonable touch. We went on the North Face of the Aiguille de l'M and Chris made very heavy weather of it : he was right, he needed the training. But we hadn't the money to hang about doing little training climbs, he'd have to get in good nick on the Eiger.

The following day we arrived in Grindelwald and then made our way up to Alpiglen where we were going to camp. Since the 1930s when the Eiger became infamous – the 'Wall of Death' – the locals, clustered round the foot of the mountain, have made it their life's work to cash in on its ghoulish appeal. Each year, thousands of tourists come to stare in awe and horror at the huge, snow-plastered wall on which so many deaths have occurred. Kleine Scheidegg has its collection of telescopes and binoculars for hire. The Eiger is the ultimate circus : there are no safety nets, no ringmasters to bring on the clowns, and the mountain doesn't pack up and move on when the season ends.

In Alpiglen, however, there is relative solitude, only the Hotel des Alpes has anything to offer the tourist. We set up our camp and waited for the Face to come into the right condition. Days turned into weeks and we fretted the time away, impatient to get to grips with the mountain. The main problem with the Eiger is the question of the condition of the North Face. Of all the North Faces in the Alps, the Eiger's seems to attract the worst weather. Over the years, I have been on the Face in all kinds of weather : I have been repulsed by torrents of water, by hailstones, by snow and wind, by mist and by combinations of them all. To climb the North Face, you've got to choose your moment, get on the mountain, get up it and then get off it as fast as possible. On occasions, the Eiger has been climbed by climbers who have not known how lucky they were to have got away with it. Conversely, great climbers have lost their lives on the wall after having used their experience and waited for weeks for the right moment, only to find that a sudden, unexpected change in the weather has brought disaster.

Chris and I lived like vegetarian monks for a fortnight and watched the Eiger. There were days when the whole Face crouched behind heavy, grey cloud, then, as the cloud dispersed, the pyramid-like bulk would emerge covered in deep, fresh snow. A couple of days of sunshine and we would be ready to go; then, as if the weather was having its own joke on us, the clouds would return.

Eventually, more out of sheer boredom than with any hope of success, we decided to have a closer look at the Face. By this time, we had been joined in Alpiglen by four Poles who were also determined to climb the Eiger. Members of the Polish Alpine Club, they were good company and showed us how to live on mushrooms and snails when our food ran out.

Chris had already been to the foot of the wall once previously. On that occasion his companion had been the redoubtable Hamish McInnes and as it had been Chris's first Alpine climb, the experience had been quite shattering.

We set off in darkness and reached the actual foot of the Wall just as it became light. Above us, 6,000 feet of near-vertical rock, snow and ice looked out of the morning mist. We made good progress up frozen snow, balancing on the points of our crampons, but it was obvious that we weren't going to get very far; there was much too much snow and ice on the Wall. We went higher than any other British party had ever managed and then were confronted by a vast, steep slab covered with ice. Somewhere under the ice was a fixed rope, for this was the famous Hinterstoisser Traverse. Fnding it buried in this way was confirmation that the Face was in bad condition.

We rappelled back down the fearsome Wall and then climbed across to the Stollenloch – an entrance to the tunnel which runs through the Eiger bearing the Jungfrau railway. We were surprised by the sudden appearance on the Face of a railway employee who offered to let us walk down the tunnel – at a price, of course. This abortive attempt on the Wall was enough to convince us both that it would take a good spell of fine weather to clear the Face. Bored with the inactivity, irritated by the Eiger atmosphere and desperately short of money, we decided to return to Chamonix.

We were accompanied by Jan Djuglosz, one of our Polish friends who was a professional mountaineer. Jan spoke good English and was a very likeable lad. Strongly built, he was, from his record, a pretty fair climber and would certainly stand the pace on anything that we wanted to do. And that was the next problem, what were we going to do? As far as I was concerned, one route stood out head and shoulders above everything else: I wanted to attempt the first ascent of the Central Pillar of Mont Blanc – the Frêney Pillar. I broached the subject to Chris and Jan and they were enthusiastic. Certainly, if we accomplished the climb, it would be better than doing the umpteenth ascent of the Eiger. If we did it...

The Frêney Pillar, unclimbed but often attempted, was a fearsome prospect. For almost ten years, Walter Bonatti had planned an ascent of this direct route to the summit of Mont Blanc. In 1959, Bonatti, with his great friend Andrea Oggioni, had made a determined attempt at the Pillar but had retreated when the weather had closed in. Then in July 1961 – shortly before Don and Chris met in Chamonix – Bonatti, Oggioni and Roberto Gallieni had joined forces with four powerful French climbers in a mass assault on the ferocious climb. One week later only Bonatti, Gallieni and the Frenchman, Pierre Mazeaud, were alive. The story of the climb was one of tragedy piled on tragedy. Atrociously bad weather conditions trapped the party on the Pillar, cutting off any chance of advance and virtually sealing off a retreat. Bonatti, with skill, heroism and powers of endurance which were almost superhuman, managed to force a way off the Pillar and through the maze of the Frêney Glacier. One by one, his companions succumbed to exhaustion and two of the Frenchmen died. Mazeaud volunteered to stay with the unconscious Oggioni while Bonatti, Gallieni and Kohlman pushed on to reach a rescue party. On the last steep descent to the Gamba Hut, Kohlman went berserk and had to be untied from the rope. He disappeared into the darkness as Bonatti and Gallieni fled for their lives. When the rescue party set out to recover any possible survivors, only Mazeaud, crouched over Oggioni's body, was alive.

One month later, as Don and Chris were whiling away the days at the foot of the Eiger, Pierre Julien and Ignazio Piussi made another attempt on the Pillar. Using a helicopter to ferry them to the summit of Mont Blanc, they descended the Peuterey Ridge to the foot of the Pillar. They made good progress up the enormous, vertical candle of rock but a mishap with their equipment, combined with a sudden worsening in the weather, caused them to hurriedly abandon their attempt. The Frêney Pillar seemed unconquerable.

We arrived in Chamonix and Chris somehow landed himself a job advertising a camera. At this stage we were willing to try anything to raise some money. I was willing to have a bash at the modelling myself but unfortunately I was considered to be too tough-looking! Jan, who had been on a course at the École Nationale du Ski et Alpinism in Chamonix where Pierre Julien was an instructor, suggested that we go along there and meet Julien with a view to obtaining some information about the Pillar. If he seemed okay, we could ask him to join us in our attempt.

Julien proved to be quite helpful. He showed us enlarged, glossy photos of the Pillar and obviously knew the area like the back of his hand. Listening to him talk, and looking at all the detailed information he provided, made me realize that there was nothing haphazard about the way the top Continental climbers approach their climbs; they didn't just say, 'Hey, let's go and have a look at such-and-such-a-thing,' and then saunter off up the hill. They made careful preparations before setting a foot in the direction of the objective. Slightly different from us, I thought.

We worked round to inviting him to join us but he refused: too much work, lost a lot of equipment on his last attempt, couldn't afford it. I smiled inwardly; Julien and Piussi had shelled out £80 for the helicopter, we could barely afford £1 each for the *télépherique* up to the Aiguille du Midi.

Chris arrived and immediately dropped a small clanger by asking Julien if, on his previous attempt, he had made any arrangements with the press to buy the story if the climb was successful. Julien looked extremely hurt and muttered something about 'the honour of the guides'. We left after thanking him for his help and Chris, unabashed, set about organizing a bit of publicity.

Now that Julien was unavailable, we looked around for a fourth member and, as luck would have it, the Gods dropped one right in our laps. Ian Clough, a Yorkshire climber, had just arrived in Chamonix after doing some hard climbing in the Dolomites. Neither Chris nor I knew him personally but we were both aware of his reputation as a first-class all-round climber. With dark, curly hair and his ready smile, Ian's amiability concealed a strength and determination which only became evident when things got tough. He was an ideal fourth man. Eventually, after one false start and delays with Chris's modelling, we were ready to go. Audrey had sent me £10 and Chris had been paid up; we were solvent – almost affluent in fact. Chris, the only one with a wallet, stowed the money away after buying four tickets on the *télépherique*.

We waited on the station in the mellow evening sunlight. Only a few people lounged about, as this was the last *télépherique* of the day. Two climbers, with tremendous bulging, Himalayan-size sacks, were leaning on the guardrails. As we eyed this impressive-looking pair, wondering who they were, Pierre Julien, attired in climbing rig-out and with an identical Himalayan-sized pack, strode through the barrier and walked towards the two climbers.

'Aye, aye,' I remarked to no one in particular.

'Monsieur Julien, *le professeur*,' said Chris.

Julien looked round and came over to us and we exchanged

wary greetings. He said that his two companions were René Desmaison and Poulet Villard, two fellow instructors and, as we knew, two formidable climbers. There could be no doubt as to their objective. We could only assume that Julien had somehow obtained leave of absence from his pressing work and that a rich relative had died.

The journey to the top of the Midi was a strange one: Desmaison and Villard surreptitiously watching us from behind their sunglasses; we studiously ignoring them. Much to our surprise, the Frenchmen didn't dismount at the Midi, but journeyed on, bound for the Torino Hut. This was peculiar because the obvious starting point for the Frêney Pillar is the Col de la Fourche Hut. Maybe they had another helicopter waiting for them, I thought.

The hut was only sparsely populated and we cooked a leisurely meal and then turned in to enjoy a few hours' sleep before our early start. On the back wall of the hut, a large, coloured picture, torn from a magazine, showed four happy climbers posed in the hut door: Guillaume, Vielle, Kohlman and Mazeaud; three dead, one still convalescing. Before I bedded down, I entered our names in the hut book, adding 'Central Pillar of Frêney' as our objective.

At midnight, the peace of the hut was disturbed when two climbers wearing white helmets entered. One of them went over to the book, took it down and shone his torch on the pages. I saw him pause briefly as he read my inscription, then he entered something in the book, turned and was gone. Curiosity got the better of me and I climbed to my feet and went over to look at the book. Neatly written, the name 'Walter Bonatti' stared back at me from the page. He and a client were on their way to the Brenva Face. I wondered what his thoughts had been on seeing our names in the book. An hour later, Chris wakened me and we prepared a brew and got ready to leave. Looking out at the night, I saw the bobbing lights of Bonatti and his client as they climbed one of the easier routes on the Brenva Face. Above me, the sky was perfectly clear though I thought the night air felt a little warm. After the brew, I looked out again and was surprised to see the two lights moving downwards at great speed. I pointed this out to Chris and we puzzled as to why the pair had abandoned the climb. The weather and the mountain were both in good condition, there seemed no obvious reason for the hasty retreat. As we packed our gear, Bonatti and his client steamed past the hut and headed down the Géant Glacier in the direction of the Torino Hut. Pushing these strange goings-on out of our minds, we set off down the hard snow to the Brenva Glacier.

On the Col Moore, a tiny hump dividing the Brenva Glacier into two arms, we had a short conference.

'It's too warm,' Chris complained. 'I can hear running water everywhere. I think we should have a go at the Route Major. We can be up and off that in a day.'

'We've come this far,' I said flatly, 'I'm going on. It's the Pillar or nothing. I've not come this far for a *voie normal*.'

Nobody objected so, putting on crampons, we crossed the other arm of the glacier and began the long, arduous ascent to the Col de Peuterey. Chris and I shared the lead and as we neared the top, the air suddenly became much colder, freezing our gloves and turning our feet to solid blocks. We stamped about on the Col, having just completed a climb which many people regard as an Alpine ascent in itself, in four hours. It was 5.30 a.m. and still dark. We melted some snow, made a brew and waited for the sun to rise and warm the Pillar.

'We've got company,' Ian commented and indicated two figures descending from the Col Moore.

'Must be Julien's lot,' I said. 'Where's the third man though?'

'I saw a tent below the Capucin,' remarked Chris. 'I wonder if there's somebody else interested?'

As we learnt later, there was somebody else interested – John Harlin and Gary Hemming, two Americans, both with good reputations as climbers. All we needed now was the Italian Scarlatti Climbing Club, the crack Dolomite climbing outfit, to turn up. Back in Chamonix it had been rumoured that the Scarlatti's members were doing hard training on granite in preparation for the Frêney Pillar.

We packed our gear and moved to the foot of the Pillar in the welcome sunshine. Looking back down the jumbled mass of the Frêney Glacier, I began to appreciate the fact that if the weather did turn nasty, a retreat would be a formidable task. The morning sky, however, was beautifully clear, looking set fair for some considerable time.

I looked at the brown rock above. There was no description of the route, of course, so I chose the most likely looking line and led off upwards. Justification of my choice of route was not long in coming: I began to discover pitons placed at regular intervals. Steadily we climbed on, gaining height quickly. The climbing was very enjoyable and far from extreme. I began to wonder when the Pillar would show its teeth. Sitting on a broad ledge, dozing in the sun, watching the red and white ropes trailing across the tawny rock, my thoughts turned inwards.

I was doing something that early in my climbing career I would never have dreamed of doing: attempting the first ascent of a major Alpine route with a party of virtual strangers. I thought of Joe and half-wished that he would suddenly appear beneath me; this climb would have been a crowning achievement to our partnership in the Alps. Still, we had drifted apart and I had been forced to climb with new partners, none of whom had ever let me down. I could hear Chris below me and my thoughts turned to him. We were an ill-assorted pair, but we balanced each other – his impetuosity, my stolidness; his volubility, my terseness. On a climb we made a sound partnership and I enjoyed climbing with him immensely. If Joe wasn't here, I could think of nobody better to share the climb with than Chris.

'Jan's slowed down to a bloody stop,' Chris broke into my reverie and joined me on the ledge. 'I think I'll rope up with him and see if I can get some life into him.'

For the last few hours, Ian had been having problems with Jan who was almost out on his feet. He had taken too much out of himself during the slog from the Col de la Fourche.

'Good idea,' I agreed, 'Ian's too easy-going to manage Jan.'

We changed round and I pushed on. For some time, we had been discovering new karabiners hanging from abseil points used by the previous parties; the climb was becoming profitable. Suddenly, I came upon two very expensive perlon ropes hanging down the rock. After some thought, I reluctantly decided to leave them there – we might need them if we had to come off in a hurry.

By late afternoon, I reached the foot of the final tower. The sight of the soaring rock came as something of a shock. There was no doubt as to what had stopped the previous attempts. For at least 500 feet, a monolithic candle of rock rose vertically to the sky. A crack split the tower for the first eighty feet or so and then – as far as I could see – there was nothing. A smaller pedestal of rock leant against the tower; climbing up to the top of this, I reached the tragic bivouac site of the Italian–French party. The small ledge was littered with the debris of their stay. When Chris and Jan joined us, we had a discussion.

'We've still an hour or two of daylight left, I suggest we have a quick recce,' said Chris.

'Okay,' I agreed. 'Hold the rope.'

The crack sported a number of pitons and I climbed steadily upwards, occasionally using étriers. Above me, the top of the tower was shrouded in mist which was slowly drifting downwards. A few hailstones bounced off the rock. I was sorely tempted to return to the bivouac ledge where I knew that Ian and Jan would be comfortably resting. Only the hope that I might find a route quickly kept me on the rock. The pitons stopped their upward trend and spread into all available cracks in every direction. Some of the pegs appeared to have been battered into solid granite, indicating how desperate Bonatti's team had been.

I made a delicate traverse to the left and investigated every possibility. Julien had told us that somewhere in this final candle was a wide, fifty-metre crack which would require large wedges. We had hauled stacks of these wedges up with us but could find no crack. I cursed Julien roundly and continued the search. I moved back and tried out to the right. Pegs littered the rock, some stuck in only a quarter of an inch, bent and mangled. The traverse was on ever-steepening rock and was difficult in spite of the pitons. I reached the edge of the candle and strained to see round the corner. Chris was shouting questions which I couldn't answer. It was hopeless; I was cold, hungry and thirsty. I banged in a piton and rappelled down to the boys.

'What do you think?' asked Chris anxiously.

'Well, if there's nothing round the corner on the right, I don't think it'll go,' I said.

'What about the fifty-metre crack?'

'There isn't even a one-metre crack,' I replied.

'Christ,' said Chris in disgust and despair.

We settled down for a sleepless night with Ian, as junior member, brewing up every hour or so. Far below us, on the Col de Peuterey, we saw the lights of a tent bivouac – presumably Julien and company. The long hours passed and slowly daylight dawned and the warming sun crept down the Pillar. There was no question of climbing until we were fully warm, so we had a leisurely breakfast and dozed in the sun.

'Four climbers heading for the couloir on the right,' Ian remarked.

'Two more going towards the Rochers Grubers,' said Chris.

As soon as we were warm, Chris climbed up to the position from where I'd rappelled the previous night. He took a stance with the aid of some slings and I climbed up and past him. This was it; there had to be something round the corner.

Very carefully, I moved slowly out round the corner. The rock was just vertical and I knew that the moves I was making would be extremely difficult to reverse. For nearly two hours, I edged my way towards the dièdre where the tower met the wall. A thin crack ran up to a small overhang ten feet above. The overhang was split by a wider crack which might just hold wide channel pegs but the rock looked rotten. Above that, and up the overhanging dièdre, ran a fine crack which led to a chimney cutting through a big overhang in the back of which were good cracks galore.

The exposure had increased enormously; I dangled from a piton above 2,000 feet of space. I noticed that the French party below had traversed from the couloir and were now on the Pillar. I brought Chris round the corner, first making sure that he brought all our wide channel pegs with him.

It was cold on the shady side of the Pillar; I envied Ian and Jan still dozing on the warm ledge.

'Large wooden wedges,' I snorted to Chris. 'This crack's too wide for the channel pegs and not wide enough for the wedges. What we want are some small wooden wedges.'

Steadily I worked away and arrived at a point in the dièdre where the crack widened and appeared to ease in angle. Seen from below, the crack looked quite reasonable and I thought that if necessary I could climb it free. I called down to Jan and asked him to ask the French if we could borrow any small wooden wedges which they might possess. The query was passed on and the answer came back: we could have them but we'd have to wait, as their last man had them in his rucksack. I made myself comfortable and continued my appraisal of the problem above. Two wedges would be enough and then I could place a piton in the bottom of the chimney. After that, there shouldn't be any trouble because the crack in the chimney was a good one.

An hour slipped by and I asked Jan if there were any wedges forthcoming.

'They won't give us any now,' replied Jan.

'Why not?' I fumed.

'They say we're going the wrong way. They're going to try on the left and they say they will need all their equipment,' Jan said.

'Send me a brew up instead then,' I said.

After a welcome drink, I decided that as there was no alternative I would have to climb the crack free. I had had ample time to study the crack, and in no time at all I had reached the chimney. When the struggle should have been over, it started. The chimney was much steeper than I had supposed and, try as I might, I could not jam my shoulders or even a knee across.

My strength was ebbing fast, partly due to the altitude, which affected one severely when anything very hard was attempted. I had a knuckle-jam between a block in the back of the chimney and the wall. If I had only taken a piton up between my teeth, I could have saved the day but all my ironmongery was way out of reach behind my back. My clumsy boots – ideal for snow and ice – would not go into the crack. I was definitely going to fall. I glanced down at my line of pegs below me. At least I wouldn't hit rock, everything around was overhanging.

'Chris?'

'Yes?'

'I'm going to come off.'

Fifty feet below me, Chris prepared himself for the impact. 'Okay, Don,' he called.

'I'll have one more try,' I thought aloud and gathered my remaining strength for a final attempt. Suddenly I was hanging from my knuckle-jam, which was slowly easing out. I looked down at the couloir below and waited. Next second, I popped out of the jam like a cork from a champagne bottle and became airborne in a jangling of pitons. Rock flashed past me and then a welcome jerk checked my fall. I was hanging upside down from a sound peg, staring into Chris's face a few feet below. My cap and hammer were still heading for the couloir.

With help from Chris, I regained the rock and stood, panting and trembling from my exertions.

'You all right?' Chris inquired.

'Aye,' I replied. 'I've lost my cap and hammer, that's all.'

'Shall I have a go?' Chris asked. He had been idling away in the cold for hours and was raring for a bit of action.

'Sure – but don't try it free,' I replied.

'If you can't do it free, I certainly can't,' said Chris. 'So don't worry, I'm going to take some chockstones, that should help.'

Chris started up and I lit a shaky cigarette.

'Hey!'

A voice floated up from below and looking down, I saw Ignazio Piussi, an old acquaintance of mine from the Dolomites. So, he was the fourth member of Julien's party. We exchanged greetings and progress reports and then he disappeared. Apparently they were having no luck on the left side of the Pillar.

There was a shout of triumph from Chris. He had conquered the chimney with the aid of two chockstones. It had been a fine piece of climbing by him and from what he was saying, it looked like the main difficulties of the Pillar were over. During his big effort I had noticed something fall from his pocket and plunge down the couloir.

'What was that that fell ?' I shouted to Chris.

'My wallet,' he replied sheepishly.

Julien was right, the Frêney was an expensive route : my hat, my hammer and now all our money.

I climbed up to join Chris and after a brief inspection of the way above, I agreed with him that the rest of the climb looked to be without serious problems. Darkness was already beginning to close in, so I shouted down to Ian and Jan and asked them to prusik up the rope. The patient pair had been on the same ledge all day.

We found a good bivouac ledge and, in the gathering gloom, we shared the last of our food and celebrated our success with some exuberant singing. I felt the exultation which always comes after a great climb. We were on the brink of bagging the current 'last great problem' in the Alps.

Another perfect day dawned and in warm sunshine we climbed the last few hundred feet to the top of the Frêney Pillar. A helicopter and a small plane buzzed around, their occupants waving and taking photographs. It looked like we were going to be in the news. Two hours later, Chris and I stood on the summit of Mont Blanc. In ten seasons of Alpine climbing, this was the first time that I had ever been on the roof of Europe. On the summit slope, pressmen greeted us and took some photographs. One of them gave us some grapefruit juice while the other detonated a smoke bomb which belched forth a great cloud of red vapour. We drank a bottle of wine that had been half-buried in the crisp snow and were slightly merry by the time we reached the Vallot Hut where Doug

Scott, a climber from Nottingham, cooked us a meal. Somehow we managed to return to Chamonix via the *télépherique* even though we had no money. We called in at Snell's, however, and he lent us some money and also put us in touch with the editor of *La Dauphine* who offered to pay for an exclusive article on the climb. We were solvent again.

*   *   *

Chris, with a few days left before he was due to start work at home, had an inspired idea. Flushed by his success with the press over the Frêney climb, he approached a *Daily Mail* man with a view to that paper financing us on yet another attempt on the Eiger. Surprisingly enough, the paper agreed and so off we went to Alpiglen.

We began the climb in hot sunshine during the late afternoon. The Face had undergone a complete transformation during the weeks that we had been away. Now, it was almost clear of snow; rivulets of water tumbled down the cracks which had been feet deep in frozen snow the last time we had been on the Face. We made good time over the warm rock; up the Difficult Crack and then across the Hinterstoisser Traverse which, without its coating of snow and ice, proved to be a steep, smooth slab. Our intention was to spend the night at the Swallow's Nest, a small ledge slightly below the First Icefield. In the morning, with an early start, we could be across the First and Second Icefields before they were raked by stones during the afternoon bombardment.

The night was warm, too warm. The sound of running water continued through the hours of darkness and when dawn came, the expected freeze-up had not taken place. The Face was in an extremely dangerous condition; as soon as we left the Swallow's Nest, we would be moving into a ceaseless fusillade of stones, large and small.

'It's no good,' I said to Chris. 'Press or no press, I'm not going on.'

'We might as well go a bit higher and give it a try,' Chris argued.

This was it: the lure of the Eiger. How many others had said just the same thing? How many others had pushed on in the hope of one thing or another and then not returned?

'No,' I said decisively. 'We're going down. There's always next year, the mountain'll still be here.'

Chris saw sense and we returned, disappointed but still alive. The fact that we hadn't got all that far up the Eiger didn't seem to worry the press. We found ourselves on the front pages again. I suppose it was what they call the 'silly season'.

In August 1961, when Don and Chris were sitting in Alpiglen, Audrey received a letter from an Irish climber called Frank Cochrane, a student at Trinity College, Dublin. In the letter, Cochrane invited Don to join an expedition to the Patagonian Andes. Organized by the Climbing Club of Trinity College, the expedition had the support, financial and otherwise, of the Irish Mountaineering Club, the firm of Guinness, the Everest Foundation, and sundry other reputable firms and organizations. Audrey forwarded the letter to Don who promptly accepted the invitation and then forgot all about it in the excitement of the Frêney climb.

The objective was to be the Aiguille Poincenot, an 11,000-foot peak in the Fitzroy Group. The party was to consist of three students from Trinity College, two Guinness employees and Don as climbing leader. The opportunity to visit Patagonia was too good to miss despite two drawbacks: the other members of the party were unknown quantities, and Don would have to sell the bike to raise £150, his contribution towards the finances of the trip.

I had read about the Fitzroy area and I was excited about the prospect of climbing there. The Patagonian Andes seemed to possess unique qualities of their own, plus a combination of all the problems found in the Himalayas and the Alps. In particular, Fitzroy and its satellite peaks were a superb blend of rock and ice climbing. Fitzroy itself had been conquered by a French party which included Lionel Terray and Guido Magnone some ten years previously. Jacques Poincenot had lost his life before the expedition even reached the mountain when he drowned in the crossing of the fast-flowing River Fitzroy. As a memorial to him, the French named the smaller, left-hand peak of the Fitzroy massif the Aiguille Poincenot.

The weeks before our expedition was due to leave flew by and letters and telegrams passed between Dublin and Craw-shawbooth in a steady stream. One event during the last few months of 1961 brought me great personal pleasure : the Bob Downes Hut, near Froggatt Edge, was officially opened. There could be no better memorial to Bob than the hut, situated as it is among the outcrops which gave him so much enjoyment.

Arriving in London, I met my companions for the first time. Frank Cochrane, the organizer, was older than I had thought, but he seemed a go-ahead sort of character and seemed to be possessed of great determination. The other members were Francis Beloe, quiet and detached; Clive Burland, a studious type, and George Narramore, an employee of Guinness who was the expedition's photography expert. Their combined climbing experience did not add up to much and I had my first doubts as to whether we had bitten off more than we could chew. The sixth member of the party was another Guinness man, Tony Kavanagh, who had left by sea with the equipment some weeks before.

At Buenos Aires, a lone figure in a bright, tartan shirt stood out among the airport crowds. A lonely, worried Tony Kav-anagh surged forward to greet us, the troubles of the world sliding from his shoulders. Nothing could go wrong now, I thought; Frank had arranged with the Argentinian Government for air transport from Buenos Aires to Patagonia. Tony in-formed us that all we had to do was collect our gear from the docks, get it to the waiting aeroplane and we would be away.

Two weeks later we had not even located our gear. The docks at Buenos Aires are vast; the officials are disinterested or evasive, the dockers are, to a man, dedicated to avoiding any-thing remotely resembling work. Somewhere in the great maze of jetties, warehouses and barges was the Expedition's equip-ment. Nobody knew where it was, nobody showed any interest in trying to find it. While Frank hurtled frantically from official to official collecting the hundred and one stamps needed to get our equipment through the Customs, the rest of us searched the labyrinthine docks.

One day, depressed by the heat and the stupidity of official-dom, I rolled back a tarpaulin on a battered barge and dis-covered some packing cases marked 'Irish Universities Andean Expedition'. Three days later, we managed to persuade the port authorities to unload it. Once unloaded, we thought, that would be it; we would be on our way once more. Then a junior clerk, mad with power, discovered that we had an official stamp missing from our collection and another day was lost. By this time, our aeroplane had given us up for lost and departed. Another three days passed before the Argentinian Air Force could provide a substitute. As a result we spent Christ-mas drinking Guinness in the hotel.

Loading the equipment into the plane at last, thrilled with the prospect of leaving Buenos Aires, we didn't even care that the Dakota loaned to us by the Argentinians was, even by their standards, pretty decrepit. One hour after take-off, we found ourselves back in Buenos Aires with engine trouble. Hours later, we set off again with instructions from the pilot ringing ominously in our ears.

'Hang on to the equipment. If it slides towards the tail, pull it forward. If it slides forward – pray.'

Our destination was Bariloche, situated in the beautiful Argentinian lake district. As the plane flew on, the arid pampas gave way to magnificent lakes and snow-covered mountains. At last, the trip was becoming worth-while.

That evening, we were entertained by the Argentinian Andino Club and a few doubts as to the feasibility of our ob-jective were expressed. In the opinion of several of the local experts, Poincenot would be harder to climb than Fitzroy had been. However, out spirits were high and no one in the party seemed to be worrying over-much.

The following day we flew on, reaching the enormous Lago Viedma in the evening. As the pilot circled, searching for the lonely airstrip, we got our first view of the Fitzroy Group. More than thirty miles away, the great, brown faces of the mountains looked magnificent, rising as they did from the flat pampas. Beyond the main massif, the needle-like point of the Cerro Torre, scene of the epic Egger–Maestri ascent, flickered and wavered as streamers of cloud floated around it. These were mountains worth coming a long way to see.

We unloaded our gear and the plane took off in a cloud of dust. We were in the middle of nowhere, dependent now on the kindness of the local *estancia* owners. We hadn't been waiting long when a dilapidated lorry roared up and a beaming gaucho greeted us with obvious pleasure. He explained that he would provide us with a roof until a lorry from Santa Cruz arrived to ferry us across the Rio de Las Vueltas, first of the major obstacles between the Poincenot and ourselves.

We lived comfortably, if fretfully, in a building constructed from corrugated iron sheets. The weather was superb and we began to wonder just how long the fine spell would last; Patagonia is not renowned for a favourable climate. At last, after seven long days, the lorry arrived and we began to close on our mountain. Reaching the Rio Fitzroy, we were met by our hired gaucho, a huge, flamboyant character named Ruffino Torre, who was quickly nick-named 'Ruffian'. Ruffino had a string of horses which would take us and our equipment to Base Camp.

The Rio Fitzroy is a fast-flowing glacial river; its depth and currents are unpredictable and crossing it is therefore a hazardous task. We were glad of the Ruffian's expertise and of the strength of his horses. By now, we were regaining our fitness and raring to get to grips with the mountain. The last stage of the approach brought us to the *estancia* owned by an elderly German named Stanhardt, who lived alone in perfect peace with his horses and dogs.

On a glorious morning, Herr Stanhardt led us to the site of the French Base Camp. I cannot remember ever being as impressed by any views as I was by those I saw on that journey. From Lago Capri, a small, vivid, blue patch of water, the panorama had everything: the lake, dense green woods, glaciers, and the clean honey-coloured ramparts and spires of the mountains. Overhead, huge condors glided effortlessly on the air currents. The beauty of the scene was breath-taking.

We set up Base Camp in a small clearing in the woods. Our time schedule was a tight one : we had to be back at the airstrip, with our equipment, on 1 February at the latest or we would miss our return air transport. Base Camp was established on 4 January, so one spell of prolonged bad weather and our attempt would be doomed.

Camp One was situated by the edge of the Lago de Tres Los at a height of around 2,500 feet. It was a good three hours' walk from Base Camp up the terminal moraine of the Tres Los glacier. From Camp One, the route lay up the glacier, past a rock rognon which the French had named 'The Luncheon Room' and then on to the col between the Rio Blanco glacier and the Piedras Blancas glacier. On the col, we built a snow-cave just as the French had done before us. Another snow-cave was built halfway up a hard snow slope underneath the col which linked the Poincenot to the Fitzroy. From there, an assault on the Poincenot could be launched.

Our chosen route of attack was the obvious one : at about 7,000 feet, a diagonal ice ramp crosses the face of the Poincenot and leads to a shoulder on the South East ridge; from there on, the route lies on rock – up the ridge to the summit. From our observations, we could see that the Ramp was about 1,200 feet long and lay at an angle of about fifty degrees. This narrow strip of ice lay across steep, granite slabs which plunged vertically down for 2,500 feet to the Rio Blanco glacier. Above the Ramp, the vast, orange East Face soared a good 1,500 feet to the sky.

Tony Kavanagh and I set out to equip the Ramp with a handrail of fixed rope – necessary if we had to make a retreat in bad weather. It took three days of hard work to make the Ramp a safe proposition. Working on it was far from pleasant; the ice was hard and the ever-present exposure nerve-wracking. The rest of the lads were ferrying loads up the mountain to provision our summit bids.

As work on the Ramp progressed, so the weather began to worsen. Sudden high winds and flurries of snow from the racing clouds were punctuating each day with increasing regularity. It began to look as if time was running out for us. Eventually, however, we were ready to try for the summit. Tony and I left Camp Three at three-thirty in the morning of 20 January. We swarmed up the Ramp in double-quick time and finally reached a formidable ice chimney which led up to the Shoulder.

As I began to cut steps up the steep ice, the weather closed in and great swirls of mist enfolded the mountain. Above me, the chimney narrowed and became overhanging. I worked my way slowly upwards, banging in pitons wherever possible. A strenuous heave, a knee-jam, and I was up; our route as far as the Shoulder was complete. Below me at the foot of the chimney, Tony was complaining about the weather. Gusts of wind were lashing powder snow into white furies. I knew that this was as far as we were going. We left food, bivouac equipment and a collection of ironmongery on the Shoulder and began our retreat. Crossing the Ramp was a nightmare; the very air seemed alive and hostile with the fierce wind driving waves of snow over us. At the end of the Ramp, we literally swam our way through masses of heaving, foaming snow. We eventually reached the ice-cave at Camp Three, wet, freezing cold and almost spent. Frank and Francis plied us with drinks and warm clothing and we prepared to sit it out through the bad weather.

Days passed and the cave became extremely uncomfortable. Heavy condensation soaked every stitch of clothing, even our sleeping bags were sodden. Outside, the storms continued and it became obvious that we would have to return to Base Camp to reorganize and replenish our supplies.

As soon as we arrived at Base Camp, the weather took up. As quickly as possible, we dried our equipment and even though time was running short we decided to make another summit bid. Tony announced that he was no longer interested in the summit, having suffered enough on our first attempt. Frank opted to take his place with me. I was very keen to beat this mountain, even if it meant driving myself and the rest of the party to the limit.

We returned to Camp Three on 25 January, prepared to set out for the summit early the next morning. George Narramore was convinced that this attempt was doomed. He indicated the falling barometer and pointed out that the wind had moved round back to the north west again. At 3 o'clock on the morning of the 26th, George was proved right. As Frank and I stood outside the cave, the sky loomed leaden above us and the wind howled round the mountain, driving the clouds at a fantastic speed. Snow was imminent; even as we stood there, the first flakes came flying past us. We crept back into the cave and prepared for another wait.

The next three days were hell on earth. The snow plastered over the entrance to the cave and we fought a continuous battle to stop ourselves from being buried alive. Once again, everything became sodden and we risked exposure. On the fourth morning we awoke to find that our air supply was too low even to allow the Primus to light. We battled our way out through snow which overnight had increased from ten to thirty feet in thickness. Outside, the storm still raged and great waves of hissing snow poured down from the slope above. It was clear that we couldn't hope to keep Camp Three open. Once again, we retreated despondently to Base Camp. Even there, the shelter of the woods had not been proof against the fierce winds. The big tent was ripped to strips of canvas, which were still anchored to the trees.

It was now 29 January. In two days' time, our equipment had to be at Herr Stanhardt's *estancia*, which was a day's march from Base Camp. Our party was depressed and apparently reconciled to defeat. I fumed and cursed the vagaries of the weather which had again taken up immediately we had arrived at Base Camp. Then, when I had almost given up hope myself, Frank came over to me as I lay in the sun.

'We've one day left, Don,' he said. 'How about if we push up to Camp Two early tomorrow morning and make an effort from there? It'll only add an hour to the approach.'

I could hardly believe my ears, I thought that even Frank had given up.

'Right,' I replied. 'It's on.'

Frank urged the others into some activity and they prepared loads to take up to Camp Two, which would supply Frank and myself with provisions for two days on the mountain.

We were ready to go at five o'clock the next morning but it looked once again as if the weather was going to foil us. The sky was heavy and the wind was rising.

'Well, that's it then,' said Frank sadly.

'Give it a few hours,' I suggested. 'You never know in this bloody climate.'

By mid-morning, sure enough the sky had cleared and it was a perfect day. Even though I got the impression that the rest of the lads thought our attempt was hopeless, we persuaded them to set off for Camp Two while we went ahead with light loads. That night, Frank and I slept soundly after praying for a fine day in the morning. Frank was obviously excited by the prospect of a last-ditch success, but I knew that we had a hard struggle ahead of us. Frank had never been higher than Camp Three and his ability as a climber was still unknown to me. I reckoned that, all-in-all, the odds were against us getting to the top.

The night sky was clear as we breakfasted at three o'clock. It looked as if for once the weather was on our side. When the sun came up in blood-red splendour, we were well on our way towards the Ramp. The going was good, as the snow was firm, and when we reached the bergschrund and the first fixed rope we found that the storms of the past week had completely filled the great crevasse, thus enabling us to cross the first difficulty with ease.

Even though Frank moved slowly and with great care across the Ramp, we reached the ice traverse leading to the difficult chimney in good time. I cut steps across the ice and brought Frank across. The chimney was packed with ice and proved difficult to climb. By the time I'd brought Frank up, it was just after mid-day and the weather didn't look too bright. The wind had got up again and a great bank of cloud loomed up in the west. Above us, the ridge – completely new ground – looked reasonable. We stood on the Shoulder and had a conference.

'I don't like the looks of the weather,' said Frank.

'We've come a fair way,' I said. 'No point in giving up until it becomes really hopeless.'

'You think we should go on then?' he asked.

'Aye,' I replied. 'I want to give it a go.'

'All right,' Frank agreed, although I could tell that he was none too enthusiastic.

The ridge appeared to consist of huge blocks piled one on top of the other. The climbing looked fair but indefinite and after a brief assault on a steep crack, I decided that if the route continued at this standard, it just wasn't on: it would be of sustained difficulty and far too time-consuming.

'What about trying the west side?' Frank suggested.

Around to the left, the west side of the ridge was exposed to the buffetings of the wind which sounded far from pleasant. Still, there was nothing for it but to give it a try. We followed a zone of ascending ledges, gaining height steadily; but soon we were clinging for dear life to the rock as the wind hit us directly. An amphitheatre seamed with cracks ran a long way up the wide ridge. Choosing a route, I began to battle my way up the series of cracks and chimneys, the wind giving me as much trouble as the rock, which was about Grade IV with the odd pitch of V. I moved as quickly as possible and was relieved to find that Frank climbed well and showed no signs of wanting to give up.

We had estimated that the ridge was about 800 feet but the hours passed and I reckoned that we had climbed well over our estimate. The wind howled continuously and occasional flurries of snow flew past like a hail of bullets. I wriggled up a small chimney, head into the fierce gale, and looked along a small ridge. There was nothing above me, we were there. I brought Frank up and straddled the ridge as he took photographs. I banged in a French piton as a memorial to Jacques Poincenot and Frank dropped an Argentinian coin into a small crack. The time was three-fifteen in the afternoon of 31 January. We had taken eleven hours to reach the summit. Could we now retrace our steps before darkness?

Our descent of the ridge was mainly accomplished by climbing, as it was impossible to throw the abseil rope down because of the wind; it simply refused to drop, waving and thrashing about, sometimes shooting vertically into the air. We eventually reached the Shoulder at seven-fifteen and darkness wasn't far off. The rope jammed in the chimney and I had to climb back up to free it, losing valuable minutes of daylight. Crossing the Ramp, I had to take extreme care because Frank was almost dead on his feet. Somehow we got across the treacherous ice and in complete darkness began the long slog down to Camp Two. Frank showed tremendous determination and guts during the whole of the hazardous descent; he was obviously on his last legs as we staggered into the haven of Camp Two after eighteen hours of continuous movement. Anyway, we'd made it; it had been an unforgettable day for me.

The ascent of the Aiguille Poincenot was immensely satisfying to Don. Against long odds, doing all of the route-finding and all of the leading, he had conquered a major peak. Also, the trip to Patagonia provided him with good experience of the conditions to which mountaineers must adapt in that wild, unpredictable corner of the world. This experience was to prove useful later in 1962 on the Paine Expedition to Chilean Patagonia.

Chris meanwhile had resigned from his job, the lure of the mountains proving stronger than the urge for security. He and Don decided to start the 1962 Alpine season with a further attempt on the Eiger. They reckoned that their combined experience of the mountain needed only to be spiced with a little weather-luck and the first British ascent of the North Face would be theirs.

We were both very fit and in good form. Before confronting the Eiger, we'd been on the West Face of the Aiguille Noire and had a little epic on the Géant. We were prepared mentally and physically for the North Wall. Our plan of attack was exactly the same as it had always been: wait for the weather, climb up to the Swallow's Nest in the late afternoon, bivouac and then finish the climb the following day. We lounged about at Alpiglen and waited for our moment.

The Face seemed in reasonable condition, with not too much snow on it. The weather was variable and perhaps a shade on the warm side which meant that there would be more water and more falling stones than usual. One afternoon, after a particularly fine morning, we set off. We made good progress up the lower part of the Face although there was too much water about for my liking. At the top of the Difficult Crack, Chris dropped his ice-axe. His climbing had been erratic and I'd been expecting something to happen. Still, better his ice-axe than him. That left us with two peg-hammers and my ice-axe, which whoever was leading would have to use. Once again, the Hinterstoisser Traverse was snowless and we reached the Swallow's Nest without further incident. We arranged our bivouac and discussed the prospects for the morning. It had to freeze during the night or the Face would be in no fit state.

The bivouac was uncomfortable; water dripped everywhere and continued to soak us right through the night. By morning, we were both reconciled to giving up. High above on the Face, stragglings of cloud were gathering and the sky was a leaden grey.

'Down then?' I asked.

'How about pushing on – at least up the icefields?' Chris said, unwilling, as always, to give up completely.

I weighed up the odds. Last year we'd turned back and got off the Face safely. Was it worth going on this time? Conditions were the same, with the weather obviously about to break. I reckoned that we could climb on for an hour or two and still get down if things got worse. I was getting sick of retreating from the Swallow's Nest anyway.

'Okay,' I replied. 'It'll give us a bit of practice.'

We cramponed our way up the First Icefield and Chris led off up the Ice Hose, which was packed with ice and running with water. His position was dodgy and I began to think about a retreat as stones were already beginning to fall. Eventually, he reached the top of the difficult pitch and brought me up. We stood at the foot of the Second Icefield and took stock of the position.

The top of the Eiger was invisible behind grey cloud. There was an ominous atmosphere, stones were zooming past and flying off the vast expanse of the Second Icefield, which itself was pock-marked by stones that had embedded themselves in the dirty ice. Also, I noticed that the volume of water was increasing. I decided that we'd had our necks out long enough. Once again, I was beginning to get that old apprehensive feeling and I'd had it too many times before not to take any notice of it. Suddenly, we heard voices from below.

'Where've they come from?' I muttered to myself.

Below us, coming up from the First Icefield, were two climbers who were shouting something in German. Eventually, we got the gist of what they were saying. They were Swiss guides, part of a rescue party, and above us were two climbers in trouble. From what they were saying, we gathered that the climbers above were British.

'I didn't know anybody else was having a go,' I said to Chris.

'They'll be the climbers we saw from Alpiglen yesterday,' Chris said.

Before we'd left Alpiglen on our attempt we'd seen, through a telescope, two climbers at the beginning of the Second Ice-field. They were moving very slowly, so slowly in fact that we hadn't been certain for a long time that they were actually climbers. We had no idea that they were British.

The Swiss wanted us to help in the rescue for it seemed that one of the pair above was injured. Without any hestitation we began to move across the icefield. It wasn't going to be an easy job for stones were now falling continuously, and progress was slowed by the necessity of cutting big steps in the ice. These steps would be essential if the injured man had to be man-handled down.

I hacked my way diagonally across the ice, pausing every now and again to scan the mountain for signs of life.

'I've seen somebody,' I called back to Chris. 'Right at the top of the ice.'

Hundreds of feet above me, and way over to the left, I picked out a tiny red dot, apparently edging downwards. He seemed an incredibly long way away. It occurred to me that if the man above was badly injured, he would never survive the manhandling that a rescue would involve and would also stand a good chance of bringing disaster on us. The icefield was alive with stones and the weather was closing in rapidly. Our posi-tion was far from pleasant.

The distance between us and the red dot didn't seem to de-crease. The grey ice soared above and below us now; we were in the middle of an icy hell. Suddenly, I heard a rushing, crack-ling noise. Looking across the icefield, I was horrified to see the figure of a man hurtling down the ice, the wind rushing through his clothes, tearing them and flapping the shreds. We watched in disbelief as the bunched-up body catapulted off the icefield and flew through space. Then, almost in slow motion, it fell out of sight.

'Ye Gods,' croaked Chris.

I swallowed, my throat dry with shock. Above, I could still see the red dot against the ice. I wondered whether the body we had just seen plunge off the Face had been the fit man. If it had, it meant that the red dot above was the injured climber. Either way, it wasn't going to be easy getting off the Face, for even if the climber above was in one piece, he would inevitably be suffering from shock. I began to climb on.

Pitch after pitch, we climbed steadily up the ice. Both of us were hit by stones, though luckily they were only small ones. After what seemed hours, we were within shouting distance of the figure in the red duvet. He stirred as Chris moved carefully towards him. The whole of the hundred and fifty foot rope ran out between Chris and myself and I prepared to climb on and join Chris.

'Stay where you are, Don,' Chris called down. 'He's coming across. He's not hurt.'

I was in an exposed position, with stones whining past. It seemed that it was only a matter of time before a big one came and found its target. Still, there was nothing for it but to stick it out. Above me, Chris and the climber, whose name was Brian Nally, were together and Chris appeared to be untangling his rope. The Eiger was now shrouded in cloud, and rain, mixed with hail, had started to fall. The Second Icefield was awash with water pouring down from above. My heart sank as I realized that most of our carefully-cut steps would be flushed away. I began to wonder if we would manage to get off the mountain.

After an age, Nally and Chris began the climb down. I saw Nally stumble as a stone caught him on his bare head. As they approached, I could see that the worst was going to happen: Nally would be a complete liability on the descent. His eyes were blank and his expression wooden. Shock, exhaustion and exposure had reduced him to a robot state. How long could we keep him moving before the mental strain became too much?

The climb back across the Second Icefield seemed interminable. The thunderstorm above descended and enveloped us and we were lashed by torrents of water while the lightning flashed around us. It was becoming a nightmare.

By the end of the Second Icefield, I realized that if we didn't move faster, our numbers were up. As we abseiled down the Ice Hose, I began to think of a method of avoiding the Hinterstoisser Traverse. During our ascent, I'd noticed a stream falling over a sheer rock face which soared upwards from the start of the Hinterstoisser. If this stream was the one flowing down the Ice Hose, it would be possible to abseil down following the stream, thus avoiding the time-consuming descent to the Swallow's Nest and the Traverse itself.

I led the way off to the left, following the stream to the point where it disappeared over a cliff that I hoped was the one we wanted. I looked over the edge and there, seventy feet below, was the start of the Hinterstoisser Traverse. I banged in a peg and abseiled down. We had cracked it, we were as good as off the Face.

It was almost as if the Eiger realized that its quarry had escaped, because the storm immediately started to ease off. Exhausted and soaked to our skins, we climbed across to the Stollenloch to a welcome from the gentlemen of the press and the Swiss guides.

Barry Brewster and Brian Nally were both competent climbers in the general sense. When the accident occurred, they had been on the mountain for over twenty-four hours. Their attempt had not gone well from the beginning: they had spent a miserable, wet night in the Swallow's Nest, lost the route the following morning – thereby wasting valuable time – and then crossed the Second Icefield through a welter of stonefalls. Brewster was leading a rock pitch in the line of the stonefall when he was hit and torn from the rock. He fell almost two hundred feet and crashed, unconscious and with a broken back, on to the ice. Nally could do nothing for him except protect him from being hit by further stones. Without thought for his own safety, Nally safeguarded Brewster through the long evening and the cold night. During the night, Brewster died.

It is impossible to say exactly what would have happened on the Eiger if Brewster had not died but had been seriously injured. One thing is certain: Don and Chris would never have been able to get both Nally and Brewster to safety. Whether the Swiss rescue party would have come to their assistance is open to question. Rescues on the Eiger are always controversial. For the Swiss guides, to venture on to the North Face when conditions are bad – which they normally are when a rescue is needed – means climbing far more difficult and dangerous than their ordinary day-to-day guiding work. They are not compelled to perform rescue operations on the North Face of the Eiger and no one can blame them for refusing to do so.

What does rather stick in the gullet in the Nally–Brewster case, is the fact that several days after the rescue, Nally was presented with a bill for a couple of hundred pounds – the cost of his rescue.

Don and Chris, tired of the Eiger and the publicity, left Alpiglen and crossed to the quiet splendour of Innsbruck, to spend three weeks on the sunlit, limestone faces at Kaisergebirge and Karwendel. At the end of August, Don returned home leaving Chris in Chamonix. Two weeks later, Chris, partnered by Ian Clough, returned to the Eiger and this time, in perfect conditions, achieved the first British ascent. Don's feelings at having missed out on this great plum after so long were typical: 'Good for them.'

23 | The Towers of Paine

Don and Chris had another commitment for 1962; they had been invited to join Barrie Page's expedition to climb the two unclimbed Towers of Paine, in Chilean Patagonia. The group comprises three vertical, granite fingers which reach heights of between 7,000 and 9,000 feet. The North Tower had been climbed by an Italian party in 1958, but the Central and South Towers had remained inviolate in spite of a series of attempts. The Central Tower in particular presented a formidable challenge. The highest of the three peaks, it was sheer on all sides, and its ascent would obviously require rock climbing of the highest standard.

The Paine Expedition got under way in October, when the party, minus one member, sailed from Liverpool. The absent member was John Streetly who lived in Trinidad and would make his own way to the Base Camp. Ian Clough, much to everybody's pleasure, had accepted an invitation to join the expedition and the climbing line-up looked extremely formidable.

Derek Walker had worked wonders with the organization; Don still considers that it was the best-fed trip he has ever been on. With Prince Philip as the patron and a fine grant from the Everest Foundation, the expedition was off to a flying start.

I got a big kick out of flying down the Andes from Santiago. We went quite close to the Fitzroy Group and got a magnificent view of the Poincenot. We arrived at Punta Arenas, the most southerly point in South America, on the Magellan Straits. It's not a very attractive place at all; stark, bare and wind-blown, with the air always heavy with sandy dust. Eric Shipton, that indefatigable wanderer, had only just left a day or two before our arrival, on his way to Tierra del Fuego.

There is an English community in Punta Arenas and they treated us very well during our week's stay, but at this stage of an expedition one is always eager to get going. I suppose the scent of adventure is so much stronger when you know that your objective is now within reach.

The Chilean Army were very helpful and it was in two of their trucks that we finally set off for the mountains. One long day of uncomfortable driving across the flat pampas eventually brought us to the Estancia Cerro Paine; a fine, hospitable sheep ranch. On the drive, we had crossed the Argentinian border and had a little bit of a barney with the frontier guards. They wanted to know whether we had permission to climb on the Central Tower of Paine, and demanded to see written proof. They'd obviously been expecting us and some higher authority, for reasons unknown to us, wanted to turn the pressure on.

The more determined their demands became, the more casual Barrie Page got. He waved pieces of paper in front of their faces and chanted: 'Central Tower of Paine, see?' Infuriatingly, Barrie wouldn't even tell us whether we had or had not got permission to climb the Central Tower. Finally, the Argentinians became as exasperated as we were and waved us on our way, delighted to be rid of us.

We arrived at the Estancia Cerro Paine at the end of a month-long spell of fine weather. Sustained good weather is unusual in Patagonia and I got that sinking feeling when I heard that we'd just missed four perfect weeks. However, the weather did hold up for another week during which time we worked furiously in establishing Base Camp and getting two camps on the mountain itself.

Our route to the Central Tower lay up the Ascencio Valley, a long, deep mixture of swamp and incredibly tough forest. Our early battles up the Valley were painful struggles as we tried to blaze a trail through the twisting, tortuous scrub. Tree roots, bushes and an infuriating creeper which grew horizontally about two feet above the ground, provided tiring and nerve-tearing obstacles.

A glacier ran into the Valley and it was at the junction of the two that we sited Camp One. From there, we had a superb view of the Towers. There too, we found traces of an Argentinian expedition which had made the second ascent of the North Tower in 1960. From Camp One we went up the glacier and round to the back of the Towers. We put a small camp on the moraine there, and began to fix ropes up to the col between the North and Central Towers. The col, which we named the Notch, was the base from which the real climbing would begin. Viewed from so near at hand, the Central Tower was a rock climber's dream; sixteen hundred feet of magnificent granite, containing every conceivable rock feature and offering limitless challenges to the climber. At the other side of the Notch, the massive walls dropped steeply away to the glacier 2,000 feet below.

Ian and I were the first to arrive at the Notch, burdened by heavy loads of gear. I eagerly surveyed the soaring rock above. To my delight, I could see a definite route with cracks, chimneys, dièdres – the lot. Now all we needed was another few days of good weather, but the increase in the strength of the wind as Ian and I retreated indicated that our luck had run out and that we were going to be delayed.

Meanwhile, John Streetly had arrived in his usual unpredictable way. Eager to get cracking, he had set out on his own from Base Camp and had proceeded to get himself completely lost. During a couple of days of solitary wanderings, he circumnavigated the three Towers and then arrived, as he himself put it, 'by sheer luck' at Camp One. Search party after seach party had combed the woods while John blithely toured round the Towers. He was eventually discovered, with much cursing and no little relief, asleep under a tarpaulin at Camp One. He didn't seem to understand what all the fuss had been about.

Maybe it was John's arrival which changed the weather. Life became almost intolerable as gale-force winds battered the whole area. The winds brought blizzards during which hard pellets of snow hurtled through the air. Climbing anything was out of the question; it took the whole of one's strength to stay upright. For a day or two, we attempted to keep two men at Camp Two, hoping for a brief break in the storm, but eventually conditions forced us to abandon the camp altogether. Camp One was equally shattered and so we gave best to the weather for the time being and retreated to the *estancia.*

The weeks dragged on and the weather seemed to worsen. Christmas came and went in a haze of booze. Then company arrived in the shape of an expedition from the Italian Alpine Club. The Italians provided an explanation for the behaviour of the Argentinian frontier guards. They too had come to climb the Central Tower. We pointed out that we were already established on this tower and that the ideal solution would be for them to do the first ascent of the South Tower. Nothing was actually mentioned about official permission, etc., but the Italians implied that we had no right to be on the Central Tower at all. I indicated, in no uncertain terms, that we were on the Central Tower, permission or not, and that if they wanted us to move off it, then they'd have to move us by force. It appeared that they had promised the Pope that they would climb the Central Tower and nothing else would do. It was news to me that the Pope was interested in climbing, but surprisingly enough they were in direct radio contact with Italy and it was obviously extremely important to somebody that they climbed the Central Tower.

Derek, acting the diplomat, suggested that it was all right with us if they did attempt the Central Tower as long as they chose a different route from ours. The Italians accepted this and gave us assurances that they would on no account trespass on our line. So everybody was happy.

After a reciprocal feast given by the Italians at their camp, contact between the two expeditions ceased, but one incident further increased the gulf between us. The Italians flew Italian and Chilean flags above their camp; naturally, we had no flags of any kind, but Vic Bray, who is something of a humorist, decided that we had to make some kind of gesture. Improvising a flagpole, Vic strung up a pair of decrepit long johns. Somehow the news of our disrespect reached the English contingent in Punta Arenas and they sent us British and Chilean flags post-haste. The empire-building spirit is not yet dead.

During our enforced lay-off, we had been working on the problem of protecting our high camps from the winds. We pooled our brains and came up with the idea of a solidly built hut, large enough to provide comfort and protection but small enough to be transported. Using timber from the *estancia* and sheets of tarpaulin, we constructed what turned out to be the ideal answer to Patagonia's furious winds. With enormous effort, we got the hut up to the site of Camp Two and erected it in the teeth of a gale. We moved Camp One – or the remains of Camp One – into the relative shelter of the woods and then started to think about climbing again.

Ian and I established ourselves in the hut and prepared to wait for a break in the weather. After one particularly violent blizzard, we were amused to see an Italian tent totally collapsed. Of the Italians themselves, there was no sign. Then, one morning, we awoke to the sound of silence : I remember sitting bolt upright and shaking Ian awake.

'Ian – listen. The wind's gone.'

Outside, the day was warm and still; perfect climbing conditions. Unfortunately we'd missed a good part of the morning by oversleeping in the unaccustomed silence. Now we had to make up for it. We literally raced up the fixed ropes to the Notch and attacked the Tower. That day, we climbed like men inspired and by nightfall we had fixed ropes up 450 feet of new ground. A summit bid required only another short spell of fine weather. Meanwhile, the Italians had not yet set foot on the Tower.

That one fine day was a real break in our favour but once again the weather closed in and we prepared to sit it out. Chris, Barrie, John and I took advantage of another lull in the weather to restock the hut and, on the off-chance that the following day might turn out to be fine, we spent the night in the hut.

The following morning was bright and clear. We got away to an early start and carrying full bivouac equipment climbed quickly up to the Notch. On the way, we passed the chaotic Italian camp but no one was astir. Much to our annoyance, we found collections of Italian gear hanging from our pitons. We had a brief discussion as to whether or not we should chuck it off the mountain but British sporting spirit got the better of us and we left it where it was.

We swarmed up the fixed ropes to a feature we'd named Big Slab, which was the highest point that we'd reached. I was leading Chris up the Big Slab when I had a most hair-raising experience. Hauling on a rope which Ian and I had left hanging down the Slab, I was amazed to feel it snap in my hand. Expecting to fall, it took me some seconds to realize that I was, in fact, sticking to the rock with pure friction. Carefully, I eased my right hand across to where the broken end of the rope dangled. Somehow I managed to tie the two ends together and with extreme caution continued to move upwards. The peculiar breakage of the rope must have been caused by the wind blowing it across a rough edge of rock.

Above the Big Slab, the Grey Dièdre stretched upwards. Chris led on, using a convenient, continuous crack and placing pitons at regular intervals. He reached an overhanging roof and suddenly, trying to reach too far over the roof, he fell awkwardly. I held my breath and prepared to receive the shock but, after falling about ten feet, he was held by a peg. It was pleasant to hear him cursing again and I let him have his say before inquiring after his health. Luckily, he was totally unhurt – more surprised than anything. A couple of minutes later, he was on a stance above the overhang.

As I was preparing to climb, I heard shouts from below. Looking down, I saw the figures of Vic, Ian and Derek far below in the gully. They were pointing and yelling, drawing my attention to the pitches above the Notch. There on the rock, complete with red crash helmets, were the Italians. They were climbing up our route.

'There are three Italians on the electron ladder,' Derek shouted.

'Aye, and there'll be three less of the Pope's mates if that wedge comes out,' I muttered to myself. 'What do they think they're going to do when they catch up with us? Climb over us? No bloody chance, this is the *voie Britannia*.'

I climbed up to Chris and we exchanged words about this new development.

'Right,' said Chris determinedly and he began the next pitch up to the foot of the Red Dièdre.

Progress was slow, pegging the whole way; it was by far the most difficult pitch of the climb. Below us, the red dots of the Italians' headgear bespecked our route; they were following our footsteps pitch by pitch.

John and Barrie, who were climbing below us, decided to turn back in order to allow us to make faster progress to the summit. All that now mattered was that at least a couple of us should get to the summit ahead of the Italians. We took a diagonal line across easier rock to a feature we named the Shoulder. There we dumped all our surplus equipment – including our bivouac gear. Only a few hundred feet of the Central Tower now remained inviolate.

'It's half-past five, Chris,' I said as we stood together on the Shoulder.

'We'll do it before dark, then come back and bivvy here,' Chris replied.

In the deepening dusk we climbed glazed slabs and icy chimneys until we reached a vertical ice chute. Without crampons and ice-axes, the chute was an impossibility and so we had to make a detour. This involved some acrobatic climbing on ver-glassed rock which led to a long chimney. At the top of the chimney, we saw that the point to which we were headed was not in fact the true summit. Farther over to the right were twin summits and we quickly changed direction and headed for them. Three times we thought that we were at the highest point and three times we found that we weren't. The climbing was still quite difficult and the frustration of moving in the gathering darkness only added to our exasperation.

Eventually, across a gap, I saw the true summit only a hundred feet away. I slid down into the gap and rapidly climbed

the rocks up to the summit. We had made it. Chris joined me
on the summit block and we grinned broadly at each other.

'Well done,' said Chris.

'I enjoyed that,' I said.

Cupping our hands to our mouths, we shouted in unison.

'Big Ned is dead.'

Far below, the shout reached the ears of the rest of our
party. 'Big Ned' – our nickname for the Central Tower – was
ours. I couldn't care less how many Italians used our route
from now on, they could bring the whole of Rome up if they
wanted.

*With time to spare before they were due to return, the boys
now turned their attention to the neighbouring mountains. Before leaving the Towers, however, Derek Walker and Ian
Clough made the third ascent of the North Tower and Don, Ian
and Barrie almost succeeded in climbing the South Tower but
were repulsed by the return of the fierce winds.*

*The complete party then launched an assault on the Cuernos,
an impressive peak tipped with black granite. Once again they
found themselves having to retreat; this time because of a
combination of snow-storms and bad rock. They had reached a
point only four hundred feet below the summit.*

*The Paine Expedition had been a great success; by climbing
the Central Tower they had picked one of the plums of the
South American ranges. It is a sad fact that Andean climbing
does not have the same glamour as Himalayan climbing and yet
mountaineering in the Andes, though different, is equally as
severe. One great advantage of Andean climbing is that the
march to the mountains is usually relatively short and easy. In
Don's next expedition, the approach to the objective almost
put paid to the whole trip before a foot was set on the mountain.*

24 | Gauri Sankar

After the Paine trip, I spent a fairly quiet year. I had a brief excursion to the Alps with Tom Patey during which I failed yet again on the Eiger but the rest of the time I spent working for my living. Lectures were now coming in at a steady rate and I began to see them as a means of making a living in between expeditions. I reckoned that with a steady round of lectures, plus income from various items of climbing equipment that I'd designed, I could at least cut routine work down to a bare minimum.

Towards the end of 1963, I contacted Dennis Gray, who was working on a Himalayan expedition which was to consist mainly of Rock and Ice members. Dennis, whose skill as an organizer is not the least of his abilities, was extremely keen on the idea of a Rock and Ice expedition. To him it seemed a logical extension of the Rock and Ice activities in Britain and the Alps. To me, it sounded like a good opportunity to return to the Himalayas.

Dennis told me that our objective was a Nepalese peak called Gauri Sankar which has often been mistaken for Everest, only forty miles away. A mountain of magnificent aspect, it can be seen from Katmandu, a hundred and thirty miles distant. Gauri Sankar had had its aspirants: Raymond Lambert, the Swiss expert, had tried and failed and the ubiquitous Japanese had also had a go but had been forced to retreat when most of their equipment was stolen. That, in fact, was one of the major problems: Gauri Sankar is dicily situated astride the present China–Nepal border, a region not noted for peace and love. Gangs of armed bandits roam the no-man's-land of the border area and they are not too particular about their choice of victims. National reputations, climbing clubs, permits, mean nothing to those lads; if you've got something, they want it.

The Nepalese Government gave their permission for us to attempt the mountain and, bandits or no bandits, the trip was on. We managed to get hold of an aerial photograph of the peak and we picked out a feasible approach route and a decent-looking line up the mountain itself. Our resulting experiences force me to place no faith whatever in aerial photography.

The party was a reasonably strong one and it included two young Rock and Ice 'stars', Terry 'Gnome' Burnell and Des Hadlum. Both were proven rock climbers but neither had been outside Europe before. Ian Howell, a climber who hailed from the Isle of Wight, was the fourth member. Ian had several good Alpine ascents to his credit and was obviously capable. Dennis himself was a fine, determined climber with plenty of experience. To give the party added strength, I suggested that Ian Clough should join us and Dennis at once agreed. Ian was a perfect expedition man : always good-humoured, adaptable, dedicated to success. All these qualities were coupled with a climbing skill – on both rock and ice – of the very highest standard.

After some bargaining, the lads bought a Land Rover to transport them cross-country to Katmandu. I didn't particularly fancy a trip I'd already done in the opposite direction and so I agreed to travel with the gear on the boat.

Because we were not too sure just how long it would take us to reach the mountain, we arrived in Katmandu a little early. The monsoon season was still going strong and our proposed journey looked like being a very uncomfortable one. It turned out to be hell.

For thirteen days we marched towards Gauri Sankar, glissading down mud slopes, perpetually wet and plagued by obnoxious leeches. The leeches got in everywhere and everything; I remember Gnome blowing his nose and finding one in

his handkerchief. They attacked our feet ceaselessly until it became necessary to remove one's boots and socks every twenty
minutes. Pulling them off the skin was useless; I used a pair of
small scissors to cut the things in half, at which they simply
dropped off. Our feet and legs became badly infected with
blood poisoning.

Our route lay up the Rongshar Gorge and by the time we
reached a village at the entrance to the Gorge, we knew that
our difficulties were only just beginning. The Nepalese porters
refused to go any farther and no amount of persuasion could
make them change their minds. Luckily, the head-man of the
village obtained some Tibetan refugees to carry our food and
gear from the village to our Base Camp, which was in a cave at
the end of the Gorge. We could just see Gauri Sankar from the
cave.

The China–Nepal border ran haphazardly through the waste-
land, forcing us to make detour after detour and limiting our
approach to the western side of the mountain. For a further
two weeks we blazed a trail, mostly through almost impassable
jungle, until we reached the foot of the West Ridge. During
this approach, we surmounted two ridges each of around
17,000 feet, descending each time to valley level. The aerial
photograph had shown but one ridge which we had thought
we wouldn't have to climb anyway. By the time we had
reached the mountain proper, our communications and supplies were stretched to the limit. We had bargained for a maximum of five camps; we had already established four and we
weren't even on the mountain.

Of course, this incredibly arduous approach had taken its toll
of the lads. All of us had suffered bad attacks of blood poisoning and the usual bouts of stomach upsets and sickness. We
were hardly in a fit condition to climb a difficult Himalayan
peak. Nevertheless, we were there to climb the mountain and
that was what we had to do.

By this point, Ian Clough and I were the only ones who were
going well enough to make any inroads at all on the mountain.
The rest of the party were weary of incessant load-carrying

and certainly not psychologically attuned for the climbing that lay ahead. The pair of us attacked the West Ridge.

The climb on to the Ridge was an epic in itself. The features of the route were very similar to those of the Eiger on about half the scale. If we were to get anywhere at all on the mountain, the whole of this 'Little Eiger' would have to be fixed-roped in order to safeguard the load-carrying. Ian and I, with Des and Gnome providing valuable assistance, spent five days putting up 2,500 feet of fixed rope. When we eventually reached the West Ridge, we were horrified to discover that it was a long, knife-edged ice ridge, impossible to climb. Our prodigious efforts had been in vain. We established a camp on the crest of the West Ridge and pondered our next steps. As far as I could see, there was a reasonable chance of success if we traversed diagonally across the North West Face in order to reach a high point on the North Ridge, which looked eminently climbable.

The North West Face was no picnic. Ian and I were stretched pretty hard by the very difficult ice climbing. We established another camp in the middle of the Face when we found, purely by chance, a fair-sized ice cavern. This camp was not the last word in comfort; sleeping in it was exactly like bedding down in a deep-freeze. Nevertheless, it did provide protection from the elements. Eventually we reached a steep rib which joined the North Ridge about a thousand feet from the summit. This was the last obstacle because the North Ridge would provide no difficult technical problems.

The last few hundred feet up to the North Ridge were the crux of the whole climb. An exceptionally steep ice gully, with smooth, green walls, provided the only feasible route. Ian and I knew that to climb this feature we would need all our skill and resource, plus a great deal of luck because the gully was an obvious avalanche chute. We put fixed ropes across a dangerously exposed ice slope leading to the gully and spent day after day working our way up the sheer ice. We were now over 22,000 feet and the climbing was of the highest possible standard. Each day we worked on the route, we knew that we were sticking our necks out. It was just a question of whether we would overcome the gully before an avalanche swept us to our deaths.

Des and one of the Sherpas joined us in the ice-cave. The Sherpa was obviously afraid when he saw what we were trying to do and he finally refused to take any further part in the climb. As Ian and I set out up the fixed ropes to spend another day in the gully, Des and the Sherpa prepared to start down.

Climbing quickly up the steep ice, I reached a bulge which was 150 feet from the easy ground above. Suddenly and apparently without good reason, I began to feel apprehensive. I glanced upwards at the clean, green ice and the blue sky. There was total silence, an ominous silence. Ian was on the other side of the gully, lost in his own thoughts. I hung the remaining ice pegs on the last running belay and returned to Ian on the stance. Then, without warning, an enormous ice avalanche crashed down the gully. Tremendous blocks smashed against the gully walls; we were engulfed in a white mist of ice particles. I was convinced that Ian, who was on the edge of the gully, had been swept off. As the white storm cleared, I was amazed to see him still on the stance, shaking the ice from himself. Below us, the great avalanche roared on its way.

'Are you all right, Don?' Ian asked.

'Aye, I'm surprised to see you still around,' I replied.

'Not half as much as I am,' said Ian laconically.

I remembered Des and the Sherpa; if they'd set off, they would now be in the direct path of the avalanche as it fanned out down the North West Face. In fact, we learnt later that they were about to leave the cave just as the avalanche occurred. It roared over the cave, leaving them completely unharmed.

Our retreat from the gully provided sensational climbing; the avalanche had removed all traces of our fixed ropes. We came across ice pegs bent like straws, all that remained of a week's work.

'Now what?' asked Ian as we sat in the safety of the ice cave.

'One more go,' I said. 'We nearly did it today. If that lot hadn't come down, I reckon we'd've got on the Ridge. We'll fix the ropes again and have one more try.'

The prospect of putting up fixed ropes again was unpleasant but necessary. To make a summit bid with any confidence, it was essential that we had a safe retreat. Almost at the limits of our endurance, we re-fixed the ropes and prepared for a final bid. Neither of us had been warm for weeks and we were in real danger of frostbite. We talked over our plans and decided that come what may, this attempt would be our last.

'If we don't make the Ridge today, that's it,' I said as we prepared to leave the ice cave.

Ian nodded his agreement. We were committed. There was nothing wrong with our determination, there was nothing lacking from our efforts, but on that final bid, we didn't even reach our previous high point. The long battle against the cold had taken too much out of us. We stood together as an icy wind whipped spindrift about us.

'I'll have to go down, Don, I'm getting frostbite,' Ian said.

I thought for a moment. 'That's it then,' I said.

'Aye,' Ian replied.

We were both bitterly disappointed but we knew that we had done our best. The irony was that, but for the Chinese border, we would have been up and off the mountain weeks before. If only we'd been allowed to approach the mountain from the Chinese side. . . .

Our retreat from the North West Face was timely, for avalanches of gigantic proportions crashed down the mountain as we left the West Ridge camp. Gauri and Sankar, two Nepalese gods, throwing their final bolts at us.

The discomfort experienced by Don during his weeks on the mountain did not end during the withdrawal. Fifty yards from the West Ridge camp, a stumble resulted in a bad cartilage injury. Anyone who has ever snapped a knee cartilage out of place knows the agony which results. Climbing down the 'Little Eiger', the cartilage went again, causing Don to black-

out. In the split-second before he became unconscious, Don saved his life by clipping on to the fixed rope. The march back to Katmandu was one long torture as the cartilage popped in and out at the slightest twist. On his return to England, Don wasted no time in having the mangled cartilage removed. Gauri Sankar had been a truly painful mountain.

In June 1965, while Don was working in a local quarry, he received a letter from John Harlin, the American climber, inviting him to take a job as a climbing instructor at the newly-founded International School of Mountaineering at Leysin in Switzerland. Although acceptance of the invitation would have meant a steady income, free living accommodation and several months' stay in the Alps, Don was still not fully confident that his knee was sufficiently healed and so he reluctantly refused Harlin's offer.

Although Don had met John Harlin only briefly, he was aware of the dynamic American's reputation. Only thirty years old, he had already exhausted several careers and reached the top in half-a-dozen different fields. He was an expert pilot – an ex-member of the U.S.A.F. formation flying team – he had worked with Balmain as a student dress designer, and he had represented the combined American Services at football. Good-looking, superbly built, he could still, at thirty, cover a hundred yards in 9.7 seconds. As a climber, he was in the top flight of American experts, with several impressive new routes to his credit – including the difficult Hidden Pillar of Frêney on Mont Blanc. Harlin believed that mountaineering was more than a sport, more even than a way of life. He was convinced that through the gospel of climbing, which he would preach in his International School, a panacea for the world's sickness would emerge. Differences of race, colour and creed would disappear in the collective search for the truth and beauty of life as revealed by the climbing of mountains. His idealism was

*proof against all cynicism and remained so until his tragic
death.*

My work in the quarry was reasonably interesting and I got
along well with the boss. Come July and I discovered that,
according to the firm's policy, I was not allowed two weeks'
holiday until I had been employed by the firm for a year. I
didn't fancy the idea of missing out on a trip to the Alps, so I
simply picked up my cards and left. I travelled over with
Derek Walker, convinced that I would be back after a fortnight. As it turned out, it was nearly two years before I came
home to stay.

The Zermatt area has never held any great fascination for
me. Whenever the subject of climbing crops up in general conversation with non-climbers, one of the first questions on the
agenda is always: 'Have you climbed the Matterhorn?' For
years, my answer had to be in the negative and I always got
the feeling that somehow, because I hadn't climbed the
damned thing, I couldn't be regarded seriously as a climber.
Derek hadn't climbed it either, so he and I decided to move
over from Chamonix to Zermatt where we knew Ian and Nikki
Clough were based.

We arrived in Zermatt to find Ian engaged in instructing and
Nikki twiddling her thumbs. The height of the tourist season
was upon us and the weather being set fair, the Matterhorn
was receiving several hundred ascents per day. Nikki said that
she would like to join us on our assault and so, not expecting
to enjoy the climb one little bit, we set out.

The Matterhorn has been described as 'a magnificent pile of
rubble'. From a distance, it presents a wonderful picture. It is
exactly what a mountain should look like: steep, imposing and
with a definite summit. The North Face, which was the first of
the great Alpine North Faces to be climbed, has not a single,
definite feature on it and did not appeal to me at all. We had
decided to climb the mountain by the ordinary route which
lies up the Nornli Ridge and via which the legendary Edward
Whymper first conquered the Matterhorn.

We climbed up to the Hornli Hut which stands next to the Hotel Belvedere at the foot of the Hornli Ridge. The Hut itself was packed to capacity but the night looked like being a reasonably fine one, so we slept in the open air.

Waking just before first light, I was amazed to see what appeared to be a continuous line of people filing up to the Hornli Ridge in the gloom.

'It's like Blackpool prom,' I remarked to Derek as we prepared a brew, and still the line continued upwards.

We were away from the Hut by just after five o'clock and dutifully took our places in the queue. A few minutes of stop, go, stop, go, however, soon had us fretting and we began to make detours to avoid the line of sweating, struggling climbers. We didn't bother to rope up as the climbing was easy to the Solvay Hut just below the shoulder.

Every now and again we came across a Swiss guide hauling his client bodily upwards. The guides have the whole thing down to a fine art; they bomb up to the Solvay, knowing full-well that few of their clients will be able to stand the pace. Collapse at the Hut is followed by a trembling descent, thus saving the guide the trouble of completing the last third of the climb while still, of course, getting his full fee.

We roped up above the Shoulder for one rather dodgy ice pitch but then reached the summit without any further trouble at about nine o'clock. It was chilly on the top but the view was worth the climb. Taken all-in-all, I had quite enjoyed it. It certainly made a change from doing a difficult ascent.

*   *   *

Leaving Derek in Zermatt, I returned to Chamonix and met up with one of the Rock and Ice lads, 'Dan Boone' alias John Fullalove. Dan has been climbing well for a number of years now but in 1965 he was only just beginning to find his feet in the Alps.

Some of the Rock and Ice members were obviously planning some fiendish plot. Broke as usual, and probably having exhausted all possible sources of income, they were working out exactly where the next meal was coming from. It had not escaped their notice that the butchers of Chamonix were in the habit of displaying barbecued chickens on stands outside their shops. They also knew that these same butchers gathered in the Nationale to play table football at a certain time of day. I left them in the Nationale with every confidence that they wouldn't starve.

That night, on the camp site, the mound of chicken bones nearly filled our tent. The following day, we set out to climb the Frendo Spur, a not-too-serious climb which, due to the conditions, turned into a minor epic. After the climb, I decided to leave Chamonix, fully intending to return home but a meeting with Dave Bathgate, the Scottish climber, resulted in him persuading me to go to Leysin. From then on, the question of returning to my quarry job never arose.

Leysin is about two hours away from Chamonix. The village is somewhat of a health resort where victims of tuberculosis and similar diseases go to convalesce and recuperate. It has attractions for the climber, though primarily it is ski country. I was very interested to see the set-up of Harlin's much-vaunted establishment. We found a number of resident climbers in the village, some of whom were working at the large American School. I was pleased to see Dougal Haston, the Scottish climber, in the village. He was about to function at the wedding of Rusty Baillie, the South African who had been Dougal's companion on the second ascent of the Eiger in 1963.

At the reception after Rusty's wedding, I met Royal Robbins, a crack American climber who was Sports Director at the American School. He told me that an acquaintance of mine, Mick Burke, was about to start work as a member of the sports staff at the school and he offered me a job there as well. Pushing aside all thoughts of returning home I accepted the offer.

The pupils were, in the main, the children of expatriate Americans. Most of them were about sixteen years of age and all possessed that disturbing quality of worldliness peculiar to American teenagers. We did a bit of climbing and some gym

work though few of the students showed much interest in anything beyond having themselves a wild time. The most difficult
part of the job was the proctoring. We were responsible for
one dormitory between us and there were many occasions
when I would have dearly loved to have belted some of the
trouble-makers.

One morning shortly after Christmas, John Harlin came to
see me.

'Would you be interested in a *direttissima* of the Eiger?' he
asked, watching me closely.

'Not particularly,' I replied. 'Why?'

I knew that Harlin had made several attempts to find a direct
line up the North Wall, notably with René Desmaison and
later, with Dougal. Personally, I couldn't see the point; a direct
line, by definition, is artificial, and in the case of the Eiger it
seemed foolishly dangerous.

'I've been promised newspaper backing and I know I can get
first-class gear,' said John.

'Who else is on it?' I asked.

'I've asked Chris. He's thinking about it,' he replied.

'Dougal?' I suggested.

'No,' said John, shaking his head.

'When are you thinking of trying it?'

John was decisive. 'This winter,' he said.

We went on to discuss the possibilities of a direct route and
the methods that might be used to make the climb feasible.
Although I wasn't interested in climbing it, I was interested in
the problems involved and I could see that John had done
hardly any serious, practical thinking himself. Talking with
him, I realized that it was in the idea of a direct line up the
toughest North Face in the Alps, that the attraction lay. It was
more than a climb to him, it was a crusade. When he left, in
spite of my down-to-earth negation of most of his ideas, he still
clung to the idea of an Alpine-style ascent taking, according to
his estimate, about ten days.

A week later, we met again in the village cinema and he
announced that the climb was definitely on and that Layton

Kor had joined him. He asked me if I had made my mind up and I said that I had and that I wasn't going. After sitting through the film in silence, he left without another word. To me, the climb seemed very risky but more important, I had no interest in the line of the ascent.

Layton Kor was an American climber of the highest calibre. Since coming to Leysin, I had done several climbs with him and I knew that on rock, Layton was as good as they come. He was possessed of a gigantic reach and knew how to use it. Being six feet four inches tall and very well built, he defied the modern idea that top-class rock climbers were, of necessity, small, wiry men. Layton was a human dynamo, who rarely, if ever, seemed to relax. I always felt that the nearer to danger he could get, the more he enjoyed himself.

At the end of January, John had second thoughts about Dougal. In between times, he had contacted Chris Bonington and Chris had turned down the offer as he thought the climb was unwarrantedly dangerous. However, Chris had taken on the job of photographing the ascent for the *Daily Telegraph*. He rang me at the school and asked me if I would climb with him on the photography mission. Thinking that it would be interesting and profitable – a combination always difficult to resist – I accepted his invitation.

Dougal arrived post-haste at Leysin at the summons from John and the full party of John, Layton and Dougal was assembled. John was still insisting on his Alpine-type tactics for the ascent, even though he now knew that each of them would have to carry almost a hundred pounds of equipment. The whole approach seemed to me to be getting more and more impracticable. John's theory that winter always produced settled weather was rubbish; winter might be more settled than summer but it is still highly unpredictable. John reckoned that each winter produced two periods of good weather, each of which lasted ten days. According to him, one such period had already occurred, therefore all he had to do was wait for the next one. In the meantime, he hired a helicopter and inspected the Face. I was amazed when, after the inspection, he informed

me that there were only three hard pitches on the whole
length of the route.

Then disaster struck. John, Layton and Dougal went ski-ing
and John fell and dislocated his shoulder. The attempt on the
mountain would have to be postponed. In some disorder, the
party returned to Leysin on 15 February. Back in Kleine
Scheidegg, a party of eight German climbers, fully-equipped
and professionally-prepared, had arrived and announced their
intention of doing a *direttissima* of the Eiger. John was soon
informed of the new arrivals.

Dougal and Layton waited in Leysin for instructions and
fretted. They knew that the German team was ready to start
the climb, and in spite of John's incapacity, the trio returned to
Kleine Scheidegg on 17 February. Also heading for Scheidegg
were dozens of pressmen and television people from all over
the world. The circus now had three rings – John, Layton and
Dougal; the German team; and the Scheidegg scandal squad.

Going up on the train from Grindelwald, John, horror-struck,
saw that the Germans were already well-established about fifteen hundred feet up the Face. The weather was still pretty
bad, and it was obvious that the Germans were extremely well-
prepared.

In fact, the Germans were a highly competent outfit. Led by
Jorg Lehne, a top-class mountaineer, they were organized down
to the last detail. The whole team had been training for the
attempt for almost two months. They were attempting the
climb with Himalayan-style tactics – establishing camps at intervals and stocking each with provisions and equipment. They
reckoned on taking eighteen days to complete the climb. John
was still attempting to do it in ten.

The presence of two rival teams competing for the same
prize was a gift for the assembled journalists. Now that the
Germans had made the first move, the press waited eagerly for
John's opening gambit. It wasn't long in coming. On Sunday, 18
February, Dougal and Layton attacked the Eiger. They climbed
the fixed ropes left by the Germans, surmounted some severe
ice pitches and then Layton began work on the First Band – a
huge, sheer cliff. The weather, which had looked bad from the

start, turned really nasty and Dougal and Layton were forced to bivouac. After a painfully cold night, they retreated to Scheidegg as the storm raged about them. Round one to the Germans.

For the next few days, the weather kept both teams off the Face. Some fraternization took place, though at this stage there was no question of combining their efforts. As the days passed, John's shoulder improved and by the time the weather took up, he was fully fit again. On 27 February, I received a phone call from Chris asking me to leave for Scheidegg immediately as the party was about to go on the Wall.

I arrived to find the whole scene somewhat chaotic. John feared that the tactics of the Germans would slow his own attempt down to a crawl. At the same time, he was worried because the Germans had taken the bad weather in their stride and had made good progress up the Wall. It was obvious that if John's plans were to be successful, he would have to make a determined effort at the first opportunity. He decided that, come what may, the following day would see his team on the Wall. Chris and I volunteered to be Sherpas, slogging up behind the climbers, carrying heavy loads to the foot of the Face. It was plain that unless Chris and I did act in a supporting role, the team would never get off the ground.

Now the competition between the two teams started in earnest, with both teams operating on the Wall. By the time the Death Bivouac was reached, the Germans were in front. Over half the Face had been conquered but at this point, the second major difficulty was encountered, and as so often happens when rivals are pitting themselves against a common enemy, the two parties found themselves working together. Much to the disappointment of the news-hounds, the competition was dwindling into a joint effort.

On 20 March, after three weeks at Scheidegg, I returned to Leysin and Mick Burke took my place with Chris. I cannot say that I was not sorry to leave the Eiger; the atmosphere in Scheidegg was not much to my liking.

A couple of days later, I rang Peter Gillman – a *Daily Telegraph* reporter who had taken on the role of team-manager to the Anglo-American team – to find out how things were going. I received a severe shock.

'I think somebody's fallen,' said an agitated Gillman. 'I was at the telescope when the phone rang. I'm sure it was a figure in red. I must get back to the telescope.'

I rang off, promising to ring again in half an hour by which time it would have been ascertained just what had happened. I sat beside the phone and waited. Supposing one of the climbers had fallen ... John's decision not to use full-weight rope on the overhanging prusiks was one of the main reasons why I considered the climb to be dangerous. By now, these fixed ropes would have taken a hammering from constant use and from the weather. I made a second phone call and learnt that Chris and Layton, taking a radio with them, were ski-ing across to where the red object had landed. Half an hour later, I rang again and asked for Peter.

'Well?'

'It's John,' said Peter. 'He's dead.'

I was stunned. The thing that I'd dreaded would happen, had happened. The comedy had turned to tragedy.

'There's nothing to say really, is there?' I said slowly.

'One of the fixed ropes broke,' said Peter.

'Are they coming down?' I asked.

'I should think so,' Peter replied. 'Wendy Bonington's coming over to Leysin to tell Marilyn Harlin but it's bound to be on the radio before she gets there. Can you go and tell her?'

'Aye, me and Audrey'll go and see her,' I said.

There was no question of thinking: 'I told you so.' I only felt a heavy sadness at this tragic blow. Harlin and I were too unalike in our philosophies ever to have become close friends, but nevertheless I felt a keen sense of loss. John Harlin had been a fine mountaineer. His enthusiasm for new projects had always been unbounded and his ability to communicate this enthusiasm to others had won him many friends. He had, for a too-brief spell, blown like a fresh breeze through the field of modern mountaineering.

Later, I rang Scheidegg again and found that the climb was

being continued; the decision had apparently been taken jointly by the German team and Dougal. Five climbers, including Dougal, were in such a position that they were almost cut off from retreat by the atrocious weather conditions. The shortest route to safety seemed to be upwards.

Undoubtedly, the feeling that Harlin himself would have wished the climb to continue influenced the decision. In John's honour, the teams decided to name the climb the John Harlin Route. On 25 March, the day of Harlin's funeral, the five climbers reached the summit. Several of them were badly frostbitten. The Eiger Direct now existed, but to me the price paid had been excessive.

26 | The Yosemite Valley

In April, Royal Robbins left the American School and Don took over his job as Sports Director until the end of the summer term. Bev Clark, Harlin's partner in the International School of Mountaineering, asked Don to manage the school during the summer and so, with Dougal as chief instructor, Don took up the position as soon as the American School closed.

That summer, the weather in the Alps was unbelievably bad and the climbing courses were far from successful because it was rarely possible to climb in the Chamonix area. As an alternative, Don began taking his eager clients down to the sea cliffs at Calanques, near Marseilles. On the penultimate climbing course of the season, a marvellous opportunity presented itself in the shape of an American called Duke Stock. Duke, basically a skier who would turn his hand to anything, was no great climber but a first-class character. He and Don hit it off straight away and when Duke returned to New York at a moment's notice, he offered Don his return ticket on a charter flight. Here was the long-awaited chance for Don to visit the granite cliffs of Yosemite National Park in California, the climbing grounds of the American tigers.

*   *   *

Yosemite was everything that Don had thought it would be. The Mecca of American rock climbers, the superb valley winds for seven miles between sheer granite walls. The rock scenery is spectacular, with El Capitan and Half Dome being particularly impressive. The whole of the valley is a National Park which presents problems to the climber in the shape of tourists

*and Park Rangers. The Californian climate also has its draw-
backs for during the long summer climbing on the valley walls
is a dehydrating business.*

*Don, accompanied by Royal Robbins, arrived in Yosemite
towards the end of September – the most beautiful time of the
year in the valley. He was quickly put on trial by the local
experts.*

The first climber I met was Chuck Pratt, who was climbing
on a crag above the road as we drove into the valley. I liked
him immediately. Short and powerfully made, he reminded me
of Joe in the way that he moved and in fact the resemblance
was even more marked when I saw him climb. It was quite
obvious that Chuck and his companions were eager to get me
on the rock. In 1966, English climbers were rare visitors to
Yosemite and whenever one did appear, the locals pulled out a
few stops in an effort to burn the new arrival off.

Chuck decided that before we did any climbing, a little
socializing wouldn't do us any harm. We bought several 'six-
packs' – six tins of beer – and sat around in the sun, chatting
and drinking. Time passed; we got through a few more beers
than we intended and dozed in the heat.

'Let's do a climb,' said Chuck suddenly.

I squinted at the bearded tanned face. Surely he couldn't be
serious. Even though I was accustomed to drinking much
stronger brews than the rather watery canned beer we were
then downing, I was none too sober and neither, as far as I
could see, was Chuck.

'Aye, might as well,' I replied without enthusiasm.

Chuck scrambled to his feet and started getting some gear. It
looked like my trial was about to begin.

Many of the climbs in Yosemite are pure exercises in rock
techniques. Having climbed a few hundred feet – or in some
cases less – one simply rappels off and that's it. The route that
Chuck proposed to take me on was just such a one. We
reached the foot of the clean, almost mirror-like granite and I
gazed upwards.

'What grade is it?' I asked.

'Oh – 5.8,' replied Chuck.

The American system of grading free climbs is totally different from ours. They use a decimal system based on the number
5. Anything about 5.6 tends to be equivalent to our Severe
grade and so on upwards. The highest grade at the time I was
in Yosemite was 5.10, so Chuck was not starting me out on
anything too easy.

I was wearing P.A.'s which I knew were not really suitable
for Yosemite climbing but I had no other footwear available.
The best kind of sole for the Yosemite rock is a corrugated one
as the rock is so smooth that the flat, rigid P.A. sole is unable to
attain the friction required. However, Chuck wanted to climb,
so that was it.

'You wanna lead?' Chuck asked with a grin.

'Get lost,' I replied.

Chuck started up. I watched with interest as he moved confidently upwards. He was so like Joe, it was uncanny. Twenty,
thirty, forty, fifty feet of rope ran out and Chuck made no
move to put on any protection. I began to wonder if he'd ever
heard of runners.

I wished that I'd stuck to the beer. Chuck continued upwards
until the rope ran out. I shook my head in disbelief. One hundred and fifty feet above me, Chuck belayed. There was not a
single runner between us.

I started to climb, the sweat squirting out. It was hard, no
doubt about it. I was overweight, full of beer and not at all fit,
but I knew that even if I'd been in the peak of condition I
would still have had to work hard. The rock was totally
different from any I had climbed on before; it was incredibly
smooth and friction was difficult to obtain. I was relieved when
I reached the grinning Chuck.

'Okay?'

'Desperate,' I said, and meant it.

We did another couple of pitches of about the same standard
– Hard Very Severe, I reckoned – and then rappelled off. I was
delighted to get back to ground level and the beer. I was a little

disturbed when, the following day, I made some comment to Chuck about the climb and he couldn't remember anything about it.

'Did we do a climb?' he asked in a puzzled voice.

I made a mental note to work out Chuck's drinking capacity to ensure that the same thing wouldn't happen again.

There is a real natural hazard in the valley – bears. Great, shambling brown bears wander through the woods and at night venture on to the camping grounds in search of food.

One night I woke to the sound of heavy breathing and, jerking upright, I looked straight into the eyes of a massive bear which was sniffing round my sleeping bag. We stared at each other for a few seconds and then, apparently deciding that I looked a bit inedible, the bear ambled off. I shudder to think what might have happened had I had some spilt food on my sleeping bag.

The storage of food was something of a problem. Most of the experienced Yosemite lads kept all their gear in kit-bags which were slung in the nearby trees. Even so, the more enterprising bears would occasionally manage to get at them, ripping the bags to pieces, scattering the tinned stuff far and wide and scoffing all the fresh food. Another form of wild life was also a consistent menace and far more subtle than the bears were. Raccoons, attractive as they may look, are great thieves and foragers; nothing is safe from them. Where bears rip and tear, raccoons untie.

A couple of days after my first experience on Yosemite rock, Chuck suggested that he and I, and a couple of his mates, Tom Garrity and Eric Beck, take a trip farther down the valley to Elephant Rock. When the suggestion was made, I sensed that this was to be no ordinary trip and I got the idea that the burning-off process was about to start.

The climb we were going to do was called the Crack of Despair and apparently it had a big reputation. The walk to Elephant Rock was also no picnic; the woods were full of poison oak, one touch of the stuff and irritating rashes sprang up in no time at all.

Tom Garrity and Eric Beck were two of the leading Yosemite climbers; Beck, only a few weeks before, had caused a great stir by soloing Half Dome, one of the great Yosemite routes. Garrity had a number of high-grade first ascents to his credit and had done the second ascent of the Crack of Despair. I reckoned I was in pretty good company.

I had been expecting a ferocious-looking climb from the conversation that had taken place, and as I stood at the foot of the rock it was obvious that the climb didn't just *look* ferocious.

Tom and Eric roped up and Tom led off up the first pitch. I watched carefully and was surprised to see that Tom seemed to be having difficulty.

'Is he off-form?' I asked Chuck.

'Nope,' replied Chuck, 'I don't think so.'

More food for thought. Eventually it was our turn and Chuck invited me to lead the first pitch. As I moved upwards, I heard a shout from above and looking up, I saw Tom hurtling through the air. Eric held him and with much cursing, Tom got back onto the rock. I was beginning to have doubts about this climb; if Tom had done the second ascent and was now capurtling off what should be familiar ground, the climbing was obviously very hard.

I concentrated on the moves ahead and, climbing quite well, I completed the pitch without too much trouble. Up above me, I was amazed to see that Eric couldn't manage the second pitch at all and that he was being hauled bodily upwards by Tom. By now it dawned on me that in their determination to burn me off, they were pushing themselves to their absolute limits.

Chuck led up the second pitch and found it hard. The rope moved up slowly, stopping every now and then as he faced a problem move. The pitch was almost entirely an awkward crack in which nothing fitted. I learnt later that on the first ascent, bongs had been used but these were now considered to be unnecessary. As soon as Chuck was safely anchored, I began the struggle. Fat and unfit, it really was a major effort but somehow I managed to do it. Above us, a series of 'squeeze chimneys' appeared – wide enough to get the body into but not wide enough to allow any bend in the body. It became a question of thrutch.

Once again I found myself glad to get off a climb. Garrity informed me that we'd just done the fourth ascent and that it was graded 5.9. A parallel crack to the left was named the Crack of Doom and Chuck, who made the first ascent – there had only been one more – said that it was 5.10 as far as he was concerned.

'Harder than this?' I asked.

'Yeah,' said Chuck.

Later, Royal and I did the third ascent and I found it no harder than the Crack of Despair.

After another two or three climbs I began to get used to the special techniques that were involved in Yosemite climbing: plenty of hand jams, foot jams, knee jams and almost every other kind of jam imaginable.

Discussing Yosemite climbing with Chuck was rather like discussing a baby with its mother. Chuck rarely climbed outside the Yosemite Valley; if he had done, I am sure that he would have made a first-class mountaineer. His attitude towards climbing was very much like mine; if he felt like doing a climb, he would do it, but if there was no real desire there, he wouldn't bother. Royal on the other hand was a true fanatic. Sometimes he almost made me feel guilty; on a particularly hot afternoon, when I didn't feel like making the effort, he would wander around trying to recruit partners. To Royal, if you were a climber then you had to climb come what may.

Late in September, members of the Alpamayo Expedition arrived in Yosemite making a detour on the way home. Des, Gnome and Ian Howell were among them and they were particularly keen to do some of the standard long routes in the valley. Together we did the North Face of the Sentinel, Half Dome and Ian, Dave Bathgate and I did the Lost Arrow Tip – a most exhilarating climb.

Back home in England, Don found himself with no alternative but to start routine work. He began to feel that once again, as when Joe had gone to Kanchenjunga, the boat had left without him. Looking round he could see that almost all of his friends and contemporaries had settled down and that the few who were still climbing had a measure of security behind them.

Joe was established in Llanberis, a thriving climbing equipment shop providing him with a good living; Ian Clough had settled in Glencoe and was running a climbing school; Chris was well-paid as a journalist and photographer. Don's income, if he did not take a regular job, was limited to lecturing fees and his cut from items of climbing gear bearing his name. Something had to be done.

Then, as had often happened in the past, talk of an expedition reached Don's ears and all thoughts of secure jobs and domesticity disappeared. Dave Bathgate, a member of the successful 1967 Alpamayo Expedition, wanted to return to the Andes in 1968. He, Ian MacEacheran and Brian Robertson — both Scots — planned to tackle the unclimbed South Face of Huandoy, a 21,000-foot peak in the Cordillera Blanc in Peru. Dave asked Don if he was interested and, of course, Don said that he was.

I hadn't been in the Peruvian Andes but in any case another idea had occurred to me. When Dave contacted me about Huandoy, I suggested to him that he and I should make a trip down the Amazon and he agreed at once. For the next few months I devoted my time to planning both the major expedition and our river trip.

The mountain itself was a real challenge. Although it had had ascents by different routes, the mountain's South Face had seen only one attempt, which had been by an American Expedition. This attempt had not got very far up the forbidding Face. We nicknamed the mountain 'The Eiger of the Andes' because Dave thought it might arouse interest and help with the necessary sponsorship.

At an altitude bordering on the oxygen barrier, the climbing would obviously be very strenuous; particularly as the top thousand feet of the Face was vertical or, in parts, overhanging. Dave was sure that the rock was excellent; but in fact it turned out to be very poor.

My three companions were all Scotsmen; Dave, of course, I had climbed with before. Ian MacEacheran was one of the young Scottish tigers; a member of the Edinburgh Squirrels, he had a very good record of winter ascents on the Ben. Far from being just an ice specialist, he was a fine rock climber, though short of big mountain experience. Brian Robertson I had met once before; he was a good aid climber who seemed to go out of his way to find difficult artificial routes.

Over the years, the money situation with regard to expeditions had worsened enormously. Now, it was extremely difficult to squeeze money from any of the old sources; it seemed that even the Everest Foundation was drying up. By limiting the party to four, we were reducing our chances of success but cutting down the cost. We all knew that the expedition would have to work on a shoe-string but I suppose that we were happy enough to go even if we'd hardly two half-pennies to rub together.

Preparing for an expedition is never easy and this was one of the most difficult in my experience. My small cottage was like a junk shop once the gear started arriving. The fact that Dave, Ian and Brian were all hundreds of miles away didn't make it any easier. However, we managed to get the gear on the boat on time, though I remember swearing that I'd never go through such a shambles again.

The usual Andean approach difficulties occurred and I can't say that any of us was really sorry when we reached Base

Camp. From close range, the impressions I had got from the photos proved to be correct: large areas of the Face were bad rock.

Four hours away from Base, we established Camp One high on the moraine. Two and a half hours from Camp One – an uncomfortable slog across the glacier – Ian and I dug a superb snow-cave at about 18,000 feet. From there on, the hard climbing would begin.

Above the cave, a long, steep, snow slope led up to the rock. For several days we worked up the slope, fixing ropes, safeguarding any possible hasty retreat. Then we began work on the rock. I reckoned I'd done my share of the graft for the time being and I returned to Base to have a short rest, replenish our stock of cigarettes and to collect any mail that had arrived.

I was at Base Camp for just over 24 hours. When I started back up the mountain, I could see the three red dots above me on the ice ramp apparently removing the fixed ropes. When we eventually met up, I was told that the climb had been abandoned. Brian and Dave had pushed up the rock as far as they could, reaching a height of just over 20,000 feet, but then they decided that further progress would be unjustifiably dangerous. They and Ian had had a short meeting and decided to call the attempt off. I cannot say that I was too pleased at the decision but there was nothing much I could do about it. If it was off, it was off. Failing on a mountain is never pleasant and though I accepted the decision as being final, I did feel that maybe we hadn't tried hard enough.

We retrieved as much of the gear as we could and returned to Lima. Brian and Ian flew off to the States to visit Yosemite and Dave and I prepared for our Amazon adventure. A twenty-four-hour bus ride over the spine of the Andes from Lima to the tiny, poverty-stricken village of Tingo Maria saw us on our way. The bus journey was as uncomfortable a ride as I can ever remember.

Tingo Maria is on the Huallaga River and it was from there that we proposed to start our journey on the water. At first, our idea had been to build a raft for ourselves but we gradually dropped the notion when we realized the futility of building anything for ourselves. The Huallaga is not a busy river compared to the Amazon but it is certainly a well-used highway. It hadn't occurred to me before, but it seems obvious that the rivers of Peru, Brazil, and indeed most South American countries, are their road-substitutes. What looks like a thin, blue line on the large-scale map is in reality a thronged thoroughfare. We soon realized that our trip was far from a journey into the unknown.

We hitched a lift in a dug-out canoe powered by an outboard motor and then on a raft. For days on end we lounged about – me in my pyjamas because they were the coolest things I had – and sweated in the almost unbearable humidity. The world drifted by us; on either side of us was the jungle, full of God knows what forms of life. Beneath our bodies the green, thick water swirled sluggishly towards the sea thousands of miles away.

Gradually the river broadened and, by the time it joined the Amazon, became much busier. Our trip was almost at an end for we were approaching Yurimagwas. From there we flew to Iquitos, an inland port where trans-Atlantic steamers actually collect passengers. At Iquitos, we were to board a river-boat for Belem at the mouth of the Amazon, 3,500 miles away. At Belem we would take a British ship back to England.

* * *

In April 1969. Alick Ormerod and I went down to Wales for a weekend to look over Cloggy and the Pass. It was rather a wild, cold couple of days, though in spite of the rough weather, Llanberis and the Pass were full of climbers. We slept Friday night at Ginger Cain's place in Deiniolen and then on a bitterly cold, windy morning we set out for Cloggy. Parking the van at Hafody Newydd, I was surprised to see that we had been followed up the track. Another van swung into the small parking-space and Joe Brown climbed out.

' 'Morning,' I said.

Apart from the odd Rock and Ice dinner, Joe and I had not met for several years. He stood, hands thrust deep in his pockets, shoulders hunched, a fag hanging from his lips.

'What are you doing up here?' he inquired.

'Having a walk,' I replied.

Joe shivered and glanced up towards Cloggy. The great cliff was shrouded in mist and it was just starting to rain.

'Ginger's wife said she thought you were going to Cloggy,' Joe said.

Ginger's wife worked as an assistant at Joe's shop. Word doesn't take long to get around.

I could see that the situation appealed to Alick. Here, after years apart, Brown and Whillans were meeting again and almost under Cloggy itself. I felt little; Joe and I were now so far apart that it seemed impossible for our partnership to be resumed and, indeed, I could see little point in attempting to renew it.

We stood in silence for a few minutes, the rain stinging our faces.

'D'you fancy a climb tomorrow?' Joe asked. 'We could go over to Anglesey; it's always sheltered on Gogarth.'

I thought for a bit. I guessed that Joe had made a big effort to come out with this invitation. Alick stood in silence waiting for the answer. I looked at Joe; he was obviously extremely fit, whereas I was vastly overweight and not at all in condition. I couldn't see myself struggling up a sea-cliff behind him.

'No, I don't think so,' I replied. 'I'm not fit.'

'Ah, you'd be all right,' Joe said.

I shook my head. 'No, not this weekend. We'll be having a booze-up – I won't feel like doing anything strenuous tomorrow,' I said.

Joe nodded but said nothing. A few minutes later, we set out to walk up the railway track to Cloggy and Joe returned to Llanberis.

'Why didn't you say you'd climb with him?' Alick asked.

'Joe's part of the past,' I said, after thinking for a minute. 'I couldn't see the point in going back.'

The following day, as we were driving up the Pass, a figure stepped out into the road and waved us down. It was Joe again and with him was the photographer, Ken Wilson.

'What a chance,' said Wilson. 'Here, get your flat-cap and a fag and let's get a picture. This is too good to miss, you and Joe, Cenotaph in the background.'

I turned to Alick. 'See what I mean?' I said.

Somehow though, Wilson brought Joe and I closer together again. We chatted for a while and parted understanding each other.

Don spent most of his time in 1969 lecturing and working on the design and production of a revolutionary climbing hammer. Earlier in the year, Chris Bonington announced his plans to lead an expedition to attempt to scale the South Face of Annapurna, and asked Don to be deputy leader. Don, realizing the significance of the proposed expedition, had no hesitation in accepting Chris's offer.

I was aware that the Annapurna trip was the most serious thing – in every sense – that I'd ever been on. As a climb, the ascent of the incredibly severe South Face would move big mountain climbing into another realm. The assault on such a mountain would necessitate rock and ice climbing of the highest standard, plus all the problems which are present in any attempt on a Himalayan peak.

The team for the Annapurna trip was one of the strongest ever assembled. Dougal Haston, Ian Clough, Martin Boysen, the American Tom Frost, Mick Burke, Mike Thompson and Nick Estcourt – all climbers of exceptional ability – accepted invitations to join. The financial side of the expedition was sewn up and, all in all, we must have been one of the best-equipped parties ever to attempt to climb a mountain.

During the months of preparation, I had plenty of time to sit and think back over my career in climbing. It seems hardly possible that I have done and seen so much. It is a long way from Nora Street to the summit of Annapurna and yet that is where my story ends. Victory over this great mountain may well have given my climbing career new impetus and yet I know that I cannot go on climbing for ever; new fields, new challenges must present themselves. As of now, I cannot say, just as I have been unable to say for the last twenty years, where I'll be this time next year. But if the next twenty years are as worth-while and exciting as the last twenty have been, I will have no complaints.

I suppose in the end it all comes down to the basic question: why do you do it? To me, the question is irrelevant; I climb, and have always done so because I enjoy it. I see around me people whose lives follow the same mundane pattern, year after year. I know that very often these people have things that I will never have – a stable home, children, money and security. Yet I wouldn't exchange my way of life for their way.

Perhaps more than the climbing, it is the people I have met who have made my life so enjoyable. First the ones who have tragically lost their lives: Tom Bourdillon, Bob Downes, John Harlin, Wilfred Noyce, Robin Smith, Tom Patey. Ian Clough, whose death ruined the triumph of Annapurna, was typical of them all: a man who would have given his life for a comrade. Mountains give; mountains take. Then there are my contemporaries – Joe, Chris, Nat Allen, John Streetly, Chuck Pratt and all the rest. I owe a great deal to all those I have mentioned – and the dozen who have somehow been left out.

Have I any ambitions left? In 1971, an international expedition is going to attempt to climb the South Face of Everest and I have been invited to join the party. I would dearly love to stand on the summit of the highest mountain in the world. After that, anything would be an anti-climax.

On 27 May 1970, Don stood on the summit of Annapurna, the highest point of his career, in both senses. It was an apt finale to twenty years of climbing. A few days later, I received a postcard from him and I can do no better than end this book with a quotation from the card:

In Base with Dougal for three days before going back up for

the final 'do'. 3,500 feet to go before the monsoon in 3 weeks.
Had some hard climbing. See you soon.

Added to the card was the laconic message:
Finished climb 27th. Aye, Don.

Glossary of Technical Terms

abseil	see *rappel*.
arete	a narrow ridge.
belay	a *belay* is a safe stance; to *belay* is to anchor safely to the rock either by clipping on to a *piton* or by using *slings* fastened in, on, or over natural rock features.
bergschrund	a *crevasse* which lies across the bottom of a snow, ice or rock slope
bong	a large, metal wedge.
col	a gap or depression linking two mountains or two high points on the same mountain.
cornice	an overhanging mass of snow found on ridges.
couloir	a large funnel-like gully. It is often a chute for stones falling from above.
crampons	steel spikes fixed on a frame which is fastened to the climber's boot.
crevasse	a fissure in the ice.
dièdre	an open-book corner.
étrier	a small ladder which is suspended from a *piton*.
gendarme	a rock tower on a ridge.
jug	a large hold.
karabiner	a snap-link used in conjunction with *pitons* and *slings*.
layback	climbing by means of side-holds in a crack with the feet placed on the wall containing the crack.

moraine	rocks and débris on the surface of a glacier or at the sides and end of the glacier.
pendulum	a move on the rope which entails swinging sideways.
perlon	artificial fibre rope.
piolet	a hammer and ice-axe on the same shaft.
pitch	one section of a climb. A *pitch* stretches from *belay* to *belay*.
piton	a spike of metal which is driven into cracks in the rock. Known as 'pegs', there are many varieties of this indispensable climbing aid.
prusik	a method of climbing directly up a fixed rope.
P.A.'s	a brand of lightweight climbing boots. There are many different varieties of climbing boot but P.A.'s and similar brands are characterized by their rigid rubber soles which are absolutely smooth so that maximum friction can be attained.
rappel	to descend by means of a doubled rope anchored on a firm *belay*. *Abseil* is the German term for the same procedure.
rognon	an island of rock on a glacier.
runner	a method of protection used by the leader on a climb. There are many ways of fixing *runners*, the most common probably being the jamming of a stone or specially manufactured metal nut into a crack. Nuts will be threaded on *slings* but if a stone is used, a *sling* will have to be wrapped around it. A *karabiner* is attached to the other end of the *sling* and the climbing rope is clipped into it. The idea of a *runner* or *running belay* as it is properly called, is to protect the leader from a long fall. In theory, he should only fall until his last-placed *runner* holds him.
sack rope	a separate rope used solely for hauling equipment up a climb.
serac	a pinnacle of ice.
slings	loops of rope or nylon tape of varying weights

and sizes. Used in conjunction with *pitons*, *kara-biners* and *runners*.

verglas   a frozen layer of water.

vibrams   a type of rubber cleated boot sole. Often used to describe the whole boot.

Index

Penguinews *and*
Penguins in Print

Every month we issue an illustrated magazine,
Penguinews. It's a lively guide to all the latest Penguins,
Pelicans and Puffins, and always contains an article on
a major Penguin author, plus other features of
contemporary interest.

Penguinews is supplemented by *Penguins in Print*, a
complete list of all the available Penguin titles – there
are now over four thousand!

The cost is no more than the postage; so why not write
for a free copy of this month's *Penguinews*? And if
you'd like both publications sent for a year, just send
us a cheque or a postal order for 30p (if you live in
the United Kingdom) or 60p (if you live elsewhere), and
we'll put you on our mailing list.

Dept EP, Penguin Books Ltd, Harmondsworth, Middlesex

Note: *Penguinews* and *Penguins in Print* are not available
in the U.S.A. or Canada

Annapurna South Face

Chris Bonington

In 1970 Chris Bonington and his team successfully battled up a seemingly impregnable mountain in the Himalayas. It was a magnificent triumph for mountaineering and good teamwork. *Annapurna South Face* tells how it was done.

'I am left ... with a sense of wonder at this feat; of admiration for the men who dared and did it' – Lord Hunt in the *Sunday Times*.

'He writes as well as he climbs' – *Times Literary Supplement*.

'This is a very good book indeed, exciting, psychologically illuminating and honest, and I read it entranced' – C. P. Snow in the *Financial Times*.

Not for sale in the U.S.A.